Concentration Camps USA

Concentration Camps USA: Japanese Americans and World War II

Roger Daniels
State University of New York at Fredonia

HOLT, RINEHART AND WINSTON, INC.
NEW YORK CHICAGO SAN FRANCISCO ATLANTA
DALLAS MONTREAL TORONTO LONDON SYDNEY

Copyright © 1971 by Holt, Rinehart and Winston, Inc.
All Rights Reserved
Library of Congress Catalog Card Number: 72-143320
ISBN: 0-03-081869-9 College
ISBN: 0-03-088474-8 Trade
Printed in the United States of America
1 2 3 4 090 9 8 7 6 5 4 3 2 1

For Judith Mandel Daniels
wife and critic

Acknowledgments

As I have been engaged in the study of the Japanese Americans for more than a decade, any attempt properly to acknowledge all my intellectual indebtedness is impossible. Teachers, colleagues, friends, members of the Japanese American community, and students have all, in many ways, enriched my understanding, such as it is, of a unique people. My debts to previous scholarship are set out in the traditional manner in the footnotes. There are, however, a few obligations which, in justice, must be noted more fully. Chief of these is to Dr. Stetson Conn, former Chief Military Historian of the United States Army, whose pioneering work on the decision for relocation is indispensable. In the summer of 1969 Dr. Conn made his personal notes available to me; as many of them cited materials that can no longer be located in the National Archives, their value was enormous. Much has been written in criticism—and some of it justified —of official, or "court," historians. Not nearly enough credit is given to the many perceptive and dedicated scholars in government service who, like Conn, do their best to "tell it like it was."

The late Joe Grant Masaoka, for many years the administrator of the Japanese American Research Project at UCLA, helped me in more ways than I can recount. He would not have agreed with some of my strictures about the Japanese American power structure, but would, I am sure, have defended my right to make them.

In the course of my research I received much help from the staffs of government archives and university libraries. The National Archives, the Federal Records Centers at Suitland, Maryland, and Denver, Colorado, The Franklin D. Roosevelt Library at Hyde Park, the Naval Historical Office in Washington, the Bancroft Library at Berkeley, the Hoover Institution Archives at Stanford, the Huntington Library in San Marino, and the Western History Center at the University of Wyoming all provided materials and the high level of cooperation that scholars have come to expect from such places. I would like to thank specially Albert Blair and Thomas E. Hohmann of the National Archives, Delbert Bishop and Robert Svenningsen of the Denver Federal Records Center, Robert Becker and James Kantor of the Bancroft Library, and Franz Lassner of the Hoover Institution. The Archivist of the United States, James B. Rhoades, gave me access to one document that had been censored by his subordinates.

As I was writing the book, I had the good fortune to direct the researches of a truly exceptional graduate student, Douglas W. Nelson. He and I explored Heart Mountain together, and I have drawn heavily on his University of Wyoming M.A. thesis. Linda Nelson was a tireless and resourceful research assistant. She, Geri Pierce, and Nancy Young typed the manuscript. The Graduate Division of the University of Wyoming provided a summer fellowship during which some of the research was done.

Many people have helped shape my manuscript into a book. Moses Rischin, the editor for this series, provided perceptive advice from the very beginning. At Holt, Rinehart and Winston, Cliff Snyder provided guidance and gave friendship. Suzanne Weiss did most of the picture research. A former colleague, Robert Wilson, read the entire manuscript and made useful criticisms.

Finally, but not least, my thanks to my wife Judith, who in this, as in all my work, has had an integral part.

Laramie, Wyoming   Roger Daniels
July 1971

Foreword

Minority history, once a euphemism disguising unpleasant or intractable social realities, has come in our time to be viewed as a source of American vitality and self-illumination. In an era when American society has been undergoing a vast realignment of its human resources, institutions, and habits of mind, Americans are more prone than ever to see that the experiences of ethnic, regional, social, economic, occupational, political, religious, intellectual, and other well-defined groups have spotlighted and personalized strategic problems in the American past.

Berkshire Studies in Minority History encompass a whole range of such group experiences. Each is intended to illuminate brightly a critical event, movement, tradition, or dilemma. By so doing, these books will individualize the problems of a complex society giving them both broad pertinence and sharp definition.

Roger Daniels has written the first study by a historian of the many facets of a repressive interlude in the history of one American ethnic group singled out for degradation in a time of national crisis. He has given full and dramatic coverage to every phase of the story beginning with the pre-Pearl Harbor history of the Japanese in the United States. He has given special attention to the resistance and protest of the evacuees, an aspect neglected or glossed over by others. Above all, he has spelled out the wider implications of the experiences of the Japanese Americans during World War II with clarity and authoritativeness. It is difficult to imagine that other Americans will ever be forced to undergo so fundamental a betrayal of everything that the nation has stood for. This book is intended both as a reminder and a warning.

San Francisco, California   Moses Rischin, *Series Editor*
July 1971   *Berkshire Studies in Minority History*

Contents

Introduction

In the early months of 1942 the United States government assembled and shipped off to concentration camps 112,000 men, women, and children, the entire Japanese American population of the three Pacific Coast states of California, Oregon, and Washington. This book is an attempt to tell their story.

It is the story of a national calamity, a calamity commonly referred to as "our worst wartime mistake." As Richard Hofstadter has pointed out, much of our history, especially textbook history, can be classified as part of a literature of "national self-congratulation." Such cannot be the case here; no American can take any pride in this sordid episode. A question may arise in some minds, however, as to the wisdom or propriety of devoting a whole volume to explicate this unhappy event. Does it really merit such an extended treatment? Even the iconoclastic Professor Hofstadter, in a two-volume text of over a thousand pages, can only spare two and a half sentences to describe the wartime evacuation.

Obviously, I feel that it does. In the first place, as the late Morton Grodzins pointed out shortly after the event, perhaps its most significant and ominous aspect was that of giving "precedent and constitutional sanctity for a policy of mass incarceration under military auspices. . . . That . . . betrayed all Americans."

In addition, the general tendency of educated Americans, including historians, to write the evacuation off as a "wartime mistake" is to obscure its true significance. Rather than a mistake—which, according to the dictionary is "an error in action, calculation, opinion or judgment caused by poor reasoning, carelessness, insufficient information . . . a misunderstanding or misconception"—the legal atrocity which was committed against the Japanese Americans was the logical outgrowth of over three centuries of American experience, an experience which taught Americans to regard the United States as a white man's country in which nonwhites "had no rights which the white man was bound to respect." These infamous words, from Chief Justice Roger B. Taney's 1857 decision in *Dred Scott* v. *Sanford*, were merely echoed by the United States Supreme Court during World War II. The evacuation, then, not only betrayed all Americans, but grew directly out of the American experience. Although it affected only a tiny segment of our population, it reflected one of the central themes of American history—the theme of white supremacy, of American racism.

But merely to describe the past and to point out its tragic flaws is not enough. Historians must not only tell what happened, they must try to explain why it happened, even though they are philosophically aware that, at the very best, such explanations are bound to be incomplete.

To examine and explain the Japanese American experience in World War II is to examine one aspect of American racism, an aspect that is, fortunately, now largely relegated to the pages of history rather than the pages of our daily newspapers. But the larger phenomenon of a generally racist society remains, and if the reader draws from the relatively "happy ending" of the Japanese American experience an analogy about the larger aspects of American racism, he will be guilty of the same kind of smug self-congratulation that allows the establishment of ten concentration camps for American citizens on American soil to be written off as a "mistake."

Neither these children nor their grandfather were much of a threat to the United States war effort, but shortly after this picture was taken they became impounded people. (*National Archives*)

THE ARCHITECTS OF EVACUATION

Secretary of War Henry L. Stimson. (*National Archives*)

Assistant Secretary of War John J. McCloy. (*National Archives*)

Major General Allen W. Gullion, the Provost Marshal General. (*U.S. Army Photo*)

Lieutenant General John L. De Witt.(*U.S. Army Photo*)

Colonel Karl R. Bendetsen. (*U.S. Army Photo*)

WESTERN DEFENSE COMMAND AND FOURTH ARMY
WARTIME CIVIL CONTROL ADMINISTRATION
Presidio of San Francisco, California
April 1, 1942

INSTRUCTIONS
TO ALL PERSONS OF
JAPANESE
ANCESTRY
Living in the Following Area:

All that portion of the City and County of San Francisco, State of California, lying generally west of the north-
line established by Junipero Serra Boulevard, Worchester Avenue, and Nineteenth Avenue, and lying generally n
of the east-west line established by California Street, to the intersection of Market Street, and thence on Market St
to San Francisco Bay.

All Japanese persons, both alien and non-alien, will be evacuated from the above designated area by 12:00 o'c
noon Tuesday, April 7, 1942.

No Japanese person will be permitted to enter or leave the above described area after 8:00 a. m., Thursday, Ap
1942, without obtaining special permission from the Provost Marshal at the Civil Control Station located at:

1701 Van Ness Avenue
San Francisco, California

The Civil Control Station is equipped to assist the Japanese population affected by this evacuation in the fol
ing ways:

1. Give advice and instructions on the evacuation.
2. Provide services with respect to the management, leasing, sale, storage or other disposition of most kin
property including: real estate, business and professional equipment, buildings, household goods, boats, automob
livestock, etc.
3. Provide temporary residence elsewhere for all Japanese in family groups.
4. Transport persons and a limited amount of clothing and equipment to their new residence, as specified b

The Following Instructions Must Be Observed:

1. A responsible member of each family, preferably the head of the family, or the person in whose name m
the property is held, and each individual living alone, will report to the Civil Control Station to receive furth
structions. This must be done between 8:00 a. m. and 5:00 p. m., Thursday, April 2, 1942, or between 8:00 a. m
5:00 p. m., Friday, April 3, 1942.

Posters were the main method of informing the Japanese American community
of what it had to do. (*Franklin D. Roosevelt Library*)

Thousands of small businesses, like this one in San Francisco, had to close on
very short notice. Eventually, most Japanese American property owners received an average of 15 cents on the dollar for their losses, without any provision for inflation or interest. (*Bancroft Library*)

CLOSING
We won't take it
to OWENS VALLEY for U.
ASAHI DYE WORKS
朝日洋服洗濯所
DYE
your faded
GARMENTS
the New
SHADES

The movement to Assembly Centers utilized all kinds of transportation. (*Above, Bancroft Library; top right, National Archives*)

Moving in was an interminable process. These evacuees are at Santa Anita racetrack. (*National Archives*)

The Assembly Center at Tanforan racetrack just after the Japanese Americans moved in. (*National Archives*)

Tanforan two months later. All the improvements were made by the evacuees themselves. (*National Archives*)

The same kind of energy made most quarters in the camps habitable. This cubicle at Heart Mountain, Wyoming, housed a Japanese American veteran of World War I and his family. (*National Archives*)

A typical landscaping by evacuees at Manzanar. (*Bancroft Library*)

Even after evacuation many Japanese Americans contributed to the war effort; these at Tule Lake are helping to dig potatoes. (*Bancroft Library*)

American children at play, Heart Mountain, November 1943. (*National Archives*)

Patriotism behind barbed wire. The Boy Scout troop at Manzanar in a Memorial Day ritual. (*Franklin D. Roosevelt Library*)

Japanese American troops in Italy bringing in German prisoners, July 1944. (*U.S. Army Photo*)

Did Truman's Action for 281 Others Also Go Astray?

After 23 Years, Nisei Le

By Helen Altonn
Star-Bulletin Writer

A Hawaii Nisei joyfully welcomed the news this week that the civil rights which he lost during World War II have been restored.

It took 23 years for the word to catch up to him.

The news, delayed more than two decades, may also affect other Nisei living here or on the Mainland.

The local man has lived in shame all this time in the mistaken belief that he had no voting rights because he had been convicted of a felony.

The Islander, now about 60, was imprisoned for draft resistance while confined in a relocation camp.

He never knew that President Harry S Truman issued a full pardon to 282 Japanese-American draft resisters in January 1948.

THE STAR-BULLETIN informed him of the pardon after learning of the astonishing situation and investigating it with the help of U.S. Sen. Daniel K. Inouye.

At this reporter's request, Inouye instituted a search through old Justice Department files, which took several weeks but finally produced evidence that a pardon had been granted.

"From the information that I have, all known Japanese-Americans who for one reason or another avoided military service during wartime internment have all been granted presidential pardons and regained full citizenship rights," Inouye said.

"To think that he's been living under that unfortunate burden," he added, regarding the Island Nisei.

AN OLD INJUSTICE—This was the first group of Japanese-American di resisters sentenced to prison from the Heart Mountain Relocation Ca

Issei parents, Mr. and Mrs. Risaku Kanaya, receiving a Silver Star posthumously awarded to their son for gallantry in action, Honolulu, 1945. (*U.S. Army Photo*)

arns of Pardon

At least one, and possibly others, has lived in shame since because he thought he had lost his civil liberties.

The first 63 draft resisters from Heart Mountain in Federal District Court, Cheyenne, Wyoming, July 1944. Most but not all of these were pardoned by President Truman in December 1947, in an amnesty of more than 1500 persons convicted of selective service violations. The publication of an excerpt from this book in the Honolulu *Star-Bulletin* in April 1971 resulted in at least one of the Heart Mountain resisters learning, for the first time, that his citizenship had been restored. For the amnesty, see *Federal Register*, p. 8731 ff., Dec. 24, 1947. (*Photograph courtesy of Mrs. E. H. Yanagisako*)

Senator Daniel Inouye (Dem.-Haw.) opening the Democratic National Convention, Chicago, August 28, 1968. (*UPI*)

1

THE JAPANESE AMERICAN EXPERIENCE
1890-1940

According to the Census of 1940 there were 126,948
Japanese Americans in the continental United States; they
comprised less than one-tenth of 1 percent of the total
population. Had they been dispersed evenly throughout the
country—as Secretary of State William Jennings Bryan once
proposed—there would have been about forty individuals in
each American county. But, like almost all other ethnic
groups throughout our history, the Japanese Americans
tended to cluster. Almost nine out of ten lived in one of
the three Pacific Coast states, with nearly three-quarters
of the total found inside the borders of California. Within
that state too, there was clustering. More than one-third
of the state's Japanese Americans were in Los Angeles
County, while six other counties (of a total of fifty-eight)
accounted for almost another third. But even in the area of
highest concentration of their population—Los Angeles
County—persons of Japanese origin were a tiny minority.
Out of every thousand Angelenos, sixteen were Japanese.[1]

---

[1] These and other population data from U.S. Census and immigration figures. Some of the nineteenth-century data used later are not
wholly accurate.

How was it then that such an infinitesimal portion of the whole population could inspire such fear and hatred in the rest of the American people? How could such a group provoke so totalitarian a response from a government dedicated to "life, liberty, and the pursuit of happiness"? These are the questions that this book seeks to answer. As will become obvious, the answers are more to be sought within the larger society than by an examination of the minority. In the final analysis, one must explain the culprits, not the victims. But an understanding of the victims is necessary. The evacuation of 1942 did not occur in a vacuum, but was based on almost a century of anti-Oriental fear, prejudice, and misunderstanding.

The immigrants from Japan who began to arrive in the United States in significant numbers after 1890 (Japan had legalized emigration only in 1885) already had two strikes against them.[2] The western United States in general and California in particular had learned to despise Orientals before this Japanese migration began. Immigration from China, starting at about the same time as the gold rush of 1849, had created an entirely new strain of American racism, from which the Japanese Americans were to suffer greatly. The anti-Orientalism of California and the West was separate from but certainly related to the general prejudice against colored people—"the lesser breeds without the law" as Kipling put it—which was endemic to white Americans from almost the very beginning of our history. Similar prejudices, usually called nativism, were exhibited even against white people if they happened not to speak English or practiced a non-Protestant variant of Christianity. But even within the general ethnocentric intolerance of American society, anti-Orientalism was something special.

The earliest Chinese immigrants were not particularly mistreated. Their outlandish costumes and unique appearance—apart from "color" most Chinese men wore their hair in long pigtails, or queues—added merely another exotic note to the polyglot cosmopolitanism of gold rush San Francisco. The fantastic boom then in progress made any addition to the labor force welcome, and these earliest immigrants found a ready-made economic niche. (The Chinese characters for California can also be translated "golden mountain.") This economic attraction—what historians of immigration call "pull"—coupled with the "push" of Chinese peasant poverty and the existence of cheap and frequent trans-Pacific sail and steamship transportation produced a steady stream of Chinese migration to the United States, as the tables on page 3 show.

Relatively speaking, the Chinese were a large fraction of the population of the West in the years after the Civil War. In 1870 Chinese

---

[2] Harry H. L. Kitano, *Japanese Americans: The Evolution of a Subculture* (Englewood Cliffs, N.J.: Prentice-Hall, 1969), p. 14.

IMMIGRATION OF CHINESE TO THE UNITED STATES

Years	No. of Immigrants
To 1860	41,443
1861–1870	64,301
1871–1880	123,823

CHINESE POPULATION, BY CENSUS

	United States	Pacific States	California
1860	34,933	–	34,933
1870	63,199	52,841	49,277
1880	104,468	87,828	75,132

comprised perhaps ·10 percent of California's population and almost a fourth of the population of its metropolis, San Francisco. The economic impact of the Chinese was even greater than their numbers would suggest, for almost all of them were adult males who competed with white work-ingmen for jobs. This competition first asserted itself in the mining districts, but became really acute after the completion of the Union–Central Pacific Railroad in 1869, which had employed some 10,000 Chinese laborers to construct its western leg. From an economic point of view the almost unanimous hostility with which far-western workingmen viewed the Chinese was quite rational. Chinese labor was cheap labor, and far-western labor had been, due to its scarcity, expensive labor. The result of this competition was a popular anti-Chinese movement, led for a while by the immigrant demagogue Dennis Kearney. His rallying cry, "The Chinese Must Go," is a good shorthand description of the whole move-ment. Originally the sole property of Kearney's third-party movement, the Workingmen's party, a Chinese exclusion policy was soon appropriated by both Democrats and Republicans, first at the state and regional levels, and then nationally.

But the protest was not solely economic. Based upon the legitimate and understandable economic grievances of western workingmen against what they considered unfair competition (one is reminded of present-day California farm workers' resentment of the importation of Mexican nationals on a temporary basis), the movement soon developed an ideology of white supremacy/Oriental inferiority that was wholly com-patible with the mainstream of American racism. Not only did "John Chinaman," as he was often called, "work cheap and smell bad," but he was also subhuman.[3] California courts refused to accept his testimony;

---

[3] On Chinese, the standard work is Elmer Sandmeyer, *The Anti-Chinese Movement in California* (Urbana, Ill.: University of Illinois Press, 1939); but see also Gunther

municipal ordinances were passed to harass him; the state legislature tried to stop his further immigration; and the California constitution itself, as rewritten in 1879, had an entire anti-Chinese section which, among other things, called upon the legislature to

> prescribe all necessary regulations for the protection of the state, and the counties and towns . . . from the burdens and evils arising from the presence of aliens who are and may become . . . dangerous and detrimental to the well-being or peace of the state, and to impose conditions upon which such persons may reside in the state, and to provide the means and modes of their removal.[4]

Apart from "legal" discrimination, the Chinese suffered greatly from individual and mob violence. Since they lived in isolated mining camps or in segregated urban ghettoes, assaults against Chinese were usually witnessed only by other Chinese, whose testimony was inadmissible in court. In a sense, California courts declared an open season on Chinese, who were subjected to everything from casual assault (cutting off a pigtail was a popular sport) to mass murder. The worst single California atrocity occurred in Los Angeles during a one-night rampage in 1871 in which a white mob shot, hanged, and otherwise murdered some twenty Chinese.[5] Other similar mob violence took place throughout the state, and indeed, throughout the West. Outside California the bloodiest outbreak took place in Rock Springs, Wyoming, in 1885 in a massacre of Chinese, originally employed as strikebreakers in a Union Pacific coal mine; twenty-eight were killed and fifteen wounded, and damage to property came to nearly $150,000.[6]

Some employers, outside the West, saw the presence of Chinese as an opportunity. They were brought to New England to break a shoemakers' strike, and some fantastic schemes were hatched to use Chinese as substitutes for newly freed and fractious Negroes on southern cotton plantations and as a solution to the vexatious "servant problem" that troubled the upper middle class in Gilded Age America.[7] But, in essence,

---

Barth, *Bitter Strength: A History of the Chinese in the United States, 1850–1870* (Cambridge, Mass.: Harvard University Press, 1964).

[4] California Constitution, 1879, Article XIX.

[5] William R. Locklear, "The Celestials and the Angels," *Southern California Quarterly*, September, 1960.

[6] Paul Crane and Alfred Larson, "The Chinese Massacre," *Annals of Wyoming*, January–April, 1940; and Arlen Ray Wilson, "The Rock Springs, Wyoming, Chinese Massacre, 1885," unpublished M.A. thesis, University of Wyoming, 1967.

[7] Frederick Rudolph, "Chinamen in Yankeedom: Anti-Unionism in Massachusetts in 1870," *American Historical Review*, October, 1947.

the Chinese question was a western question, and largely a California problem at that.

The West, however, could not solve the problem; to put an end to immigration from China, federal power was required, and by the early 1870s western legislatures and western political parties were petitioning Congress to end Chinese immigration and adopting planks calling for Chinese exclusion. An exclusion bill passed both houses of Congress in Rutherford B. Hayes's administration, but received a Presidential veto. In 1882, however, Chester Alan Arthur reluctantly bowed to Congressional feeling and signed a compromise exclusion bill, barring all Chinese for ten years. The ten-year ban was renewed by Congress in 1892 and then made "permanent" under the progressive administration of Theodore Roosevelt in 1902. A regional problem had required a national solution; that solution was certainly easier to achieve than it might have been for two quite separate reasons. It was easy for most Americans to extend their feelings about the inferiority of the Negro to all "colored races"; in addition, China was a weak, defenseless nation, and the protests of its government did not have to be taken seriously. Chinese exclusion represented the first racist qualification of American immigration policy, although it would not be the last. In addition, the whole anti-Chinese episode in our history served as a kind of prophetic prologue for what would befall immigrants from Japan.

Significant immigration from Japan actually started about 1890. The census of that year enumerated 2039 Japanese in the entire country, more than half of them in California. According to the not always accurate immigration data of the federal government, about 25,000 immigrants came in the 1890s, 125,000 in the peak period of immigration between 1901 and 1908, and then about 10,000 a year until the Immigration Act of 1924 barred further immigration from Japan. During the entire period fewer than 300,000 Japanese were recorded as entering the United States. In comparison to the total immigration picture—between the end of the Civil War and 1924 some 30 million immigrants came to the United States—this is a very small number indeed. But even the 300,000 figure greatly overstates what some publicists liked to call the "yellow flood." Cheap and rapid trans-Pacific transportation made it possible for a number of individuals to go back and forth many times. Others were students and "birds of passage," that is, sojourners rather than immigrants. A brief population table will put the demographic data into clearer perspective (see table on page 6). Yet, as we shall see, this tiny population became the focus of local agitation, national concern, and international negotiation and insult. But before we consider the furor that was raised over them, we ought to look at the immigrants themselves.

Immigrants from Japan (hereafter called Issei, from the combination

	Japanese in U. S.	United States Population	Japanese in California	California Population
1890	2,039	63,000,000	1,147	1,200,000
1900	24,326	76,000,000	10,151	1,500,000
1910	72,157	92,000,000	41,356	2,400,000
1920	111,010	106,000,000	71,952	3,400,000

of the Japanese words for "one" and "generation"; their children, the American-born second generation, are Nisei; and the third generation are Sansei) came to the United States for exactly the same kinds of reasons that other immigrants came: for economic opportunity and to escape severe economic and social dislocations at home. The Japan which they left was rapidly undergoing its own industrial revolution. (According to W. W. Rostow, the Japanese economy "took off" between 1878 and 1900.)[8] Unlike many other contemporary immigrant groups however, emigration for the Issei did not mean rejection of the old country. Most of them maintained an interest and a pride in the accomplishments of Japan, a pride that they publicly exhibited on such traditional occasions as the Emperor's birthday or on the occurrence of special events like Admiral Togo's victory over the Russian fleet during the Russo-Japanese War.

For many of the Issei generation, the United States itself was not the first stop. The first significant trans-Pacific migration of Japanese was to the kingdom of Hawaii, where they provided cheap agricultural labor on the semifeudal sugar plantations of the American economic elite.[9] During the period of heaviest immigration (1900–1908) more than 40,000 of the Japanese entering the United States came via Hawaii. The attraction of the United States vis-à-vis Hawaii was simple: wages were higher, hours were shorter, and economic opportunity more abundant. But whether they came by way of Hawaii or directly from Japan, the Issei generation started at the bottom of the economic ladder. Few came with any significant amount of capital; the vast majority were young adult males without family ties. One Issei recently told an interviewer:

> I grew up in a farm in Japan. My father owned a fairly large piece of land, but it was heavily mortgaged. I remember how hard we all had to work, and I also remember the hard times. I saw little future in farm work; my older brothers would later run the farm, so at my first good chance I went to work in Osaka. Later I came to California

---

[8] Walt W. Rostow, *The Stages of Economic Growth: A Non-Communist Manifesto* (London: Cambridge University Press, 1960).

[9] Hilary Conroy, *The Japanese Frontier in Hawaii, 1868–1898* (Berkeley and Los Angeles: University of California Press, 1953).

and worked as a laborer in all kinds of jobs. However, for the first five years I had to work in the farms, picking fruit, vegetables, and I saved some money. Then I came to live in the city permanently.[10]

This immigrant's experience was, if not typical, common. Most of the Issei came from the Japanese countryside rather than the city; most seem to have come from somewhere above the lowest socioeconomic strata of the population; and most exhibited that combination of energy and ambition which has made the Japanese Americans the most upwardly mobile nonwhite minority in the United States.[11] (If the Japanese had been white Protestants, the tendency would be to attribute their success to what Max Weber and others have called "the Protestant Ethic." That is, that the "Puritan traits" of honesty, industry, zeal, punctuality, frugality, and regularity advanced the growth of capitalism by promoting rational, systematic economic conduct. Apart from the Japanese, the American ethnic group that best exemplifies these traits are the Jews.) Whatever its cause, the spectacular economic achievement of the Issei generation—especially within agriculture—was an important causal component of the animosity it engendered.

This achievement can be best seen in California, where the bulk of the Issei settled. By 1919 about half of the state's 70,000 Japanese were engaged in agriculture. They controlled over 450,000 acres of agricultural land, some of it among the most fruitful in the state. Although this amounted to only 1 percent of the state's land under cultivation, the labor-intensive agricultural techniques which the Issei brought from Japan produced about 10 percent of the dollar volume of the state's crops. The historian of Japanese American agriculture, Masakazu Iwata, has ably summarized the contribution the Issei made.

> [First] they filled the farm labor vacuum and thus prevented a ruinous slump. . . . [Then] as independent farm operators, the Japanese with their skill and energy helped to reclaim and improve thousands of acres of worthless lands throughout the State, lands which the white man abhorred, and made them fertile and immensely productive. They pioneered the rice industry, and planted the first citrus orchards in the hog wallow lands in the San Joaquin Valley. They played a vital part in establishing the present system of marketing fruits and vegetables, especially in Los Angeles County,

---

[10] Kitano, *Japanese Americans*, p. 16.

[11] Roger Daniels, "Westerners from the East: Oriental Immigrants Reappraised," *Pacific Historical Review*, November, 1966. See also John Modell, "The Japanese American Family: A Perspective for Future Investigations," *Pacific Historical Review*, February, 1968.

and dominated in the field of commercial truck crops. From the perspective of history, it is evident that the contributions of the Issei. . . . were undeniably a significant factor in making California one of the greatest farming states in the nation.[12]

Most of the Issei farmers achieved a steady but unspectacular prosperity; one Japanese immigrant, however, had a career that reads like a Horatio Alger story. George Shima (he Americanized his name) came to the United States directly from Japan in 1889 at the age of twenty-six with less than $1000 in capital. The son of a relatively prosperous Japanese farm owner, he worked first as a common laborer and then rather quickly became a labor contractor who specialized in marketing the services of his countrymen to white agriculturalists. He invested his profits in hitherto unused land, starting with a leasehold on 15 acres. Working in partnership with other Issei, Shima created his own agricultural empire, specializing in potatoes, then a new crop in California. By 1909 the press was referring to him as the "Potato King" of California. By 1913, when a Japanese graduate student surveyed his holdings, Shima controlled nearly 30,000 acres directly, and, through marketing agreements, handled the produce raised by many of his compatriots. By 1920 it was estimated that he controlled 85 percent of California's potato crop, valued at over $18 million that year. He employed over 500 persons in a multiracial labor force that included Caucasians. When he died, in 1926, the press estimated his estate at $15 million; his pallbearers included such dignitaries as James Rolph, Jr., the mayor of San Francisco, and David Starr Jordan, the chancellor of Stanford University. In 1909 he bought a house in one of the better residential sections of Berkeley, California, close to the university. A protest movement, led by a professor of classics, demanded that he move to an Oriental neighborhood. Shima held his ground, although he did erect a large redwood fence around the property, as he told the press, "to keep the other children from playing with his." Even an Issei millionaire could not escape the sting of discrimination.[13]

Most of the Issei, whether they lived in the city or the country, did not offend the housing mores of the majority; they lived the segregated life typical of American minority groups. Those who did not go directly into agriculture usually started out as common laborers or domestic servants. Like their rural fellow immigrants, they too demonstrated up-

---

[12] Masakazu Iwata, "The Japanese Immigrants in California Agriculture," *Agricultural History*, 1962.

[13] This and the subsequent pages on the anti-Japanese movement are condensed from Roger Daniels, *The Politics of Prejudice: The Anti-Japanese Movement in California and the Struggle for Japanese Exclusion* (Berkeley and Los Angeles: University of California Press, 1962; paperback edition, New York: Atheneum, 1968).

ward social and economic mobility. Starting with almost token wages—in 1900, $1.50 a week plus board was standard—these immigrants quickly learned English and the "ropes," and moved into better-paying jobs, although several thousand remained domestic servants. Since California trade unions almost universally barred Orientals from membership, work in manufacturing, the building trades, and many other occupations was closed to them. The typical pattern for urban Issei was to establish a small business—a laundry, a restaurant, a curio shop—or to go to work for an Issei businessman who was already established. A great many of these businesses catered to the immigrant community; others provided specialized services to whites (for example, contract gardening) or served as retail marketing outlets for Japanese agriculturalists, usually specializing in produce or flowers. A smaller group—and one that was to arouse special concern after Pearl Harbor—went into commercial fishing; more than any other group of Issei entrepreneurs the fishermen were in direct economic competition with white businessmen. Most other Issei formed a complementary rather than a competing economy. Their businesses employed almost exclusively members of their own ethnic community at lower wages and longer hours than generally prevailed.

If Californians and other westerners had been the rational "economic men" of nineteenth-century classical economic theory, there would have been no anti-Japanese movement. The Issei subeconomy neither lowered wages nor put white men out of work. Its major effect, in fact, was a lowering of the cost of fresh fruit and vegetables for the general population, and Issei agriculture was one of the bases which allowed California's population to expand as rapidly as it did, from less than 1.5 million in 1900 to almost 7 million in 1940. But race prejudice, of course, is not a rational phenomenon, even though in some instances, as in the anti-Chinese movement, it does have a certain economic rationale.[14] Nothing more clearly indicates the nonrational, inherited nature of California's anti-Japanese movement than the fact that it started when there were fewer than a thousand Japanese in the entire state.

The anti-Japanese war cry was first raised by elements of the San Francisco labor movement in 1888, and for the first two decades of agitation labor took the lead, as it had done against the Chinese.[15] In 1892 the demagogue Dennis Kearney returned to the hustings and unsuccessfully tried to base a political comeback on the slogan "The Japs Must Go!" and in the same year a San Francisco newspaper launched a self-styled journalistic "crusade" against the menace of Japanese immigration. These

---

[14] For a discussion of rationality and prejudice, see Isabella Black, "American Labour and Chinese Immigration," *Past and Present*, July, 1963, and my comments in the April, 1964, issue.

[15] *Coast Seaman's Journal* (San Francisco), July 25, 1888.

first moves were abortive: in 1892 probably not one Californian in ten had even seen a Japanese. But they were indicative of things to come. Just eight years later the real anti-Japanese movement began. At a meeting sponsored by organized labor, the Democratic mayor of San Francisco, James Duval Phelan, effectively linked the anti-Chinese and anti-Japanese movements. The major purpose of the meeting was to pressure Congress to renew Chinese exclusion, but Phelan pointed out a new danger:

> The Japanese are starting the same tide of immigration which we thought we had checked twenty years ago. . . . The Chinese and Japanese are not bona fide citizens. They are not the stuff of which American citizens can be made.

Another speaker at the same meeting was the distinguished sociologist Edward Alysworth Ross, then teaching at Stanford University. Ross rang some changes on Phelan's remarks and made a common analogy with the protective tariff: If we keep out pauper-made goods, he asked, why don't we keep out the pauper? In those years few academics championed the cause of labor (Ross would soon lose his job at Stanford because of his economic views), but most of those who did were opposed to immigrants in general and Oriental immigrants in particular. Although their grounds for this objection were ostensibly economic, most flavored their arguments with racist appeals. The same could be said for most American socialists in the years before 1920. From staid Victor Berger of Milwaukee to flamboyant Jack London of California, socialists insisted that the United States must be kept a white man's country.

These arguments of the left quickly found echoes in the more traditional segments of the political spectrum. During the summer of 1900 all three major political parties—Republicans, Democrats, and Populists—took stands against "Asiatic" immigration, and at the end of the year the national convention of the American Federation of Labor asked Congress to exclude not only Chinese, but all "Mongolians."

Agitation of this sort continued sporadically until 1905; in that year the anti-Japanese movement escalated significantly. The reasons for the escalation are to be sought both inside and outside the United States. On the world scene, the startling triumph of Japan over czarist Russia in both land and naval battles effectively challenged, for the first time, white military supremacy in Asia and raised the specter of the yellow peril. At home, heightened immigration of Japanese—45,000 came between 1903 and 1905—made the "threat" of Japanese immigration much more real than it had been five years before. In February the San Francisco *Chronicle*, a conservative Republican paper and probably the most influential on the Pacific Coast, began a concerted and deliberate anti-Japanese campaign.

The first front-page streamer, THE JAPANESE INVASION, THE PROBLEM OF THE HOUR, set the tone for the whole campaign. In addition to the usual economic and racial arguments, arguments that stressed a lowering of the standard of living and the impossibility of assimilation, the *Chronicle* injected two new and ugly elements into the agitation: sex and war. The paper insisted that Japanese were a menace to American women and that "every one of these immigrants . . . is a Japanese spy."

A little more than a week after the *Chronicle*'s campaign started, both houses of the California legislature unanimously passed a resolution asking Congress to limit the further immigration of Japanese. Included in a long bill of particulars were statements that

> Japanese laborers, by reason of race habits, mode of living, disposition and general characteristics, are undesirable. . . . Japanese . . . do not buy land [or] build or buy houses. . . . They contribute nothing to the growth of the state. They add nothing to its wealth, and they are a blight on the prosperity of it, and a great and impending danger to its welfare.

The legislature was obviously reacting in a sort of racist conditioned reflex, a reflex conditioned by decades of anti-Chinese rhetoric. Within a few years the tune of the anti-Japanese song would change: the new refrain would stress not Japanese pauperism but Japanese landholding. The 1905 legislature had one other distinction: it limited itself to an anti-Japanese resolution. For the next forty years, every session of the California legislature would attempt to pass at least one piece of anti-Japanese legislation.

A major factor in the introduction of these bills was the existence of anti-Japanese organizations and pressure groups which sprang up throughout the state from 1905 on. In May of that year the first of these organizations, the Asiatic Exclusion League, was set up. In effect, the League and its immediate successors were appendages of the powerful San Francisco labor movement. But the anti-Japanese movement appealed to more than labor; in December 1905, two California Republican congressmen, using League arguments, introduced similar Japanese exclusion bills into Congress. Although these bills never got out of committee, they produced one significant reaction: a leading southern politician, Oscar W. Underwood of Alabama, pledged that on this race question the South would support the Pacific Coast.

Despite this momentary national attention, the anti-Japanese movement failed to attract any publicity outside the Pacific Coast in 1905. When national and international notoriety did come, in the very next year, it was not immigration but school segregation that drew the spotlight. In May 1905, in response perhaps to the *Chronicle*'s continuing crusade, the San Francisco School Board announced that it intended sometime in the future to order Japanese pupils—native and foreign-born —removed from the regular schools and placed in the already existing school for Chinese. The stated reason was so that "our children should not be placed in any position where their youthful impressions may be affected by association with the Mongolian race." (The use of the term "Mongolian" was dictated by an old California school law which permitted exclusion of children of "filthy or vicious habits," or "suffering from contagious diseases," and segregation in separate schools of American Indian children and those of "Chinese or Mongolian descent." The law made no provision for Negro children.) But like so many pro-integration statements of intent today, these segregationist sentiments were left purely verbal, and no national or international notice was taken of them.

A year and a half later, the school board acted, and ordered the segregation to take place. In the meantime the famous San Francisco earthquake and fire of April 18, 1906, had taken place, and, in the chaotic conditions that followed, the anti-Japanese movement changed from peaceful if bigoted protest to direct action. Japanese restaurants, laundries, and other business establishments were picketed and boycotted, and in many instances businessmen, employees, and even white customers, were physically abused. By the fall of 1906 assaults upon individual Japanese were too frequent to have been accidental. Most of those who suffered were humble immigrants, but a distinguished party of visiting Japanese seismologists was stoned and otherwise attacked in various parts of northern California. More typical was the complaint of a laundry proprietor, as put forth in the stilted English of an employee of the Japanese consulate:

> I am proprietor of Sunset City Laundry. Soon after the earthquake the persecutions became intolerable. My drivers [of slow, horse-drawn laundry wagons] were constantly attacked on the highway, my place of business defiled by rotten eggs and fruit; windows were smashed several times. . . . The miscreants are generally young men, 17 or 18 years old. Whenever the newspapers attack the Japanese these roughs renew their misdeeds with redoubled energy.

Apparently there were never any convictions of whites for assault on Japanese during this period, although several Japanese were punished when they tried to defend themselves. It was in this atmosphere that the San Francisco School Board promulgated its segregation order on October 11, 1906. It was apparently unnoticed in the rest of the United States, and even the San Francisco papers gave it very little space. But nine days later the segregation order was front-page news in the Tokyo newspapers, and from that moment on the anti-Japanese movement was both a national and an international problem.

The Japanese government, always solicitous about the welfare of its citizens abroad, naturally protested. (Hilary Conroy has pointed out that the chief motivation for this solicitude "was the protection of her own prestige as a nation".)[16] These protests, raising as they did the question of American-Japanese friendship, naturally disturbed many Americans, but few were disturbed as mightily as President Theodore Roosevelt. Roosevelt had been aware of the growing anti-Japanese agitation on the West Coast and as early as 1905 had privately expressed his disgust with the "idiots" of the California legislature. In response to the Japanese protests of October 1906, he dispatched a Cabinet member to investigate the school situation in San Francisco and privately assured the Japanese government of American friendship. But even before the report was in, Roosevelt publicly denounced the San Francisco proposal. In his annual message of December 2, 1906, the President asserted, falsely, that Japanese were treated, in most of the United States, just as most Europeans were treated. He went on to denounce the action of the school board as a "wicked absurdity" and then proposed that the naturalization laws—which provided for the naturalization of "free white persons and persons of African descent"—be amended to permit the naturalization of Japanese.

Roosevelt thus differentiated sharply between Chinese and Japanese. As we have seen, he signed the Chinese Exclusion Act of 1902, and strongly reiterated his opposition to Chinese immigrants in 1905. The reason Roosevelt discriminated between Orientals was because of the different relative military strengths of China and Japan. As he himself put it in his 1906 message, "the mob of a single city may at any time commit acts of lawless violence that may plunge us into war." Japan was strong, so its immigrants must be treated with respect; China was weak, so its immigrants could be treated as the mob desired. But, it should be noted, Roosevelt quickly retreated from his advanced position on Japanese naturalization; he soon discovered that Congress would not permit it, and he never again publicly proposed it.

Shortly after his annual message, Roosevelt received and published the report on San Francisco schools from his Secretary of Commerce and Labor Victor H. Metcalf. It was something of an anticlimax for most of the nation to discover that the whole furor had been raised over a grand total of ninety-three Japanese students distributed among the twenty-three public schools of San Francisco. Twenty-five of these students had been born on American soil, and since they were American citizens, the federal government could do nothing for them. Separate but equal facilities had

[16] Conroy, *Japanese Frontier*, p. 140.

been condoned by the United States Supreme Court in *Plessy* v. *Ferguson* (1896), so segregation of American citizens was perfectly legal. But for the sixty-eight school children who were subjects of the empire of Japan, the government could do something. They were protected by a stronger shield than the Constitution: the 1894 treaty between Japan and the United States, which guaranteed reciprocal "most favored nation" residential rights to nationals of both countries. Secretary of State Elihu Root himself, working with Department of Justice lawyers, prepared a federal desegregation suit directed against the San Francisco School Board.

At the same time, however, the federal authorities entered into discussions with the Japanese government designed to alleviate what they considered the real problem—continued immigration from Japan. In a complicated series of maneuvers Roosevelt, at a personal interview at the White House, persuaded the San Francisco School Board to revoke the offending order, managed to restrain the California legislature from passing anti-Japanese legislation relating to schools and other matters, and began an exchange of notes with Japan which collectively became known as the Gentlemen's Agreement of 1907–1908. The Japanese government agreed to stop issuing to laborers passports that would be good in the continental United States (Japanese labor was still wanted on Hawaiian sugar plantations), but it was agreed that passports could be issued to laborers who had already been to the United States and, most significantly, "to the parents, wives and children of laborers already there."

Roosevelt and his subordinates apparently failed to realize that under the provisions of the Gentlemen's Agreement thousands of Japanese men resident in the United States would send for wives, and that these newly married couples would increase and multiply. They presented the Gentlemen's Agreement to the hostile California public as exclusion. When, under its terms, the Japanese population of California continued to grow, first largely from the immigration of women and then from natural increase, Californians and others concerned about the Japanese problem insisted that they had been betrayed by their government in Washington. Instead of easing racial tension in California, the Roosevelt administration, in the final analysis, exacerbated it.[17] The subsequent sessions of the California legislature, in 1909 and 1911, witnessed persistent attempts, usually led by Democrats, to pass anti-Japanese legislation. The measures were defeated, one way or another, by Republican majorities in both houses under pressure from national Republican administrations concerned about the possible effects of this legislation on relations between Japan and the

---

[17] Many diplomatic historians take a more favorable view of Roosevelt's efforts. See, for example, Raymond A. Esthus, *Theodore Roosevelt and Japan* (Seattle: University of Washington Press, 1966).

United States. In 1913, however, a different situation prevailed. Republicans still controlled the California government, but the Democratic administration of Woodrow Wilson was in charge nationally. California Republicans, who during three elections had suffered Democrats' slurs about their national party's position on the Japanese question—in the 1908 election one Democratic slogan was "Labor's choice [is] Bryan—Jap's choice [is] Taft"—now saw a chance to make political capital and embarrass their opponents. In this whipsaw of the politics of prejudice the Japanese issue once again became an international affair.

By 1913 California politics had become dominated by progressive Republicans, and one of the chief architects of progressivism, Hiram W. Johnson, sat in the governor's chair. Two years previously, cooperating with a national administration of his own party, he had "sat upon the lid" and prevented passage of significant anti-Japanese measures. With a Democratic administration, Johnson quite early foresaw, as he wrote his most trusted adviser, a "unique and interesting" situation and "one out of which we can get a good deal of satisfaction." What the wily Johnson foresaw came about. A popular antialien land bill, designed to forbid "aliens ineligible to citizenship" (that is, Asians) from purchasing land, moved rapidly through the California legislature, with Johnson doing some behind-the-scenes stage-managing. Johnson arranged a public hearing in the spacious Assembly chamber in Sacramento, and seems also to have planned a "spontaneous" demonstration by farmers. The leading "farmer" was, in fact, a former Congregational clergyman, Ralph Newman, who made an appeal that ended:

> Near my home is an eighty-acre tract of as fine land as there is in California. On that tract lives a Japanese. With that Japanese lives a white woman. In that woman's arms is a baby. What is that baby? It isn't a Japanese. It isn't white. It is a germ of the mightiest problem that ever faced this state; a problem that will make the black problem of the South look white.

The specter of interracial marriage or sex, although often raised by extremists, was not really a significant factor; Japanese rarely married or cohabited outside their own ethnic group. What had changed was the perceived nature of the Japanese threat. No longer the pauper immigrant, but an increasingly successful entrepreneur, Newman's image—the Japanese possessing the white woman—could be interpreted as the sexualization of a different kind of usurpation, the yellow man's taking of what the white man conceived to be his rightful place in society. With this kind of send-off, the anti-Japanese land bill seemed assured of passage.

Back in Washington, Woodrow Wilson and his Secretary of State

William Jennings Bryan were faced with persistent diplomatic protest in the very first weeks of their administration. They were reluctant to intervene, as both Roosevelt and Taft had, for three reasons. First, they feared, correctly, that the Republican California administration would reject their pleas. Second, each of them had expressed and still held distinct anti-Japanese sentiments. Third, both of them, like most Democrats of their time, held strongly Jeffersonian states' rights views, and were much more reluctant to intervene in the internal affairs of a state than were their Hamiltonian Republican predecessors. But national power brings responsibility, and Wilson and Bryan at least made an effort to moderate the California action. Bryan went all the way to California, addressed the legislature, caucused with followers, all to no avail. The Alien Land Act passed both houses overwhelmingly and was quickly signed by Johnson.

Although passage of the Alien Land Law of 1913 was a great psychic triumph for the Californians—after almost a decade they had finally thwarted Washington—it served very little real purpose, as the more astute California politicians (including Hiram Johnson) knew at the time. Japanese land tenure was not seriously affected by the law; although it prohibited further ownership by Japanese aliens, it did permit leasing. It was quite simple for the attorneys who represented Japanese interests in California to evade the alleged intent of the law in many ways. The simplest was through incorporation so that control was ostensibly held by whites. For the growing number of Issei who had American-born children, things were even easier; they simply transferred the stock or title to their citizen children whose legal guardianship they naturally assumed.

When the truth about the impotence of the bill dawned on many Californians, their bitterness against the Japanese and their own government merely increased. The years that followed, however, were years of war, and during part of that time Japan was on our side, or at least fighting the same enemy, Germany. During those years anti-Japanese activity, organized and spontaneous, was at a minimum. The years after the war, however, saw the anti-Japanese movement go over the top and move from triumph to triumph.

How representative of white California were the exclusionists? The best possible measure of the popularity of the anti-Japanese position came in 1920, when a stronger Alien Land Act, one that prohibited leasing and sharecropping as well as land purchase, was put on the California ballot as an initiative. It passed by a margin of more than 3 to 1. Few of the more than six hundred thousand California citizens who voted for the measure can have been in any way actual or potential competitors with Japanese farmers; the measure carried every county in the state, and did well in both urban and rural areas. The simple fact of the matter was that Californians had come to hate and fear Japanese with a special intensity.

Late in 1919 this hate and fear became focused in one omnibus anti-Japanese organization—the Oriental Exclusion League. Although it had a vast number of cooperating organizations, four of them provided the real clout: the California Federation of Labor, the American Legion, the State Grange, and the Native Sons and Daughters of the Golden West. This curious coalition agreed on little else—the Legion and organized labor were almost always on opposite sides of the fence—but it did formulate an anti-Japanese program about which they could all agree. They had five basic demands, four of which were quickly achieved.

1. Cancellation of the Gentlemen's Agreement
2. Exclusion of picture brides
3. Rigorous exclusion of Japanese as immigrants
4. Maintaining the bar against naturalization of Asians
5. Amending the Federal Constitution to deny citizenship even to native-born Asians

The picture brides, about whom the nativists were so bitter, need some explanation. Under the Gentlemen's Agreement, as we have seen, Japanese men already in the United States were given the right to bring in wives. The Japanese government was reasonably careful about granting such passports, and usually went far beyond the terms of the agreement. To ensure that these women immigrants would not become public charges, the husband or prospective husband was often required to present evidence to a Japanese consulate in California showing that he could support a wife, before her passport would be issued. In many instances the prospective bridegroom would return to Japan and bring back a bride. In other instances, however, friends and relatives at home would do the selecting for him. A proxy wedding would take place; a picture of the bride would be sent to California, followed, eventually, by the bride herself. As shocking as this seemed to the American ideal of romantic love, marriages arranged in such a manner were quite common in Japan and not infrequent among some European immigrant groups. The matchmakers, or go-betweens, took pride in their work, and, in fact, their reputations depended upon the success of the marriages they arranged. To the Japanese this seemed natural; to most Americans, unnatural; but to many Californians this age-old method of mate selection seemed just another aspect of a massive and diabolical plot to submerge California under a tide of yellow babies.

The California reaction to the picture brides, to the creation of yellow American citizens, can only be described as paranoid. One leading exclusionist, V. S. McClatchy, former publisher of the Sacramento *Bee* and a director of the Associated Press, once assembled "indisputable facts and figures" which demonstrated that America's Japanese population, unless checked, would reach 318,000 in 1923, 2 million in 1963, and 100 million in 2063. One female exclusionist was sure that California was being "Japanized" in the same way as the South was being "Negroized"; she warned her fellow Californiennes about "Japanese casting furtive glances at our young women." Cora W. Woodbridge, a state legislator and an officer of the California Federation of Women's Clubs, dismissed the Issei woman as "a beast of burden up to the time of the birth of her child [who], within a day or two at most, resumes her task and continues it from twelve to sixteen hours a day." Even more outrageous to the convinced exclusionists were the white allies of the Japanese, who were called "Jap-lovers" and "white-Japs, who masquerade as Americans, but, in fact, are servants of the mikado." All this emotion, remember, was generated at a time when there were only 70,000 Japanese in the state; they amounted to one Californian in fifty. But Californians were convinced that they were threatened. After passage of the 1920 Alien Land Act, which inhibited the growth of Issei agriculture but did not cripple it, the state had used all its alternatives. As had been the case with the anti-Chinese movement, the goals of the exclusionists could only be achieved with federal power.

California, of course, had allies. Most other western states, but particularly Oregon and Washington, had anti-Japanese movements of their own and passed similar alien land laws. In addition, most southern senators and representatives stood ready to support their fellow "beleaguered" whites. But a western and southern bloc cannot carry Congress. National support had to be organized. Much of the support came from two of the major California pressure groups. At the national level both the American Legion and the American Federation of Labor worked hard for exclusion. But even more crucial support came, however indirectly, from Japan itself. Sometime between the beginning of the Russo-Japanese War and the end of World War I the Japanese became, in the eyes of most Americans, villains. Aggressive actions by Japan, particularly its demands against China and its conflict with the United States in Siberia during the short-lived occupation of parts of Soviet East Asia, helped cause American public opinion to turn against Japan, thus providing more support for the exclusionist position.

But at least equally important was the growing racist feeling in the United States, a feeling exacerbated by both the postwar retreat from internationalism and the domestic upsurge against "un-American" ideas and individuals. Intellectual racists like Lothrop Stoddard and Madison Grant warned of a "rising tide of color" that menaced white civilization; the second Ku Klux Klan, focusing its attack on Catholics, Jews, and foreigners, gained brief power and pseudorespectability in much of the Midwest and some of the East. These two factors, added to the persistent anti-Japanese propaganda and organizational activity of the western exclusionists, eventually created a climate of opinion that made exclusion possible.

Perhaps the key organizational meeting, at the national level, was held in the caucus room of the United States House of Representatives on April 20, 1921. Called by Senator Hiram Johnson and the rest of the California delegation, it united one senator and one representative from each of twelve other western states into an informal executive committee to push exclusion through Congress. The group insisted that the West was being "invaded." Their argument is worth quoting at length.

> The process of invasion has been aptly termed "peaceful penetration." The invasion is by an alien people. They are a people unassimilable by marriage. They are a people who are a race unto themselves, and by virtue of that very fact ever will be a race and a nation unto themselves, it matters not what may be the land of their birth.
>
> Economically we are not able to compete with them and maintain the American standard of living; racially we cannot assimilate them. Hence we must exclude them from our shores as settlers in our midst and prohibit them from owning land. Those already here will be protected in their right to the enjoyment of life, liberty, and legally acquired property. . . .
>
> The alternative [to exclusion] is that the richest section of the United States will gradually come into the complete control of an alien race. . . . A careful study of the subject will convince anyone who will approach it with an open mind that the attitude of California, and other states . . . is not only justifiable but essential to the national welfare.[18]

But before this powerful Congressional group could get into action, the Supreme Court of the United States made things a little easier for the exclusionists. As we have seen, Japanese and other Asians were considered aliens ineligible to citizenship. This presumption stemmed, not from any constitutional bar, but from the naturalization statute, which, after the Dred Scott decision of 1857 and the Fourteenth Amendment, had been rewritten to permit naturalization of "white persons" and aliens of African descent. Although in some jurisdictions—most significantly Hawaii—courts had naturalized Japanese and other aliens, prevailing practice had been to bar them. This practice was challenged by Takao Ozawa, born in Japan but educated in the United States. The court conceded that he was "well qualified by character and education for citizenship."

Ozawa's counsel, George W. Wickersham, who had been Attorney

---

[18] House Document No. 89, 67th Cong., 1st Sess. (1921), p. 4.

General under William Howard Taft, argued that in the absence of any specific Congressional provision barring Japanese, they were eligible for citizenship, and he pointed out that the original language, which went back to 1790, had spoken of "free white persons." The original intent of Congress, Wickersham insisted, had not in any way been aimed at Japanese or other Asians. The court unanimously rejected Wickersham's argument, and confirmed the denial of citizenship to Ozawa.[19] This decision meant that Congressional exclusionists could now safely use the time-honored "aliens ineligible to citizenship formula" and did not have to resort to a special Japanese exclusion act, as had been the case with the Chinese.

For tactical reasons, the exclusionists bided their time; exclusion of Japanese would come, not through special action, but as a part of the general restriction of immigration which the nativist climate of the 1920s made a foregone conclusion.

What became the National Origins Act of 1924 originated in the House of Representatives in late 1923. After much backing and filling the House Committee on Immigration—under the chairmanship of a West Coast representative, Albert Johnson of Washington—came up with a frankly racist quota system whose basic aims were to reduce greatly the volume of immigration in general and to all but eliminate "non-Anglo-Saxon" immigration from eastern and southern Europe. As reported by the Committee and passed by the House, the bill also contained a section barring all "aliens ineligible to citizenship." (Had the quota system, which was based on the number of individuals from each country reported in the 1890 census, been applied to Japan, the result would have been a maximum of 100 immigrants a year.)

In the Senate, however, exclusionists did not control the Immigration Committee, and the bill reported to that body provided for a Japanese quota. While the debate was in progress Secretary of State Charles Evans Hughes suggested to Japanese Ambassador Masanao Hanihara that a letter from him containing an authoritative description of the Gentlemen's Agreement would be helpful in combating the drive for exclusion, which neither government wanted. Hanihara complied. In the course of the letter to Hughes, which was made public, Hanihara spoke accurately of the possible results of exclusion as opposed to a token quota.

> I have stated or rather repeated all this to you rather candidly and in a most friendly spirit, for I realize, as I believe you do, the grave consequences which the enactment of the measure retaining [the

---

[19] For an analysis of *Ozawa* and similar cases, see Milton R. Konvitz, *The Alien and the Asiatic in American Law* (Ithaca, N.Y.: Cornell University Press, 1946), pp. 81 ff.

aliens ineligible to citizenship] provision would inevitably bring upon the otherwise happy and mutually advantageous relations between our two countries.

At the time Hanihara's note was made public by Hughes, it seemed possible that the Senate, usually more sensitive to the international implications of its actions, would reject the exclusion provisions of the House bill. But in a shrewd but utterly unprincipled tactical stroke, Senator Henry Cabot Lodge of Massachusetts, seizing upon the phrase "grave consequences," made the language of the Japanese ambassador's friendly note seem to be a "veiled threat." "The United States," he insisted, "cannot legislate by the exercise by any other country of veiled threats." Once the matter had been made a question of national honor, reason flew out the window. Senators who had previously expressed themselves as favorable to a Japanese quota or a continuation of the Gentlemen's Agreement, now, for what they said were patriotic reasons, joined the exclusionist side of the debate. On the key roll call, the Senate vote was 76–2 against the Japanese.

With the passage of the Immigration Act of 1924 all but one of the basic demands of the anti-Japanese movement had been met. Although many individual exclusionists continued to agitate for a constitutional amendment that would deprive Nisei of their citizenship, such an amendment was never seriously considered by Congress. But, after a campaign of nearly a quarter century, exclusion had been achieved, the immigration question had been settled. The exclusionists were exultant: "I am repaid for my efforts," wrote former California Senator James D. Phelan who had been an exclusionist from the beginning; "the Japs are routed."

But left in the wake of the rout was a sizable immigrant community with a growing number of citizen offspring. At the time of the Gentlemen's Agreement male Issei had outnumbered females by better than 7 to 1; the years of largely female immigration after 1908 had somewhat redressed that balance, but many thousands of older Issei were doomed to bachelorhood if they remained in America. Despite the halt in immigration, the Japanese population of the United States continued to rise (the slight drop in total population between 1930 and 1940 would soon be reversed by the births of Sansei, which were just beginning), as the table indicates:

JAPANESE POPULATION, CONTINENTAL UNITED STATES

	Total	Alien	Native	% Native
1920	111,010	81,383	29,672	26.7
1930	138,834	70,477	68,357	49.2
1940	126,947	47,305	79,642	62.7

The Japanese American community was thus really becoming two communities in the years after 1920: the Issei community, alien and somewhat Japan-centered, and the Nisei community, native and distinctly American-oriented. As the years passed, the first grew steadily older and smaller—absolutely and relatively—while the second matured and saw its influence grow. But during most of these years the overwhelming majority of Nisei were children. In a typical Issei family, children were born in the years 1918–1922 to a thirty-five-year-old father and a twenty-five-year-old mother; this meant that the numerically most significant group of Nisei were coming of age between the years 1939 and 1943. Even without any external crisis, generational conflict surely would have arisen between the Issei and their children. As John Modell has observed:

[The Nisei] had inherited from his parents a remarkable desire to succeed in the face of hardship, but had also learned the American definition of success, by which standard the accommodation made by his parents could not be considered satisfactory.[20]

The older immigrant generation and their American children had many conflicts, but essentially these conflicts were over life style. The Issei, like many immigrant groups before and since, tried to re-create a Japanese society in America, but the image of Japan which most of them held was static. They remembered, as immigrants usually do, the Japan of their youth, not the emerging, industrializing Japan of the twenties and thirties. Since the United States deliberately tried to keep them separate by both law and custom, the Issei were probably better insulated against Americanization than were contemporary immigrant groups from Europe. Within the Issei community almost all the institutions—the press, the church, and the other associational groups—were Japan- and Japanese-language centered. At the same time, membership in a broad spectrum of Americanizing institutions was denied to them. Had the immigrant generation been eligible for naturalization and at least potential voters, certain opportunities would have been open to them.

On the other hand, despite their own cultural isolation, the Issei insisted that their children not only accept education but excel in it. The Nisei thus went to school and were subjected to the most powerful Americanizing influence; fortunately for them, their number in any school was generally so small that the classrooms they attended were truly integrated. Therefore, they participated, from early childhood, in at least a part

---

[20] John Modell, "Class or Ethnic Solidarity: The Japanese American Company Union," paper read at the Pacific Coast Branch Meeting, American Historical Association, August, 1968.

of American society; despite the general anti-Orientalism of western American society, the schools themselves seem to have been, almost without exception, more than fair to the Nisei children. At least part of the explanation for this was the exceptional behavior and aspiration of the Nisei children; from the very first they charmed their American teachers and ranked quite high in scholastic achievement. That these achievements were not always appreciated by the rest of society is perhaps best illustrated by the case of John Aiso, now a judge in Los Angeles. He was the Los Angeles winner in the American Legion oratorical contest one year, but the authorities of that organization sent the second place finisher, a Caucasian, to represent Los Angeles in the national finals in Washington.

Outside school, however, the Nisei faced a society that rejected them regardless of their accomplishments. Fully credentialed Nisei education majors, for example, were virtually unemployable as teachers in the very schools in which they had excelled. Whatever their skills, most Nisei were forced into the ethnic economic community; their parents expected and accepted this—shouldn't children follow in the footsteps of their parents? —but the Nisei resented and chafed at the low wages, long hours, and lack of status which jobs in the ethnic community entailed. As one Nisei wrote, in 1937:

> I am a fruitstand worker. It is not a very attractive nor distinguished occupation. . . . I would much rather it were doctor or lawyer . . . but my aspiration of developing into such [was] frustrated long ago. . . . I am only what I am, a professional carrot washer.[21]

The almost total lack of economic opportunity outside the ethnic community had closed down the horizons for this young man. He went on to say that the zenith of his aspirations was to save some money and get a business of his own, which would probably be a fruit or vegetable market. Other Nisei were similarly "trapped" in agriculture, gardening, curio shops, and other aspects of the economic ghetto. Despite what Modell calls their "American definition of success," all but a very few of the maturing Nisei generation found that their "safest recourse" was within the ethnic economic structure.

There was generational political and cultural conflict as well. Most of the Issei identified with Japan. Their organizations—for example, the Japanese Chamber of Commerce of Los Angeles—tended to support or at least find a rationale for Japanese aggression. In a 1931 publication the Chamber complained of "China's oppressive policy toward the Japanese" and insisted that the purpose of Japanese troops in Manchuria was "purely

---

[21] Taishi Matsumoto, "The Protest of a Professional Carrot Washer," *Kashu Mainichi*, April 4, 1937, as cited by Modell, "Class or Ethnic Solidarity."

to protect the life and property of our countrymen" and that "we possess no political ambition." Similar treatment was given to what the Japanese liked to call the "China incident" of the mid-1930's.[22]

The Nisei did not share in these sentiments. It was not so much a case of opposing the interests of Japan, although there were a few members of both the immigrant and second generation who participated in such anti-Japanese activities as picketing Japanese ships in the late 1930s. It was simply that the vast majority of the Nisei were almost wholly America-oriented and simply did not concern themselves with things Japanese. As early as the 1920s they began to form their own organizations; there were Japanese American Young Republicans and Young Democrats and even some all-Japanese American Legion posts. What was to become the most important of the Nisei organizations—the Japanese American Citizens League (JACL)—formally came into being in 1930 and had arisen out of a number of local and regional organizations of the second generation.

Even if there had been no war crisis, the JACL was on a collision course with the organizations of the older generation. Since it was an organization for citizens, the older generation was barred; since it stressed Americanization and minimized even cultural ties with Japan, its goals were somewhat repugnant to many of the Issei, especially to the community leaders. The JACL creed, written in 1940, perhaps best expresses the orientation of the more articulate Nisei on the eve of World War II, and is worth quoting in full.

I am proud that I am an American citizen of Japanese ancestry, for my very background makes me appreciate more fully the wonderful advantages of this nation. I believe in her institutions, ideals and traditions; I glory in her heritage; I boast of her history; I trust in her future. She has granted me liberties and opportunities such as no individual enjoys in this world today. She has given me an education befitting kings. She has entrusted me with the responsibilities of the franchise. She has permitted me to build a home, to earn a livelihood, to worship, think, speak and act as I please—as a free man equal to every other man.

Although some individuals may discriminate against me, I shall never become bitter or lose faith, for I know that such persons are not representative of the majority of the American people. True, I shall do all in my power to discourage such practices, but I shall do it in the American way—above board, in the open, through courts of law, by education, by proving myself to be worthy of equal treatment

---

[22] Japanese Chamber of Commerce, *The Present Situation in Manchuria and Shanghai* (Los Angeles, ca. 1931).

and consideration. I am firm in my belief that American sportsman-
ship and attitude of fair play will judge citizenship and patriotism
on the basis of action and achievement, and not on the basis of
physical characteristics. Because I believe in America, and I trust she
believes in me, and because I have received innumerable benefits
from her, I pledge myself to do honor to her at all times and all
places; to support her constitution; to obey her laws; to respect her
flag; to defend her against all enemies, foreign and domestic; to
actively assume my duties and obligations as a citizen, cheerfully and
without any reservations whatsoever, in the hope that I may become
a better American in a greater America.[23]

This hypernationalism, as we have seen, did not spring from the
Nisei experience or accurately reflect the current status of the second
generation. It was, rather, an expression of expectations, a hopeful vision
of what the future would be like. As many historians of immigration have
observed, when the second generation becomes patriotic, quite often it
tries to become 200 percent American. A good part of this overreaction is
compensation and a conscious rejection of an alien heritage that is seen as
retarding the aspirations of the second-generation group concerned.
Another factor is surely the belief, conscious or unconscious, that if only
it protests its loyalty loudly enough, the majority will come to believe its
protestations. In addition, of course, many of the Nisei had become so
thoroughly Americanized that they actually believed the creed as written,
although one wonders how the "professional carrot washer" with his
frustrated ambitions felt about the "wonderful advantages . . . liberties
and opportunities such as no individual enjoys in this world today."
    But, whatever its basic cause or motivation, the superpatriotism of
the JACL availed the Nisei little. They were prepared to defend America
"against all her enemies," but when war came America identified them as
the enemy. They tried, in many ways with success, to be better Americans
than most of their white fellow citizens, but when the chips were down
their countrymen saw only the color of their skin and remembered only
that their parents had come from the land of the rising sun.

---

[23] Written by Mike Masaoka some time in 1940, it was published in the *Congressional Record* for May 9, 1941, p. A2205.

2

PEARL HARBOR AND THE YELLOW PERIL

If the attack on Pearl Harbor came as a devastating shock to most Americans, for those of Japanese ancestry it was like a nightmare come true. Throughout the 1930s the Nisei generation dreaded the possibility of a war between the United States and Japan; although some in both the Japanese and American communities fostered the illusion that the emerging Nisei generation could help bridge the gap between the rival Pacific powers, most Nisei, at least, understood that this was a chimera. As early as 1937 Nisei gloom about the future predominated. One Nisei spoke prophetically about what might happen to Japanese Americans in a Pacific war. Rhetorically he asked his fellow Nisei students at the University of California:

> . . . what are we going to do if war does break out between United States and Japan? . . . In common language we can say "we're sunk." Even if the Nisei wanted to fight for America, what chances? Not a chance! . . . our properties would be confiscated and most likely [we would be] herded into prison camps—perhaps we would be slaughtered on the spot.[1]

---

[1] *Campanile Review* (Berkeley), Fall, 1937.

As tensions increased, so did Nisei anxieties; and in their anxiety some Nisei tried to accentuate their loyalty and Americanism by disparaging the generation of their fathers. Newspaper editor Togo Tanaka, for example, speaking to a college group in early 1941, insisted that the Nisei must face what he called "the question of loyalty" and assumed that since the Issei were "more or less tumbleweeds with one foot in America and one foot in Japan," real loyalty to America could be found only in his own generation. A Los Angeles Nisei jeweler expressed similar doubts later the same year. After explaining to a Los Angeles *Times* columnist that many if not most of the older generation were pro-Japanese rather than pro-American, he expressed his own generation's fears. "We talk of almost nothing but this great crisis. We don't know what's going to happen. Sometimes we only look for a concentration camp."[2]

While the attention of Japanese Americans was focused on the Pacific, most other Americans gave primary consideration to Europe, where in September 1939 World War II had broken out. Hitler's amazing blitzkrieg against the west in the spring of 1940—which overran, in quick succession, Denmark and Norway and then Holland, Belgium, Luxembourg, and France—caused the United States to accelerate its defense program and institute the first peacetime draft in its history. Stories, now known to be wildly exaggerated, told of so-called fifth column and espionage activities, created much concern about the loyalty of aliens, particularly German-born aliens, some 40,000 of whom were organized into the overtly pro-Nazi German-American Bund. As a component part of the defense program, Congress passed, in 1940, an Alien Registration Act, which required the registration and fingerprinting of all aliens over fourteen years of age. In addition, as we now know, the Department of Justice, working through the Federal Bureau of Investigation, was compiling a relatively modest list of dangerous or subversive aliens—Germans, Italians, and Japanese—who were to be arrested or interned at the outbreak of war with their country. The commendable restraint of the Department of Justice's plans was due, first of all, to the liberal nature of the New Deal. The Attorney General, Francis Biddle, was clearly a civil libertarian, as befitted a former law clerk of Oliver Wendell Holmes, Jr.

Elsewhere in the government however, misgivings about possible fifth column and sabotage activity, particularly by Japanese, were strongly felt. For example, one congressman, John D. Dingell (D-Mich.), wrote the President to suggest that Japanese in the United States and Hawaii be used as hostages to ensure good behavior by Japan. In August 1941, shortly after Japanese assets in the United States were frozen and the Japanese made it difficult for some one hundred Americans to leave Japan, Dingell

---

[2] Tom Treanor, "The Home Front," Los Angeles *Times*, August 6, 1941.

suggested that as a reprisal the United States should "cause the forceful detention or imprisonment in a concentration camp of ten thousand alien Japanese in Hawaii. . . . It would be well to remind Japan," he continued, "that there are perhaps one hundred fifty thousand additional alien Japanese in the United States who [can] be held in a reprisal reserve."[3]

And, in the White House itself, concern was evidenced. Franklin Roosevelt, highly distrustful of official reports and always anxious to have independent checks on the bureaucracy, set up an independent "intelligence" operation, run by John Franklin Carter. Carter, who as the "Unofficial Observer" and "Jay Franklin" had written some of the most brilliant New Deal journalism and would later serve as an adviser to President Harry S Truman and Governor Thomas E. Dewey, used newspapermen and personal friends to make special reports. In early November he received a report on the West Coast Japanese from Curtis B. Munson. His report stressed the loyalty of the overwhelming majority, and he understood that even most of the disloyal Japanese Americans hoped that "by remaining quiet they [could] avoid concentration camps or irresponsible mobs." Munson was, however, "horrified" to observe that

> dams, bridges, harbors, power stations etc., are wholly unguarded. The harbor of San Pedro [Los Angeles' port] could be razed by fire completely by four men with hand grenades and a little study in one night. Dams could be blown and half of lower California could actually die of thirst. . . . One railway bridge at the exit from the mountains in some cases could tie up three or four main railroads.[4]

Munson felt that despite the loyalty or quiescence of the majority, this situation represented a real threat because "there are still Japanese in the United States who will tie dynamite around their waist and make a human bomb out of themselves."[5] This imaginary threat apparently worried the President too, for he immediately sent the memo on to Secretary of War Henry L. Stimson, specifically calling his attention to Munson's warnings about sabotage. In early December, Army Intelligence drafted a reply (which in the confusion following Pearl Harbor was never sent) arguing, quite correctly as it turned out, that "widespread sabotage by Japanese is not expected . . . identification of dangerous Japanese on the West Coast is reasonably complete."[6] Although neither of these nor other similar

---

[3] Dingell to FDR, August 18, 1941, Franklin D. Roosevelt Library, Hyde Park, Official File 197.

[4] Munson's Report enclosed in Memo, FDR-Stimson, November 8, 1941, Franklin D. Roosevelt Library, Hyde Park, "Stimson Folder."

[5] *Ibid.*

[6] Stetson Conn, "Notes," Office, Chief of Military History, U.S. Army. Illuminating but fragmentary details of the Carter intelligence operations may be found in the Carter Mss., University of Wyoming.

proposals and warnings was acted upon before the attack on Pearl Harbor, the mere fact that they were suggested and received consideration in the very highest governmental circles indicates the degree to which Americans were willing to believe almost anything about the Japanese. This belief, in turn, can be understood only if one takes into account the half century of agitation and prophecy about the coming American-Japanese war and the dangers of the United States being overwhelmed by waves of yellow soldiers aided by alien enemies within the gates.

This irrational fear of Oriental conquest, with its racist and sex-fantasy overtones, can be most conveniently described as the "yellow peril," a term probably first used by German Kaiser Wilhelm II about 1895. As is so often the case, the phenomenon existed long before the name. Between 1880 and 1882 three obscure California publicists produced works describing the successful invasion and conquest of the United States by hordes of Chinese. These works were undoubtedly concocted to stimulate and profit from the initial campaign for Chinese exclusion, successfully consummated in 1882. There is no evidence that they were taken seriously by any significant number of people; in that period, after all, China was a victim, not a predator. But, by the end of the century, a potential predator had appeared; in 1894 formerly isolated and backward Japan won its first modern naval battle, defeating the Chinese off the Yalu River. The very next year, that prince of Jingoes, Henry Cabot Lodge, then a Republican congressman from Massachusetts, warned Congress that the Japanese "understand the future . . . they have just whipped somebody, and they are in a state of mind when they think that they can whip anybody." In 1898, during the discussion of the American annexation of Hawaii, Senator Cushman K. Davis (R-Minn.), chairman of the Senate Foreign Relations Committee, warned his colleagues that the mild controversy with Japan over Hawaii was merely "the preliminary skirmish in the great coming struggle between" East and West.

These still nascent fears about Japan were greatly stimulated when the Japanese badly defeated Russia in the war of 1904–1905, the first triumph of Asians over Europeans in modern times. The shots fired at Mukden and in the Straits of Tushima were truly shots heard round the world. Throughout Asia the Japanese victory undoubtedly stimulated nationalism and resistance to colonialism; in Europe, and particularly in the United States, it greatly stimulated fears of conquest by Asia. Shortly after the end of that war the "yellow peril" was adopted by its most significant American disseminator, newspaper mogul William Randolph Hearst. Although the theme of possible Japanese attack had been initiated by a rival paper, the San Francisco *Chronicle*, it was Hearst's San Francisco *Examiner*, as well as the rest of his chain, which made the theme of danger from Asia uniquely its own. Although there are earlier scattered references to the external Japanese threat, the real opening salvo of what the chain later called its thirty-five-year war with Japan began in the *Examiner* on December 20, 1906. Its front page that day proclaimed

JAPAN SOUNDS OUR COASTS
Brown Men Have
Maps and Could
Land Easily

The next year the Hearst papers printed the first full-scale account of a Pacific war between the United States and Japan. Richmond Pearson Hobson, who had translated an inept but heroic exploit in the Spanish-American War into a seat in Congress (he was an Alabama Democrat), was the author of the two-part Sunday Supplement fantasy. Under the headline JAPAN MAY SEIZE THE PACIFIC COAST, Hobson wrote, "The Yellow Peril is here." Unless a really big navy were built, Hobson calculated, an army of "1,207,700 men could conquer the Pacific Coast." He predicted that Japan would soon conquer China and thus "command the military resources of the whole yellow race."

An even more elaborate military fantasy—or rather a series of fantasies—was concocted by "General" Homer Lea. Lea was a Sinophile who served as a military adviser to Sun Yat Sen. There is no evidence, despite the claims of naïve publicists, that he ever commanded troops in battle. His most important literary work, *The Valor of Ignorance*, was published in 1909 and reissued, with an effusive introduction by Clare Booth Luce, shortly after Pearl Harbor. It foretold, in great detail, a Japanese conquest of the Philippine Islands, quickly followed by a landing on the Pacific Coast and the occupation of California, Oregon, and Washington. Lea, who felt that only professional armies could fight, insisted that the small American army would be no match for the Japanese. In florid prose, he described the results of this conquest.

> Not months, but years, must elapse before armies equal to the Japanese are able to pass in parade. These must then make their way over deserts such as no armies have ever heretofore crossed; scale the entrenched and stupendous heights that form the redoubts of the desert moats; attempting, in the valor of their ignorance, the militarily impossible; turning mountain gorges into the ossuaries of their dead, and burdening the desert winds with the spirits of their slain. The repulsed and distracted forces to scatter, as heretofore, dissension throughout the Union, breed rebellions, class and sectional insurrections, until this heterogenous Republic, in its principles, shall disintegrate, and again into the palm of re-established monarchy pay the toll of its vanity and its scorn. [pp. 306–307]

Hearst, Hobson, and Lea were all essentially conservative, social darwinistic racists. But the yellow peril was popular on the left as well. The English Fabian Socialist H. G. Wells, perhaps the greatest English-speaking science fiction writer, is best known for his fantasy about a Martian invasion. But in his *War in the Air* (1908) Orientals rather than Martians were the bogeymen. In the novel Wells rather accurately predicts World War I, and has the United States, France, and Great Britain locked in a death struggle with Germany. Then, without warning, Japan and China indiscriminately attack the white powers almost destroying civilization in the process. A character comments, "the Yellow Peril was a peril after all."

Even during World War I, when Japan fought Germany, anti-Japanese military propaganda did not cease; the publication of the infamous Zimmermann telegram of early 1917 which proposed a German-Mexican-Japanese alliance against the United States further inflamed American, and particularly Pacific Coast, feeling, even though Japan, interested in annexations in the Pacific and on the East Asian Mainland, clearly wanted to have nothing to do with it. During and after the war a number of anti-Japanese movies, which often showed the Japanese actually invading or planning to invade the United States, were produced and shown in theaters throughout the country; some of the most noxious were made by the motion picture arm of the Hearst communications empire. Sunday supplements and cheap pulp magazines featured the "yellow peril" theme throughout the 1920s and 1930s and a mere inventory of "yellow peril" titles would cover many pages. It is impossible, of course, to judge with any accuracy the impact or influence of this propaganda, but it seems clear that well before the actual coming of war a considerable proportion of the American public had been conditioned not only to the probability of a Pacific war with Japan—that was, after all, a geopolitical fact of twentieth-century civilization—but also to the proposition that this war would involve an invasion of the continental United States in which Japanese residents and secret agents would provide the spearhead of the attack. After war came at Pearl Harbor and for years thereafter many Japanophobes insisted that, to use Wells's phrase, "the Yellow Peril was a peril after all," but this is to misunderstand completely Japan's intentions and capabilities during the Great Pacific War. The Japanese military planners never contemplated an invasion of the continental United States, and, even had they done so, the logistical problems were obviously beyond Japan's capacity as a nation. But, often in history, what men believe to be true is more important than the truth itself because the mistaken belief becomes a basis for action. These two factors—the long racist and anti-Oriental tradition plus the widely believed "yellow peril" fantasy—when triggered by the traumatic mechanism provided by the attack on Pearl

Harbor, were the necessary preconditions for America's concentration camps. But beliefs, even widely held beliefs, are not always translated into action. We must now discover how this particular set of beliefs— the inherent and genetic disloyalty of individual Japanese plus the threat of an imminent Japanese invasion—produced public policy and action, the mass removal and incarceration of the West Coast Japanese Americans.[7]

* * *

As is well known, despite decades of propaganda and apprehension about a Pacific war, the reality, the dawn attack at Pearl Harbor on Sunday, December 7, 1941, came as a stunning surprise to most Americans. Throughout the nation the typical reaction was disbelief, followed by a determination to close ranks and avenge a disastrous defeat. Faced with the fact of attack, the American people entered the war with perhaps more unity than has existed before or since. But if a calm determination to get on with the job typified the national mood, the mood of the Pacific Coast was nervous and trigger-happy, if not hysterical. A thousand movies and stories and reminiscences have recorded the solemnity with which the nation reacted to that "day of infamy" in 1941. Yet, at Gilmore Field, in Los Angeles, 18,000 spectators at a minor league professional football game between the Hollywood Bears and the Columbus Bulldogs "jumped to their feet and cheered wildly when the public address system announced that a state of war existed between Japan and the United States."

The state's leading paper, the Los Angeles *Times* (Dec. 8, 1941), quickly announced that California was "a zone of danger" and invoked the ancient vigilante tradition of the West by calling for

> alert, keen-eyed civilians [who could be] of yeoman service in coop-
> erating with the military authorities against spies, saboteurs and fifth
> columnists. We have thousands of Japanese here. . . . Some, perhaps
> many, are . . . good Americans. What the rest may be we do not
> know, nor can we take a chance in the light of yesterday's demonstra-
> tion that treachery and double-dealing are major Japanese weapons.

Day after day, throughout December, January, February, and March, almost the entire Pacific Coast press (of which the *Times* was a relatively restrained example) spewed forth racial venom against all Japanese. The term Jap, of course, was standard usage. Japanese, alien and native-born, were also "Nips," "yellow men," "Mad dogs," and "yellow vermin," to name only a few of the choicer epithets. *Times* columnist Ed Ainsworth

---

[7] For a fuller treatment of the "yellow peril," see Roger Daniels, *The Politics of Prejudice* (Berkeley and Los Angeles: University of California Press, 1962), pp. 65–78.

cautioned his readers "to be careful to differentiate between races. The Chinese and Koreans both hate the Japs more than we do. . . . Be sure of nationality before you are rude to anybody." (*Life* Magazine soon rang some changes on this theme for a national audience with an article— illustrated by comic strip artist Milton Caniff, creator of *Terry and the Pirates* and, later, *Steve Canyon*—which purported to explain how to tell "Japs" from other Asian nationalities.) The sports pages, too, furnished their share of abuse. Just after a series of murderous and sometimes fatal attacks on Japanese residents by Filipinos, one sports page feature was headlined FILIPINO BOXERS NOTED FOR COURAGE, VALOR.

Newspaper columnists, as always, were quick to suggest what public policy should be. Lee Shippey, a Los Angeles writer who often stressed that *some* Japanese were all right, prophetically suggested a solution to California's Japanese problem. He proposed the establishment of "a number of big, closely guarded, closely watched truck farms on which Japanese-Americans could earn a living and assure us a steady supply of vegetables." If a Nazi had suggested doing this with Poles, Shippey, a liberal, undoubtedly would have called it a slave labor camp. But the palm for *shrecklichkeit* must go to Westbrook Pegler, a major outlet of what Oswald Garrison Villard once called "the sewer system of American journalism." Taking time off from his vendettas with Eleanor Roosevelt and the American labor movement, Pegler proposed, on December 9, that every time the Axis murdered hostages, the United States should retaliate by raising them "100 victims selected out of [our] concentration camps," which Pegler assumed would be set up for subversive Germans and Italians and "alien Japanese."

Examples of newspaper incitement to racial violence appeared daily (some radio commentators were even worse). In addition, during the period that the Japanese Americans were still at large, the press literally abounded with stories and, above all, headlines, which made the already nervous general public believe that military or paramilitary Japanese activists were all around them. None of these stories had any basis in fact; amazingly, there was not one demonstrable incident of sabotage committed by a Japanese American, alien or native-born, during the entire war. Here are a few representative headlines.

JAP BOAT FLASHES MESSAGE ASHORE

ENEMY PLANES SIGHTED OVER CALIFORNIA COAST

TWO JAPANESE WITH MAPS AND ALIEN LITERATURE SEIZED

JAP AND CAMERA HELD IN BAY CITY

VEGETABLES FOUND FREE OF POISON

CAPS ON JAPANESE TOMATO PLANTS POINT TO AIR BASE

JAPANESE HERE SENT VITAL DATA TO TOKYO

CHINESE ABLE TO SPOT JAP

MAP REVEALS JAP MENACE

Network of Alien Farms Covers

Strategic Defense Areas over Southland

JAPS PLAN COAST ATTACK IN APRIL WARNS CHIEF OF KOREAN SPY BAND[8]

In short, any reading of the wartime Pacific Coast press—or for that matter viewing the wartime movies that still pollute our television channels —shows clearly that, although a distinction was continually being made between "good" and "bad" Germans (a welcome change from World War I), few distinctions were ever made between Japanese. The evil deeds of Hitler's Germany were the deeds of bad men; the evil deeds of Tojo and Hirohito's Japan were the deeds of a bad race. While the press was throwing fuel on the fires of racial animosity, other faggots were contributed by politicians, federal officials, and, above all, the military. The governor of California, Culbert L. Olson, a liberal Democrat, had insisted, before Pearl Harbor, that Japanese Americans should enjoy all their rights and privileges even if war with Japan came, and correctly pointed out that equal protection under the law was a "basic tenet" of American government. But Olson's constitutional scruples were a casualty of Pearl Harbor: on December 8, the governor told the press that he was thinking of ordering all Japanese, alien and citizen, to observe house arrest "to avoid riot and disturbance."[9]

The Department of Justice, working through the FBI and calling on local law enforcement officials for assistance and detention, began roundups of what it considered "dangerous" enemy aliens. Throughout the nation this initial roundup involved about 3000 persons, half of whom were Japanese. (All but a handful of these lived on the Pacific Coast.) In other words the federal officials responsible for counterespionage thought that some 1500 persons of Japanese ancestry, slightly more than 1 percent of the nation's Japanese population, constituted some kind of threat to the nation. Those arrested, often in the dead of night, were almost universally of the immigrant, or Issei, generation, and thus, no matter how long they had lived here, "enemy aliens" in law. (It must be kept in mind that American law prohibited the naturalization of Asians.) Those arrested were community leaders, since the government, acting as it so often

---

[8] Headlines and quotations from the Los Angeles *Times*, December 8, 1941–February 23, 1942, *passim*; similar material may be found in almost any West Coast paper for the period.

[9] Robert E. Burke, *Olson's New Deal for California* (Berkeley and Los Angeles: University of California Press, 1953), p. 201.

does on the theory of guilt by association, automatically hauled in the officers and leading lights of a number of Japanese organizations and religious groups. Many of these people were surely "rooting" for the Emperor rather than the President and thus technically subversive, but most of them were rather elderly and inoffensive gentlemen and not a threat to anything. This limited internment, however, was a not too discreditable performance for a government security agency, but it must be noted that even at this restrained level the government acted much more harshly, in terms of numbers interned, toward Japanese nationals than toward German nationals (most known members of the German-American Bund were left at liberty), and more harshly toward Germans than to Italians. It should also be noted, however, that more than a few young Nisei leaders applauded this early roundup and contrasted their own loyalty to the presumed disloyalty of many of the leaders of the older generation.

In addition to the selective roundup of enemy aliens, the Justice Department almost immediately announced the sealing off of the Mexican and Canadian borders to "all persons of Japanese ancestry, whether citizen or alien." Thus, by December 8, that branch of the federal government particularly charged with protecting the rights of citizens was willing to single out one ethnic group for invidious treatment. Other national civilian officials discriminated in other ways. Fiorello La Guardia, an outstanding liberal who was for a time director of the Office of Civilian Defense as well as mayor of New York, pointedly omitted mention of the Japanese in two public statements calling for decent treatment for enemy aliens and suggesting that alien Germans and Italians be presumed loyal until proved otherwise. By implication, at least, Japanese were to be presumed disloyal. Seventeen years earlier La Guardia had been one of three congressmen who dared to speak in favor of continuing Japanese immigration, but in December 1941 he could find nothing good to say about any Japanese.

Even more damaging were the mendacious statements of Frank Knox, Roosevelt's Republican Secretary of the Navy. On December 15 Secretary Knox held a press conference in Los Angeles on his return from a quick inspection of the damage at Pearl Harbor. As this was the first detailed report of the damage there, his remarks were front-page news all across the nation. Knox spoke of "treachery" in Hawaii and insisted that much of the disaster was caused by "the most effective fifth column work that's come out of this war, except in Norway."[10] The disaster at Pearl Harbor, as is now generally acknowledged, was caused largely by the unpreparedness and incompetence of the local military commanders, as Knox already knew. (The orders for the relief of Admiral Kimmel were already

---

[10] Knox Press Conference transcript, December 15, 1941, Knox Collection, Office of Naval History, Washington Navy Yard.

being drawn up.) But the secretary, who, as we shall see, harbored deep-felt anti-Japanese prejudices, probably did not want the people to lose faith in their Navy, so the Japanese population of Hawaii—and indirectly all Japanese Americans—was made the scapegoat on which to hang the big lie. (Knox, it should be remarked, as a Chicago newspaper publisher in civilian life, had a professional understanding of these matters.)

But the truly crucial role was played by the other service, the United States Army. The key individual, initially, at least, was John L. De Witt, in 1941 a lieutenant general and commander of the Western Defense Command and the 4th Army, both headquartered at San Francisco's Presidio. Despite these warlike titles, De Witt, who was sixty-one years old and would be retired before the war's end, was essentially an administrator in uniform, a staff officer who had specialized in supply and had practically nothing to do with combat during his whole Army career. Even before Pearl Harbor, De Witt had shown himself to be prejudiced against Japanese Americans. In March 1941, for example, he found it necessary to complain to Major General William G. Bryden, the Army's Deputy Chief of Staff, that "a couple of Japs" who had been drafted into the Army, were "going around taking pictures." He and Bryden agreed to "just have it happen naturally that Japs are sent to Infantry units," rather than to sensitive headquarters or coast defense installations. De Witt's prejudices, in fact, extended all along the color line. When he discovered that some of the troops being sent to him as reinforcements after Pearl Harbor were Negro, he protested to the Army's chief of classification and assignment that

> you're filling too many colored troops up on the West Coast. . . .
> there will be a great deal of public reaction out here due to the Jap
> situation. They feel they've got enough black skinned people around
> them as it is. Filipinos and Japanese. . . . I'd rather have a white
> regiment. . . .[11]

Serving under De Witt, in December 1941, as the corps commander in charge of the defense of Southern California, was a real fighting man, the then Major General Joseph W. Stilwell, the famed "Vinegar Joe" of the heartbreaking Burma campaigns. His diary of those days, kept in pencil in a shirt-pocket notebook, gives an accurate and pungent picture of the hysteria and indecisiveness that prevailed at De Witt's headquarters and on the Coast generally.

---

[11] Telephone conversations: De Witt to Bryden, March 13, 1941, Office, Chief of Staff Binder #11; De Witt and General Green, January 31, 1942, Office, Chief of Staff Binder #2, both from Stetson Conn, "Notes."

Dec. 8
Sunday night "air raid" at San Francisco . . . Fourth Army
kind of jittery.
Dec. 9
. . . Fleet of thirty-four [Japanese] ships between San Francisco and
Los Angeles. Later—not authentic.
Dec. 11
[Phone call from 4th Army] "The main Japanese fleet is 164 miles
off San Francisco." I believed it, like a damn fool. . . .
    Of course [4th Army] passed the buck on this report. They
had it from a "usually reliable source," but they should never have
put it out without check.
Dec. 13
Not content with the above blah, [4th] Army pulled another at
ten-thirty today. "Reliable information that attack on Los Angeles
is imminent. A general alarm being considered. . . ." What
jackass would send a general alarm [which would have meant
warning all civilians to leave the area including the workers in the
vital Southern California aircraft industry] under the circumstances.
The [4th] Army G–2 [Intelligence] is just another amateur,
like all the rest of the staff. Rule: the higher the
headquarters, the more important is *calm*.[12]

Stilwell's low opinion of General De Witt was apparently shared by
others within the Army; shortly after Vinegar Joe's transfer to Washington
just before Christmas, he noted that Lieutenant General Lesley J. McNair,
Deputy Commander, Army Ground Forces, had told him that "De Witt
has gone crazy and requires ten refusals before he realizes it is 'No.' "[13]
De Witt, it must be understood, was a cautious, conservative officer in the
twilight of his career. He saw, throughout the Army, younger men being
promoted into key posts; his contemporary, Lieutenant General Walter C.
Short, the Army commander in Hawaii, was in disgrace. With misplaced
concreteness De Witt apparently decided that there would be no Pearl
Harbors on the West Coast. It is interesting to note that the cautious
De Witt, in safe San Francisco, was more alarmed by the famous "war
warning" telegram of November 27 than was Short in exposed Honolulu,
and had the former been the Hawaiian commander, the Army at least,
might have been in a more advanced state of readiness. But after Pearl
Harbor, caution turned into funk; no one who reads the transcripts of

---

[12] Theodore H. White, ed., *The Stilwell Papers* (New York: William Sloane Associates, 1948), pp. 3–23; and Stilwell Diaries, The Hoover Institution.
[13] *Ibid.*

De Witt's telephone conversations with Washington or examines his staff correspondence can avoid the conclusion that his was a headquarters at which confusion rather than calm reigned, and that the confusion was greatest at the very top.

It was in this panic-ridden, amateurish Western Defense Command atmosphere that some of the most crucial decisions about the evacuation of the Japanese Americans were made. Before examining them, however, it should be made clear that the nearest Japanese aircraft during most of December were attacking Wake Island, more than 5000 miles west of San Francisco, and any major Japanese surface vessels or troops were even farther away. In fact, elements of the Luftwaffe over the North Atlantic were actually closer to California than any Japanese planes. California and the West Coast of the continental United States were in no way seriously threatened by the Japanese military. This finding does not represent just the hindsight of the military historian; the high command of the American army realized it at the time. Official estimates of Japanese capabilities made late in December concluded correctly that a large-scale invasion was beyond the capacity of the Japanese military but that a hit-and-run raid somewhere along the West Coast was possible.

In the days just after Pearl Harbor there was no concerted plan for mass incarceration. As evidence of this, on December 9 General Brehon Somervell, the Army's G–4 (Supply), ordered the construction of "facilities for the internment of alien enemies and other prisoners of war"; the three facilities authorized within De Witt's Western Defense Command had a total capacity of less than 2000, a figure consistent with the number of enemy aliens the FBI was in the process of rounding up.[14] But De Witt and his nervous headquarters staff, ready to believe anything, soon began to pressure Washington for more drastic action against the presumably dangerous enemies in their midst.

The first proposal by the Army for any kind of mass evacuation of Japanese Americans was brought forward at a De Witt staff conference in San Francisco on the evening of December 10. In the language of a staff memo, the meeting considered "certain questions relative to the problem of apprehension, segregation and detention of Japanese in the San Francisco Bay Area." The initial cause of the meeting seems to have been a report from an unidentified Treasury Department official asserting that 20,000 Japanese in the Bay Area were ready for organized action. Apparently plans for a mass roundup were drawn up locally, and approved by General Benedict, the commander of the area, but the whole thing was

---

[14] General Somervell, Memo for the Adjutant General, "Construction of Facilities for the Internment of Alien Enemies . . . ," December 9, 1941, Adjutant General's Office 14.311, National Archives.

squelched by Nat Pieper, head of the San Francisco office of the FBI, who laughed it off as "the wild imaginings" of a former FBI man whom he had fired. The imaginings were pretty wild; the figure of 20,000 slightly exceeded the total number of Japanese men, women, and children in the Bay Area. But wild or not, De Witt's subordinate reported the matter to Washington with the recommendation that "plans be made for large-scale internment." Then on December 19 General De Witt officially recommended "that action be initiated at the earliest practicable date to collect all alien subjects fourteen years of age and over, of enemy nations and remove them" to the interior of the United States and hold them "under restraint after removal" to prevent their surreptitious return.[15] (The age limit was apparently derived from the federal statutes on wartime internment, but those statutes, it should be noted, specified males only.)

De Witt was soon in touch with the Army's Provost Marshal General, Allen W. Gullion, who would prove to be a key figure in the decision to relocate the Japanese Americans. Gullion, the Army's top cop, had previously served as Judge Advocate General, the highest legal office within the Army. He was a service intellectual who had once read a paper to an International Congress of Judicial Experts on the "present state of international law regarding the protection of civilians from the new war technics." But, since at least mid-1940, he had been concerned with the problem of legally exercising military control over civilians in wartime. Shortly after the fall of France, Army Intelligence took the position that fifth column activities had been so successful in the European war in creating an internal as well as an external military front that the military "will actually have to control, through their Provost Marshal Generals, local forces, largely police" and that "the Military would certainly have to provide for the arrest and temporary holding of a large number of suspects," alien and citizen.

Gullion, as Judge Advocate General, gave his official opinion that within the United States, outside any zone of actual combat and where the civil courts were functioning, the "Military . . . does not have jurisdiction to participate in the arrest and temporary holding of civilians who are citizens of the United States." He did indicate, however, that if federal troops were in actual control (he had martial law in mind), jurisdiction over citizen civilians might be exercised.[16] Although martial law was never declared on the Pacific Coast, Chief of Staff George C. Marshall did

---

[15] Stetson Conn, "Japanese Evacuation from the West Coast," pp. 116–18, in Stetson Conn, Rose C. Engleman, and Byron Fairchild, *United States Army in World War II: The Western Hemisphere: Guarding the United States and Its Outposts* (Washington: Government Printing Office, 1964).

[16] Memo, Gullion to Assistant Chief of Staff (G–1), "Internment of Enemy Aliens," August 12, 1940, JAG 383.01, National Archives.

declare the region a "Theater of Operations" on December 11. This declaration, which was not made with the Japanese Americans in mind, created the legal fiction that the Coast was a war zone and would provide first the Army and then the courts with an excuse for placing entirely blameless civilian citizens under military control.

By December 22 Provost Marshal General Gullion, like any good bureaucrat, began a campaign to enlarge the scope of his own activities, an activity usually known as empire building. He formally requested the Secretary of War to press for the transfer of responsibility for conduct of the enemy alien program from the Department of Justice to the War Department. This recommendation found no positive response in Stimson's office, and four days later Gullion was on the telephone trying to get General De Witt to recommend a mass roundup of all Japanese, alien and citizen. Gullion told the Western Defense commander that he had just been visited by a representative of the Los Angeles Chamber of Commerce urging that all Japanese in the Los Angeles area be incarcerated. De Witt, who would blow hot and cold, was, on December 26, opposed. He told Gullion that

> I'm very doubtful that it would be common sense procedure to try and intern 117,000 Japanese in this theater. . . . An American citizen, after all, is an American citizen. And while they all may not be loyal, I think we can weed the disloyal out of the loyal and lock them up if necessary.[17]

De Witt was also opposed, on December 26, to military, as opposed to civilian, control over enemy aliens. "It would be better," he told Gullion, if "this thing worked through the civil channels."[18]

While these discussions and speculations were going on all about them, the West Coast Japanese in general and the citizen Nisei in particular were desperately trying to establish their loyalty. Many Japanese communities on the Coast were so demoralized by the coming of war that little collective action was taken, especially in the first weeks after Pearl Harbor. But in Los Angeles, the major mainland center of Japanese population, frantic and often pitiful activity took place. Most of this activity revolved around the Japanese American Citizens League, an organization, by definition, closed to Issei, except for the handful who achieved citizenship because of their service in the United States armed forces during World War I. Immediately following Pearl Harbor the Japanese American Citizens League (JACL) wired the President, affirming their loyalty; the

---

[17] Stetson Conn et al., *United States Army in World War II* . . . , *loc. cit.*
[18] *Ibid.*

White House had the State Department, the arm of government usually used to communicate with foreigners, coolly respond by letter that "your desire to cooperate has been carefully noted." On December 9 the JACL Anti-Axis Committee decided to take no contributions, in either time or money, from noncitizens, and later, when special travel regulations inhibited the movement of aliens, it decided not to help Issei "in securing travel permits or [giving] information in that regard." In addition, Nisei leaders repeatedly called on one generation to inform on the other.

On the very evening of Pearl Harbor, editor Togo Tanaka went on station KHTR, Los Angeles, and told his fellow Nisei:

> As Americans we now function as counterespionage. Any act or word prejudicial to the United States committed by any Japanese must be warned and reported to the F.B.I., Naval Intelligence, Sheriff's Office, and local police. . . .

Before the end of the week the Los Angeles Nisei had set up a formal Committee on Intelligence and had regular liaison established with the FBI.[19] These patriotic activities never uncovered any real sabotage or espionage, because there was none to uncover. Nor did it provide the protective coloration that the Nisei hoped it would; race, not loyalty or citizenship, was the criterion for evacuation. It did, however, widen the gap between the generations, and would be a major cause of bitterness and violence after the evacuation took place.

---

[19] Minutes of the Japanese American Citizens League Anti-Axis Committee, John Anson Ford Mss., Box 64, Huntington Library.

3

THE DECISION FOR MASS EVACUATION

December 1941 was a month of calamities which saw West Coast opinion harden against the Japanese; during January, as the war news got worse and worse and it became apparent that the Japanese audacity at Pearl Harbor would not be quickly avenged, the national climate of opinion, and Congressional opinion in particular, began to veer toward the West Coast view. That this climate had to be created is shown by an examination of the *Congressional Record*. Not only was there no concerted strong feeling exhibited against the Japanese Americans, but in the first weeks after Pearl Harbor members of the California delegation defended them publicly. (The only trace of hostility shown by a California solon in early December was a telephone call that the junior senator, Democrat Sheridan Downey, made to the Army on the night of December 7 suggesting that De Witt prompt Governor Olson to declare some sort of curfew on "Japs.") On December 10, for example, Bertrand W. Gearhart, a four-term Republican congressman from Fresno and an officer of the American Legion, read a telegram professing loyalty to the United States from an Issei leader in his district whom Gearhart described as an "American patriot."

Five days later, when John Rankin (D-Miss.), the leading nativist in the lower house, called for "deporting every Jap who claims, or has claimed, Japanese citizenship, or sympathizes with Japan in this war," he was answered by another Californian, Leland M. Ford, a Santa Monica Republican:

> These people are American-born. They cannot be deported . . . whether we like it or whether we do not. This is their country. . . . [When] they join the armed forces . . . they must take this oath of allegiance . . . and I see no particular reason at this particular time why they should not. I believe that every one of these people should make a clear, clean acknowledgement.[1]

Despite the lack of Congressional concern, by the end of December momentum was gathering for more drastic action against the Japanese and against enemy aliens generally. On December 30 the Justice Department made the first of many concessions to the military, concessions that had little to do either with due process or the realities of the situation. On that date Attorney General Biddle informed the Provost Marshal General's office that he had authorized the issuance of search warrants for any house in which an enemy alien lived, merely on the representation that there was reasonable cause to believe that there was contraband on the premises. Contraband had already been defined to include anything that might be used as a weapon, any explosive (many Issei farmers used dynamite to clear stumps), radio transmitters, any radio that had a shortwave band, and all but the simplest cameras. For the next few months thousands of houses where Japanese lived were subjected to random search. Although much "contraband" was found (most of it in two Issei-owned sporting goods stores), the FBI itself later stipulated that none of it was sinister in nature and reported that there was no evidence at all that any of it was intended for subversive use. But the mere fact of these searches, widely reported in the press, added to the suspicion with which the Japanese were viewed. These searches, like so much of the anti-Japanese movement, were part of a self-fulfilling prophecy: one is suspicious of the Japanese, so one searches their houses; the mere fact of the search, when noticed ("the FBI went through those Jap houses on the other side of town"), creates more suspicion.

For individual Japanese families, these searches intensified the in-security and terror they already felt. One fifteen-year-old girl in San Jose, California reported what must have been an all-too-routine occurrence:

---

[1] Telephone conversation, Bendetsen and Meredith, December 7, 1941, Provost Marshal General, Record Group 389, National Archives: *Congressional Record*, 77th Cong., pp. 9603, 9808–09; see also pp. 9631 and 9958.

One day I came home from school to find the two F.B.I. men at our front door. They asked permission to search the house. One man looked through the front rooms, while the other searched the back rooms. Trembling with fright, I followed and watched each of the men look around. The investigators examined the mattresses, and the dresser and looked under the beds. The gas range, piano and sofa were thoroughly inspected. Since I was the only one at home, the F.B.I. questioned me, but did not procure sufficient evidence of Fifth Columnists in our family. This made me very happy, even if they did mess up the house.[2]

Concurrent with its more stringent search order, the Department of Justice and the Provost Marshal General's office decided to send representatives to De Witt's headquarters in San Francisco; the two men sent— James Rowe, Jr., Assistant Attorney General and a former Presidential assistant, and Major (later Colonel) Karl R. Bendetsen, chief of the Aliens Division, Provost Marshal General's office—were key and mutually antagonistic figures in the bureaucratic struggle over the fate of the West Coast Japanese. Rowe, during his short visit in California, exercised a moderating influence on the cautious General De Witt, who often seemed to be the creature of the last strong personality with whom he had contact. Bendetsen represented a chief (Gullion) who wanted not only exclusion of the Japanese from the West Coast but also the transfer of supervisory authority over all enemy aliens in the United States from the civilian control of the Department of Justice to the military control of his office. Bendetsen soon became the voice of General De Witt in matters concerning aliens, and was well rewarded for his efforts. A graduate of Stanford Law School, he had gone on to active duty as a captain in 1940, and in the process of evacuating the Japanese he would gain his colonel's eagles before he turned thirty-five. After Bendetsen's arrival, Gullion arranged with De Witt that the West Coast commander go out of normal channels and deal directly with the Provost Marshal on matters concerning aliens. The result of this seemingly routine bureaucratic shuffle was highly significant; as Stetson Conn has pointed out, the consequence of this arrangement was that "the responsible Army command headquarters in Washington [that is, Chief of Staff George C. Marshall and his immediate staff] had little to do during January and February 1942 with the plans and decisions for Japanese evacuation."[3]

Telephone conversations and correspondence between De Witt's

---

[2] Contained in a collection of letters from Poston, Bancroft Library.

[3] Stetson Conn, "The Decision to Evacuate the Japanese from the Pacific Coast," in Kent Roberts Greenfield, ed., *Command Decisions* (New York: Harcourt, 1959), p. 92.

headquarters and the Provost Marshal General's office in late December and early January reveal the tremendous pressures that the soldiers were putting on the civilians. According to General Gullion, the Justice Department's representatives, James Rowe, Jr., and Edward J. Ennis, were apologetic about the slowness of the Justice Department, an apparent criticism of their chief, the Attorney General. At about the same time Gullion was complaining that "the Attorney General is not functioning" and threatened to have Secretary Stimson complain to the President. De Witt was, as usual, vacillating. Within the same week he told the Provost Marshal General's office that "it would be better if . . . this thing worked through the civil channels," but a few days later insisted that "I don't want to go after this thing piece meal. I want to do it on a mass basis, all at the same time."[4]

The arrival of Bendetsen at De Witt's San Francisco headquarters seemed to strengthen the West Coast commander's resolve. Before Bendetsen left Washington he had drafted an Executive Order transferring authority over aliens to the War Department, but the Provost Marshal General's office felt that since the Justice Department's representatives were so apologetic, it "wasn't quite fair" to take over without giving them a chance to come up to the Army's standards. Shortly after his arrival in San Francisco, Bendetsen drafted a memo that quickly became the guideline for De Witt's policy. It called for an immediate and complete registration of all alien enemies, who were to be photographed and fingerprinted. These records were to be kept in duplicate, one set to be kept in the community in which the alien resided, the other in a central office. The purpose was to set up what Bendetsen called a "Pass and Permit System." Doubtful that the Attorney General would agree to this, Bendetsen's memo concluded with what had become the refrain of the Provost Marshal General's men: if Justice won't do it, the War Department must.

The next day, January 4, in a conference at his Presidio headquarters attended by Rowe, Bendetsen, and representatives of other federal departments and officials in local government, De Witt made some of his position clear, stressing, as he always did to civilians, what he called the military necessity.

> We are at war and this area—eight states—has been designated as a theater of operations. I have approximately 240,000 men at my disposal. . . . [There are] approximately 288,000 enemy aliens . . . which we have to watch. . . . I have little confidence that the enemy aliens are law-abiding or loyal in any sense of the word. Some of them yes;

---

[4] Telephone conversations, Gullion and De Witt, December 26, 1941; and De Witt and Lerch, January 1, 1942, Stetson Conn, "Notes," Office, Chief of Military History, U.S. Army.

many, no. Particularly the Japanese. I have no confidence in their
loyalty whatsoever. I am speaking now of the native born Japanese—
117,000—and 42,000 in California alone.[5]

One result of this conference was that the Department of Justice
agreed to go further than it had previously: enemy aliens were to be re-
registered under its auspices, the FBI would conduct large-scale "spot"
raids, something De Witt was particularly eager for, and, most significantly, a large number of restricted, or Category A, zones would be
established around crucial military and defense installations on the Pacific
Coast. Entry to these zones would be on a pass basis. Assistant Secretary
of War John J. McCloy later described this program as "the best way to
solve" the West Coast alien problem.

> . . . establish limited restricted areas around the airplane plants, the
> forts and other important military installations . . . we might call
> these military reservations in substance and exclude everyone—whites,
> yellows, blacks, greens—from that area and then license back into
> the area those whom we felt there was no danger to be expected
> from . . . then we can cover the legal situation . . . in spite of the
> constitution. . . . You may, by that process, eliminate all the Japs
> [alien and citizen] but you might conceivably permit some to come
> back whom you are quite certain are free from any suspicion.[6]

In addition to the Category A zones, there were to be Category B
zones, consisting of the rest of the coastal area, in which enemy aliens
and citizen Japanese would be allowed to live and work under rigidly
prescribed conditions. Although De Witt and the other Army people
were constantly complaining about the slowness of the Justice Department,
they quickly found that setting up these zones was easier said than done.
De Witt did not forward his first recommendations for Category A areas
to the War Department until January 21, more than two weeks after the
San Francisco conference.

On January 16 Representative Leland Ford, the Santa Monica Republican who had opposed stern treatment for the Japanese on the floor
of the House in mid-December, had changed his mind. Ford had received

---

[5] Notes on January 4, 1942, conference, Stetson Conn, "Notes."

[6] Telephone conversation, McCloy and De Witt, February 3, 1942, Assistant Secretary of War, Record Group 107, National Archives. For clarity, certain portions of
McCloy's rambling conversation have been transposed. To the final remark quoted
above, De Witt responded, "Out here, Mr. Secretary, a Jap is a Jap to these people
now."

a number of telegrams and letters from California suggesting removal of Japanese from vital coastal areas—the earliest seems to have been a January 6 telegram from Mexican American movie star Leo Carillo—and by mid-January had come around to their point of view. He urged Secretary of War Henry L. Stimson to have "all Japanese, whether citizens or not, . . . placed in inland concentration camps." Arguing that native-born Japanese either were or were not loyal to the United States, Ford developed a simple test for loyalty: any Japanese willing to go to a concentration camp was a patriot; therefore it followed that unwillingness to go was a proof of disloyalty to the United States. Stimson and his staff mulled over this letter for ten days, and then replied (in a letter drafted by Bendetsen, now back from the Pacific Coast) giving the congressman a certain amount of encouragement. "The internment of over a hundred thousand people," Stimson wrote, "involves many complex considerations." The basic responsibility, Stimson pointed out, putting the finger on his Cabinet colleague Francis Biddle, has been delegated to the Attorney General. Nevertheless, the Secretary continued, "the Army is prepared to provide internment facilities in the interior to the extent necessary." Assuring Ford that the Army was aware of the dangers on the Pacific Coast, Stimson informed him that the military were submitting suggestions to the Justice Department, and advised him to present his views to the Attorney General.[7]

The same day that Ford wrote Stimson, January 16, another federal department became involved in the fate of the West Coast Japanese. Agriculture Secretary Claude Wickard, chiefly concerned with increasing farm production—"Food Can Win the War" was his line—called a meeting in his office at which the War, Labor, Navy, Justice, and Treasury Departments were represented. He had become alarmed over investigative reports from his agents on the West Coast, who were concerned both about the fate of the Japanese and the threat to food production. Wickard had been informed that although violence against the Japanese farmers was an isolated phenomenon, greatly exaggerated by the press, nevertheless it was quite clear that the Japanese rural population was "terrified."

> They do not leave their homes at night, and will not, even in the daytime, enter certain areas populated by Filipinos. The police authorities are probably not sympathetic to the Japanese and are giving them only the minimum protection. Investigation of actual attacks on Japanese have been merely perfunctory and no prosecutions have been initiated.[8]

[7] Letters, Ford to Stimson, January 16, 1942, and Stimson to Ford, January 26, 1942, Secretary of War, Record Group 107, National Archives.

[8] Memo, January 10, 1942, by J. Murray Thompson et al.

The federal officials then concluded that the whole "propaganda campaign" against the Japanese was essentially a conspiracy designed to place Japanese-owned and -leased farm lands into white hands; the real aim was to "eliminate Japanese competition." Wickard's West Coast representatives urged him to take positive steps both to maintain agricultural production and to preserve and protect the property and persons of the Japanese farmers.

Wickard's action was not exactly along the lines recommended by the men in the field. He did urge immediate federal action "so that the supply of vegetables for the military forces and the civilian population will not be needlessly curtailed." But Wickard also felt that the fears and suspicions of the general public—particularly the West Coast public— should be taken into account. He seemed to envision a sort of large agricultural reservation in the central valleys of California on which the Japanese could "carry on their normal farming operations" after being removed from "all strategic areas." In this way, Wickard felt, the country could protect itself from "possible subversive Japanese activities," provide "limited protection to all Japanese whose conduct is above suspicion," and at the same time "avoid incidents that might provide an excuse for cruel treatment for our people in Japanese occupied territory." As for the agricultural lands in the coastal area which the Japanese had tilled, Wickard suggested that Mexicans might be brought in to replace them.[9]

Also, by mid-January, the urban Japanese, if not terrorized as were their rural cousins, were feeling more and more hopeless and demoralized. An occasional militant like James Y. Sakamoto, a Japanese American Citizen League (JACL) official in Seattle, could indignantly protest against Representative Ford's evacuation proposal which went out on the Associated Press wire on January 21.

"This is our country," Sakamoto pointed out, "we were born and raised here . . . have made our homes here . . . [and] we are ready to give our lives, if necessary, to defend the United States." Ford's drastic measures, he insisted, were not in the best interests of the nation. But even a Nisei leader like Sakamoto felt compelled to admit that there was some kind of subversive danger from the older generation of Japanese. The Seattle Nisei, he stated, were "actively cooperating" with the authorities "to uncover all subversive activity in our midst" and, if necessary, he concluded, the Nisei were "ready to stand as protective custodians over our

[9] Letter, Wickard to Stimson, January 16, 1942, in Records of the Secretary of Agriculture, Foreign Relations 2–1. Aliens-Refugees 1942, Record Group 16, National Archives. For a fascinating glimpse of how the evacuation looked to a liberal Department of Agriculture staffer, see Laurence Hewes, *Boxcar in the Sand* (New York, 1957), pp. 151–175.

parent generation to guard against danger to the United States arising from their midst."[10] One of the standard complaints quite properly raised by Americans in denouncing totalitarian regimes is that their police states turn children against their parents; it is rarely remarked that, in this instance at least, such too was the function of American democracy.

But for those really in charge, the agonizing distinctions between father and son, between alien and citizen, were essentially irrelevant. By mid-January, perhaps as a way of answering the points made by Representative Ford, Chief of Staff George C. Marshall ordered the Provost Marshal General's office to prepare a memorandum on the West Coast Japanese situation. Bendetsen, the natural drafter for such a report, called General De Witt to ask what his attitude would be if "the Department of Justice still fails to do what we think they ought to do?" De Witt, who felt that things would work out, was nevertheless apprehensive about the continuing potentialities for sabotage and other subversive activities. "We know," he told Bendetsen, "that they are communicating at sea. . . ." De Witt actually knew no such thing, as no evidence existed of such communication, but he undoubtedly believed it. Then, in a classic leap in what Richard Hofstadter has styled the paranoid style, the West Coast commander insisted that "the fact that we have had [not even] sporadic attempts at sabotage clearly means that control is being exercised somewhere." Here then was the "heads I win, tails you lose" situation in which this one Army officer was able to place more than 100,000 innocent people. There had been no acts of sabotage, no real evidence of subversion, despite the voices that De Witt kept hearing at sea. Yet, according to this military logician, there was a conspiracy afoot not to commit sabotage until America dropped its guard. Ergo, evacuate them quickly before the conspiracy is put into operation.[11]

The next day, January 25, the long-awaited report on the attack on Pearl Harbor made by the official committee of inquiry headed by Supreme Court Justice Owen J. Roberts was released to the press just in time for the Sunday morning papers, though it is dated two days earlier. In addition to its indictment of the general conditions of unreadiness in the Hawaiian command, the board reported, falsely, as it turned out, that the attack was greatly abetted by Japanese spies, some of whom were described as "persons having no open relations with the Japanese foreign service." It went on to criticize the laxity of counterespionage activity in the Islands, and implied that a too close adherence to the Constitution had seriously inhibited the

[10] Sakamoto's statement enclosed in letter, William Hosokawa to Cordell Hull, January 23, 1942, Secretary of War, Record Group 107, National Archives.

[11] Telephone conversation, Bendetsen and De Witt, January 24, 1942, Provost Marshal General, Record Group 389, National Archives.

work of the Federal Bureau of Investigation.[12] The publication of the report was naturally a sensation; it greatly stimulated already prevalent rumors that linked the disaster to wholly imaginary fifth column activities by resident Japanese. Perhaps the most popular was the yarn that University of California class rings had been found on the fingers of Japanese pilots shot down in the raid. Even more ridiculous was the story that the attacking pilots had been aided by arrows, pointing at Pearl Harbor, which had been hacked into the cane fields the night before by Japanese workers. The absurdity of this device—a large natural harbor containing dozens of war vessels, large and small, is highly visible from the air—seems to have occurred to few. The Roberts Report provided a field day for those who had long urged more repressive measures and a more effective secret police unfettered by constitutional restrictions. Congressmen like Martin Dies of Texas, then head of the House Committee on Un-American Activities, insisted, in and out of Congress, that if only people had listened to them, the disaster at Pearl Harbor could have been averted. More significantly, it gave an additional argument to those who were pressing for preventive detention and must have given pause to some who had been urging restraint.

On January 25 Secretary Stimson forwarded to Attorney General Biddle recommendations that General De Witt had made four days earlier, calling for total exclusion of enemy aliens from eighty-six Category A zones and close control of enemy aliens in eight Category B zones on a pass and permit system. As this proposal involved only aliens, the Justice Department quickly agreed and made the first public, official announcement of a mass evacuation on January 29, to be effective almost a month later, on February 24.[13] This relatively modest proposal would have moved only about 7000 aliens in all, and fewer than 3000 of these would have been Japanese. At about the same time it announced the appointment of Tom C. Clark (who later became Attorney General under Truman and then an Associate Justice of the Supreme Court) as Co-Ordinator of the Alien Enemy Control Program within the Western Defense Command. Clark flew to the West Coast the next day.

A few days before Stimson's recommendation to Biddle, the top echelons of military command, for the first time, began to become aware of the kinds of proposals that were emanating from De Witt's headquarters. General Mark W. Clark (then a brigadier on the General Staff

---

[12] The entire report is published in *Pearl Harbor Attack: Hearings Before the Joint Committee on the Investigation of the Pearl Harbor Attack*, Pt. 39, pp. 1–21 (Washington, 1946). The quotation is from p. 12.

[13] Justice Department Press Release, January 29, 1942, in *House Report No. 2124*, 77th Cong., 2d Sess., p. 302. Thirty-two basic documents relating to the evacuation are conveniently assembled here.

and later a major commander in the European Theater) was instructed to prepare a memorandum for the President on the subject of "enemy aliens" in the Western Theater of Operations. The day after Stimson's letter to Biddle requesting the announcement of Category A and B areas, General Clark recommended that no memorandum be sent unless the Attorney General's action should "not be all that is desired." Clark's memorandum was read by Chief of Staff George C. Marshall, who noted on it "hold for me until Feb. 1." The top brass was satisfied with a very modest program, involving the forced removal, without detention, of a very few aliens. Clark's memorandum made no mention of citizens at all.[14]

But if the top brass were satisfied, De Witt, Bendetsen, and Gullion were not. And neither were the leading public officials in California. On January 27 De Witt had a conference with Governor Culbert Olson and related to Washington, probably accurately:

> There's a tremendous volume of public opinion now developing against the Japanese of all classes, that is aliens and non-aliens, to get them off the land, and in Southern California around Los Angeles —in that area too—they want and they are bringing pressure on the government to move all the Japanese out. As a matter of fact, it's not being instigated or developed by people who are not thinking but by the best people of California. Since the publication of the Roberts Report they feel that they are living in the midst of a lot of enemies. They don't trust the Japanese, none of them.[15]

Two days later, De Witt talked with Olson's Republican Attorney General Earl Warren. (De Witt thought his name was Warner.) The California Attorney General, who was then preparing to run for governor against Olson in November, was in thorough agreement with his rival that the Japanese ought to be removed. This was not surprising. Warren was heir to a long anti-Japanese tradition in California politics and the protégé of U. S. Webb, a long-time Attorney General of California (1902–1939) and the author of the 1913 California Alien Land Act. Warren had been intimately associated with the most influential nativist group in the state, the Joint Immigration Committee, but shortly after he became Attorney General in 1939 he prudently arranged to have his name taken off the Committee's letterhead, although he continued to meet with them and receive copies of all documents and notices. Because of his later prominence, some have tried to make too much of Warren's very minor role in

---

[14] Memo, Mark W. Clark to Deputy Chief of Staff, January 26, 1942, The Adjutant General, Record Group 407, National Archives.

[15] Telephone conversation, De Witt and Bendetsen, January 29, 1942. Provost Marshal General, Record Group 389, National Archives.

pressing for an evacuation. He did add his voice, but it was not yet a very strong one and it is almost inconceivable that, had any other politician held his post, essentially the same result would not have ensued.[16]

On the very day of Biddle's formal announcement of the A and B zones, De Witt and Bendetsen worked out a more sweeping scheme, which Bendetsen would present to an informal but influential meeting of congressmen the next day. After a rambling conversation—De Witt was rarely either concise or precise—Bendetsen, always the lawyer in uniform, summed it up neatly:

BENDETSEN. . . . As I understand it, from your viewpoint summarizing our conversation, you are of the opinion that there will have to be an evacuation on the west coast, not only of Japanese aliens but also of Japanese citizens, that is, you would include citizens along with alien enemies, and that if you had the power of requisition over all other Federal agencies, if you were requested you would be willing on the coast to accept responsibility for the alien enemy program.

DE WITT. Yes I would. And I think it's got to come sooner or later.

BENDETSEN. Yes sir, I do too, and I think the subject may be discussed tomorrow at the congressional delegation meeting.

DE WITT. Well, you've got my viewpoint. You have it exactly.[17]

The next day, January 30, the Japanese question was discussed in two important meetings, one in the White House and one on Capitol Hill. In the Cabinet meeting fears were expressed about the potentially dangerous situation in Hawaii. General Marshall penned a short memo to General Dwight D. Eisenhower, then a member of his staff, telling him that Stimson was concerned about "dangerous Japanese in Hawaii." Justice Roberts had told the War Secretary that "this point was regarded by his board as most serious." Several Cabinet members, but particularly Navy Secretary Frank Knox, were greatly disturbed at what they considered the laxity with which the Hawaiian Japanese were treated. As early as December 19, a previous Cabinet meeting had decided that all Japanese aliens in the Hawaiian Islands should be interned, and put on some island other than Oahu, where the major military installations were located.[18]

---

[16] Telephone conversation, De Witt and Gullion, January 30, 1942, Provost Marshal General, Record Group 389, National Archives.

[17] Telephone conversation, De Witt and Bendetsen, January 29, 1942, Provost Marshal General, Record Group 389, National Archives.

[18] Memo, General Marshall to General Eisenhower, January 30, 1942, Secretary of War, Record Group 107, National Archives; Conn, "The Hawaiian Defenses After Pearl Harbor," p. 207, in Stetson Conn, Rose C. Engleman, and Byron Fairchild,

At the other end of Pennsylvania Avenue, the focus was on the West Coast Japanese. Bendetsen, along with Rowe and Ennis from the Justice Department, attended a meeting of the Pacific Coast House delegation. (A joint meeting between the congressmen and the six senators was already scheduled for the following Monday.) The subject was what to do about the Japanese. Although Bendetsen officially reported to his superiors that he "was present as an observer," it is clear from his telephone conversations with General De Witt, both before and after the meeting, that he went as an advocate for the policies that he and his boss, General Gullion, had been proposing. Bendetsen called De Witt right after the meeting and told him what they both considered good news.

> They asked me to state what the position of the War Department was. I stated that I could not speak for the War Department. . . . They asked me for my own views and I stated that the position of the War Department was this: that we did not seek control of the program, that we preferred it be handled by the civil agencies. However, the War Department would be entirely willing, I believed, [to assume] the responsibility provided they accorded the War Department, and the Secretary of War, and the military commander under him, full authority to require the services of any federal agency, and required that that federal agency was required to respond.[19]

De Witt liked this. "That's good," he responded. "I'm glad to see that action is being taken . . . that someone in authority begins to see the problem." What he particularly liked was the delegation to himself of full power over civilian agencies. He had had problems with civilians already, particularly civilians in the Federal Bureau of Investigation whose West Coast agents, as we have seen, refused to respond positively to De Witt's imaginary alarms and excursions. As De Witt envisioned it, "Mr. [J. Edgar] Hoover himself as head of the F.B.I. would have to function under the War Department exactly as he is functioning under the Department of Justice."

Bendetsen, naturally, encouraged De Witt to grab for power. "Opinion is beginning to become irresistible, and I think that anything you recommend will be strongly backed up . . . by the public." De Witt and Bendetsen agreed that protestations of loyalty from the Nisei were utterly worthless. As De Witt put it:

United States Army in World War II: The Western Hemisphere: Guarding the United States and Its Outposts (Washington: Government Printing Office, 1964).

[19] Telephone conversation, Bendetsen and De Witt, January 30, 1942, Provost Marshal General, Record Group 389, National Archives.

"There are going to be a lot of Japs who are going to say, 'Oh, yes, we want to go, we're good Americans and we want to do everything you say,' but those are the fellows I suspect the most."

"Definitely," Bendetsen agreed. "The ones who are giving you only lip service are the ones always to be suspected."[20]

The Congressional recommendations were immediately sent to Secretary Stimson by the senior California representative, Clarence Lea, a Santa Rosa Democrat first elected in 1916. Although they did not specifically call for removal of American citizens of Japanese ancestry, the delegation did ask that mass evacuation proceed for "all enemy aliens and their families," which would have included most of the Nisei.[21] Later the same day, Provost Marshal General Gullion called De Witt to get some details straight. He was chiefly interested in how far De Witt proposed to move the evacuees. De Witt did not know, but he did point out to Gullion that within California "one group wanted to move them entirely out of the state," whereas another wanted "them to be left in California." After receiving these assurances from De Witt, Gullion began to wonder where the Army was going to put 100,000 people, and, perhaps for the first time, fleetingly realized that "a resettlement proposition is quite a proposition."[22] The following day, Bendetsen, acting for his chief, had the Adjutant General dispatch telegrams to Corps Area commanders throughout the nation asking them about possible locations for large numbers of evacuees. Bendetsen suggested some possible sites: "agricultural experimental farms, prison farms, migratory labor camps, pauper farms, state parks, abandoned CCC camps, fairgrounds."[23]

By the end of the month De Witt was able to make his position a little clearer. When Bendetsen asked whether or not he contemplated moving citizens, De Witt was emphatic.

I include all Germans, all Italians who are alien enemies and all Japanese who are native-born or foreign born . . . evacuate enemy aliens in large groups at the earliest possible date . . . sentiment is being given too much importance. . . . I think we might as well eliminate talk of resettlement and handle these people as they should be handled . . . put them to work in internment camps. . . . I place

---

[20] *Ibid.*

[21] Letter, Lea to Stimson, January 30, 1942, Secretary of War, Record Group 107, National Archives.

[22] Telephone conversation, De Witt and Gullion, January 30, 1942, Provost Marshal General, Record Group 389, National Archives.

[23] Bendetson, Memo for the Adjutant General, January 31, 1942, The Adjutant General, Record Group 407, National Archives.

the following priority. . . . First the Japanese, all prices [?*sic*] . . . as the most dangerous . . . the next group, the Germans . . . the third group, the Italians. . . . We've waited too long as it is. Get them all out.[24]

On Sunday, February 1, exactly eight weeks after Pearl Harbor, Assistant Secretary of War John J. McCloy, Gullion, and Bendetsen went to a meeting in Attorney General Francis Biddle's office. Biddle, who was seconded by James Rowe, Jr., Edward J. Ennis, and J. Edgar Hoover, had been concerned about the increasing pressure for mass evacuation, both from the military and from Congress, and about a crescendo of press criticism directed at his "pussyfooting," some of which was undoubtedly inspired by the military. Biddle presented the Army men with a draft of what he hoped would be a joint press release. Its crucial sentences, which the military refused to agree to, were

The Department of War and the Department of Justice are in agreement that the present military situation does not *at this time* [my emphasis] require the removal of American citizens of the Japanese race. The Secretary of War, General De Witt, the Attorney General, and the Director of the Federal Bureau of Investigation believe that appropriate steps have been and are being taken.

Biddle informed McCloy and the others that he was opposed to mass evacuation and that the Justice Department would have nothing to do with it. Rowe, remembering his early January visit to De Witt's headquarters, said that the West Coast commander had been opposed to mass evacuation then and wondered what had changed his mind. According to Gullion, Rowe, after some uncomplimentary remarks about Bendetsen, complained about the hysterical tone of the protests from the West Coast, argued that the western congressmen were "just nuts" on the subject, and maintained that there was "no evidence whatsoever of any reason for disturbing citizens." Then Biddle insisted that the Justice Department would have nothing at all to do with any interference with civilians. Gullion, admittedly "a little sore," said: "Well, listen, Mr. Biddle, do you mean to tell me if the Army, the men on the ground, determine it is a military necessity to move citizens, Jap citizens, that you won't help us?"

After Biddle restated his position, McCloy, again according to Gullion, said to the Attorney General: "You are putting a Wall Street lawyer in a helluva box, but if it is a question of the safety of the country

---

[24] Telephone conversations, De Witt and Gullion, January 31, 1942, and De Witt and Gullion and Bendetsen, February 1, 1942, Provost Marshal General, Record Group 389, National Archives.

[and] the Constitution. . . . Why the Constitution is just a scrap of paper to me."

As the meeting broke up, it was agreed that the Army people would check with the "man on the ground," General De Witt. As soon as they got back to their office, Gullion and Bendetsen made a joint phone call to the West Coast commander. They read him the proposed press release and, when the crucial sentences were reached, De Witt responded immediately: "I wouldn't agree to that." When asked specifically whom he did want to evacuate, the answer was "those people who are aliens and who are Japs of American citizenship." Then Gullion cautioned De Witt:

> Now I might suggest, General, Mr. McCloy was in the conference and he will probably be in any subsequent conference . . . he has not had all the benefit of conversations we have had with you—if you could give us something, not only in conversation but a written thing . . . stating your position.

De Witt agreed to do this. Then Bendetsen summarized the Justice Department's point of view:

> . . . they say . . . if we recommend and it is determined that there should be an evacuation of citizens, they said hands off, that is the Army's job . . . they agree with us that it is possible from . . . a legal standpoint. . . . They agree with us that [the licensing theory] could be . . . the legal basis for exclusion. . . . However we insist that we could also say that while all whites could remain, Japs can't, if we think there is military necessity for that. They apparently want us to join with them so that if anything happens they would be able to say "this was the military recommendation."

De Witt stated, "they are trying to cover themselves and lull the populace into a false sense of security."

When questioned about the details of the evacuation, De Witt blustered: "I haven't gone into the details of it, but Hell, it would be no job as far as the evacuation was concerned to move 100,000 people."[25]

Actually, of course, it was a tremendous job, and even in such a relatively simple matter as the designation of Category A (prohibited to aliens) and Category B (restricted to aliens) zones, De Witt's staff had botched the job. Bendetsen had to call Western Defense Command headquarters and point out that although they had permitted limited use by

---

[25] *Ibid.* and telephone conversation, Gullion and Mark W. Clark, February 4, 1942, Provost Marshal General, Record Group 389, National Archives.

enemy aliens of the San Francisco–Oakland Bay Bridge (the bridge itself was Category B), all the approaches to the bridge were classified Category A, and thus prohibited.[26]

Two days after the conference in Biddle's office both Assistant Secretary of War McCloy and General George C. Marshall made separate calls to De Witt. McCloy, and presumably Stimson and Marshall, had become concerned that De Witt and the Provost Marshal's office were committing the Army to a policy that the policy makers had not yet agreed to. McCloy was blunt:

> ... the Army, that means you in the area, should not take the position, even in your conversations with political figures out there [favoring] a wholesale withdrawal of Japanese citizens and aliens from the Coast. . . . We have about reached the point where we feel that perhaps the best solution of it is to limit the withdrawal to certain prohibited areas.

Then, incredibly to anyone who has read the transcripts of his conversations with Gullion and Bendetsen (which were apparently not then available to McCloy), General De Witt denied that he had done any such thing: "Mr. Secretary . . . I haven't taken any position."[27]

This, of course, was a palpable lie. What the cautious commander knew, however, was that he had never put any recommendations on paper, and that General Gullion was not likely to produce the telephone transcripts because they showed him and his subordinates pressing for a policy that had not yet been officially sanctioned.

General Marshall's call was terse and businesslike; the extract of it which he furnished to the Secretary of War is worth quoting in full, both because of what it does and what it does not say.

> MARSHALL. Is there anything you want to say now about anything else? Of course we're on an open phone.
>
> DE WITT. We're on an open phone, but George I can talk a little about this alien situation out here.
>
> MARSHALL. Yes.
>
> DE WITT. I had a conference yesterday [February 2] with the Governor [Olson] and several representatives of the Department of Justice [Tom C. Clark] and the Department of Agriculture with a

---

26 Telephone conversation, Bendetsen and Colonel Stroh, February 2, 1942, Provost Marshal General, Record Group 389, National Archives.

27 Telephone conversation, McCloy and De Witt, February 3, 1942, Assistant Secretary of War, Record Group 107, National Archives.

view to removal of the Japanese from where they are now living to other portions of the state.

MARSHALL. Yes.

DE WITT. And the Governor thinks it can be satisfactorily handled without having a resettlement somewhere in the central part of the United States and removing them entirely from the state of California. As you know the people out here are very much disturbed over these aliens, and want to get them out of the several communities.

MARSHALL. Yes.

DE WITT. And I've agreed that if they can get them out of the areas limited as the combat zone, that it would be satisfactory. That would take them about 100 to 150 miles from the coast, and they're going to do that I think. They're working on it.

MARSHALL. Thank you.

DE WITT. The Department [of Justice] has a representative out here and the Department of Agriculture, and they think the plan is an excellent one. I'm only concerned with getting them away from around these aircraft factories and other places.

MARSHALL. Yes. Anything else?

DE WITT. No, that's all.

MARSHALL. Well, good luck.[28]

That same day, February 3, there was an hour-and-a-half meeting between Stimson, McCloy, Gullion, and Bendetsen. (It is not clear whether the phone conversations between McCloy and De Witt and Marshall and De Witt preceded, followed or straddled this meeting.) The next day Provost Marshal Gullion reported, somewhat dejectedly: ". . . the two Secretaries [Stimson and McCloy] are against any mass movement. They are pretty much against it. And they are also pretty much against interfering with citizens unless it can be done legally."[29]

What had apparently happened was that De Witt, understanding from the McCloy and Marshall phone calls that the War Department was, as he put it, "afraid that I was going to get into a political mess," and under great pressure from Governor Olson and Tom C. Clark to allow a limited, voluntary, compromise evacuation within California, trimmed his position accordingly. Clark, a strong and vigorous personality, seemed to have great influence over the general, who described him as "a fine

---

[28] Telephone conversation, Marshall and De Witt, February 3, 1942, Secretary of War, Record Group 107, National Archives.

[29] Telephone conversation, Gullion and Mark W. Clark, February 4, 1942, Provost Marshal General, Record Group 389, National Archives.

fellow . . . the most cooperative and forceful man I have ever had to deal with. He attacks a problem better than any civilian I have ever had contact with."[30]

Clark was clearly playing an independent role, and his position was somewhere between that of the Provost Marshal's office and that held by his own chief, the Attorney General. The plan that he sponsored or supported in the February 2 conference in Sacramento with Governor Olson and De Witt called for a conference between Governor Olson and leading Japanese Americans which would result in a voluntary resettlement in the central valleys of California where the Japanese could augment agricultural production. As De Witt explained the Clark-Olson plan to an unhappy Gullion:

> Well, I tell you, they are solving the problem here very satisfactorily. . . . I have agreed to accept any plan they propose to put those people, Japanese Americans and Japanese who are in Category A area in the Category B area on farms. . . . We haven't got anything to do with it except they are consulting me to see what areas I will let them go into. . . . Mr. Clark is very much in favor of it . . . the people are going to handle it locally through the Governor and they are going to move those people to arable and tillable land. They are going to keep them in the state. They don't want to bring in a lot of negroes and mexicans and let them take their place. . . . They just want to put them on the land out of the cities where they can raise vegetables like they are doing now.[31]

The Provost Marshal General's men were disgusted with this turn of events. Not only were their plans being thwarted by the civilians who ran the Army—Stimson and McCloy, who were thinking in terms of creating "Jap-less" islands of security around a few key installations like the Consolidated-Vultee aircraft plant in San Diego, the Lockheed and North American plants in Los Angeles, and the Boeing plant in Seattle—but even their former ally, General De Witt, the all-important man on the ground who alone could make authoritative statements about "military necessity," had now deserted their cause. As Colonel Archer Lerch, Gullion's deputy, put it:

> I think I detect a decided weakening on the part of Gen. De Witt, which I think is most unfortunate. . . . The idea suggested to Gen.

---

[30] Telephone conversation, De Witt and Bendetsen, February 7, 1942, Provost Marshal General, Record Group 389, National Archives.

[31] Telephone conversation, De Witt and Gullion, February 5, 1942, Provost Marshal General, Record Group 389, National Archives.

De Witt in his conference with Gov. Olson, that a satisfactory solution must be reached through a conference between the Governor and leading Jap-Americans, savors too much of the spirit of Rotary and overlooks the necessary cold-bloodedness of war.[32]

If pressure for evacuation within the Army seemed to be weakening, stronger and stronger outside forces were being brought into play. On February 2 and 3, in separate meetings, representatives and senators from all three Pacific Coast states agreed to coordinate their efforts. Serving as coordinator of these anti-Japanese efforts was Senator Hiram W. Johnson of California, who, in the mid-1920s, had masterminded a similar joint Congressional effort which brought about elimination of a Japanese quota in the Immigration Act of 1924. Johnson was actually more concerned about the defense of the West Coast—he feared a Japanese invasion—and complained bitterly to one of his political intimates that "the keenness of interest in the Japanese question far overshadowed the general proposition of our preparedness."[33]

Back in California, Governor Culbert Olson went on the air on February 4; his speech could only have further inflamed public opinion. Disseminating false information that probably came from his conference two days previously with General De Witt and Tom Clark, he warned the already frightened people of California that

> it is known that there are Japanese residents of California who have sought to aid the Japanese enemy by way of communicating information, or have shown indications of preparation for fifth column activities.

Loyal Japanese, he insisted, could best prove their loyalty by cooperating with whatever the authorities asked them to do. Then, in a vain attempt to reassure the public, he went on to say that everything would be all right. He told of his conference with De Witt and announced, without of course giving any specifics, that

> general plans [have been] agreed upon for the movement and placement of the entire adult Japanese population in California at productive and useful employment within the borders of our state, and under such surveillance and protection . . . as shall be deemed necessary.[34]

---

[32] Conn, "Japanese Evacuation from the West Coast," p. 128.

[33] Letters, Johnson to Rufus Holman, February 3, 1942; and Johnson to Frank P. Doherty, February 16, 1942, Johnson Mss., Pt. III, Box 19, Bancroft Library.

[34] Speech text, February 4, 1942, Carton 5, Olson Mss., Bancroft Library.

The next day the mayor of Los Angeles, Fletcher Bowron, outdid the governor in attempting to arouse passions. After pointing out that the largest concentration of Japanese was in Los Angeles, he turned on the venom:

> Right here in our own city are those who may spring to action at an appointed time in accordance with a prearranged plan wherein each of our little Japanese friends will know his part in the event of any possible attempted invasion or air raid.

He then argued that not only Japanese aliens but citizens of Japanese descent, some of whom were "unquestionably . . . loyal," represented a threat to Los Angeles. Disloyal Nisei, he argued, would loudly proclaim their patriotism. "Of course they would try to fool us. They did in Honolulu and in Manila, and we may expect it in California." Bowron's answer, of course, was mass internment for all Japanese, citizens and aliens alike. From favorable references to Tom Clark, he seems to have been willing to go along with the De Witt–Olson–Clark plan of labor camps within California. Bowron also tried to take care of constitutional and ethical scruples:

> If we can send our own young men to war, it is nothing less than sickly sentimentality to say that we will do injustice to American-born Japanese to merely put them in a place of safety so that they can do not harm. . . . We [in Los Angeles] are the ones who will be the human sacrifices if the perfidy that characterized the attack on Pearl Harbor is ever duplicated on the American continent.

In a follow-up statement the next day, Bowron put forth the interesting proposition that one of the major reasons that Japanese could not be trusted was that Californians had discriminated against them:

> The Japanese, because they are unassimilable, because the aliens have been denied the right to own real property in California, because of [immigration discrimination against them], because of the marked differences in appearance between Japanese and Caucasians, because of the generations of training and philosophy that makes them Japanese and nothing else—all of these contributing factors set the Japanese apart as a race, regardless of how many generations have been born in America. Undoubtedly many of them intend to be loyal, but only each individual can know his own intentions, and when the final test comes, who can say but that "blood will tell"?

We cannot run the risk of another Pearl Harbor episode in Southern California.[35]

And, that same week, in Sacramento, Attorney General Earl Warren presided over a meeting of some one hundred and fifty law enforcement officers, mostly sheriffs and district attorneys. According to a federal official who attended the meeting:

> In his opening remarks, Mr. Warren cautioned against hysteria but then proceeded to outline his remarks in such a fashion as to encourage hysterical thinking. . . . Mr. [Isidore] Dockweiler, Los Angeles District Attorney . . . , asserted that the United States Supreme Court had been packed with leftist and other extreme advocates of civil liberty and that it was time for the people of California to disregard the law, if necessary, to secure their protection. Mr. Dockweiler finally worked himself into such a state of hysteria that he was called to order by Mr. Warren. . . . The meeting loudly applauded the statement that the people of California had no trust in the ability and willingness of the Federal Government to proceed against enemy aliens. One high official was heard to state that he favored shooting on sight all Japanese residents of the state.[36]

Despite relative calm in the press until the end of January, a government intelligence agency (the civilian Office of Government Reports) informed Washington that "word of mouth discussions [continue] with a surprisingly large number of people expressing themselves as in favor of sending all Japanese to concentration camps." By the end of January, the press "flared up again" with demands growing "that positive action be taken by the Federal Government. This awakening of the press has increased the verbal discussions that never ceased." By early February the Los Angeles *Times*, never friendly to the Japanese Americans, as we have seen, could no longer find human terms to describe them. All Japanese Americans, the *Times* insisted editorially, were at least potentially enemies: "A viper is nonetheless a viper wherever the egg is hatched—so a Japanese-American, born of Japanese parents—grows up to be a Japanese, not an American."

Henry McLemore, the nationally syndicated columnist, put into

---

[35] Bowron speech and statement in *Congressional Record*, February 9, 1942, pp. A547–48.

[36] Material on the meeting of law enforcement officers from California reports of the Office of Government Reports for January and February, 1942, Record Group 44, Washington National Records Center, Suitland, Md.

words the extreme reaction against Attorney General Francis Biddle, whom Californians (probably with some prompting from the military and militant congressmen) had made the chief target of their ire. Biddle, McLemore reported, couldn't even win election as "third assistant dog catcher" in California. "Californians have the feeling," he explained, "that he is the one in charge of the Japanese menace, and that he is handling it with all the severity of Lord Fauntleroy."[37]

With this kind of encouragement in the background, Provost Marshal Gullion and his associates continued to press for mass action against the West Coast Japanese despite the fact that the officers of General Headquarters, directly under Marshall, were now trying to moderate anti-Japanese sentiment among members of Congress. On February 4, an impressive array of military personnel attended the meeting of West Coast congressmen: Admiral Harold R. Stark, Chief of Naval Operations; Brigadier General Mark W. Clark of General Headquarters (who had become Marshall's "expert" on the West Coast Japanese, even though just hours before he was to appear at the meeting he had to ask Bendetsen, "Now what is this Nisei?"); Colonel Hoyt S. Vandenberg of the Army Air Corps; and Colonel Wilton B. Persons, Chief of the (Congressional) Liaison Branch. According to Colonel Persons' report, Senator Rufus Holman of Oregon was the chief spokesman, and in pressing for an evacuation, he stressed the point that the people on the West Coast were "alarmed and terrified as to their person, their employment, and their homes." Clark then gave the congressmen the first truly military appraisal of the situation that they had received. Summarizing General Headquarters' findings, he told them that they were "unduly alarmed" and speculated that, at worst, there might be a sporadic air raid or a commando attack or two, and that while an attack on Alaska "was not a fantastic idea," there was no likelihood of a real onslaught on the West Coast states.[38]

The day after General Clark's moderate presentation, the Provost Marshal began to try to bring Assistant Secretary of War McCloy around to his point of view. On February 5 he wrote McCloy that although De Witt had changed his mind, he (Gullion) was still of the view that mass evacuation was necessary. The De Witt–Olson–Tom Clark idea of voluntary cooperation with Japanese American leaders, the Provost Marshal General denounced as "dangerous to rely upon. . . ." In a more detailed memo the following day (February 6) he warned McCloy of the possible grave consequences of inaction:

---

[37] *Ibid.*

[38] Memo for record by Persons, February 6, 1942, Stetson Conn, "Notes," Office, Chief of Military History, U.S. Army.

If our production for war is seriously delayed by sabotage in the West Coastal states, we very possibly shall lose the war. . . . From reliable reports from military and other sources, the danger of Japanese inspired sabotage is great. . . . No half-way measures based upon considerations of economic disturbance, humanitarianism, or fear of retaliation will suffice. Such measures will be "too little or too late."

This shrewd appeal—"too little and too late" was a journalistic slogan that all too accurately described the general tenor of anti-Axis military efforts to that date—was followed by a concrete program that had been drawn up by Gullion and Bendetsen, and that the Provost Marshal General formally recommended. Somewhat short of total evacuation, it still would have involved moving the vast majority of West Coast Japanese. The plan consisted of four steps, as follows:

Step 1. Declare restricted areas from which all alien enemies are barred. [This had already been done by Biddle, although it would not go into effect until February 24.]
Step 2. Internment east of the Sierra Nevadas of all Japanese aliens, accompanied by such citizen members of their families as may volunteer for internment. [Since a majority of the Nisei were minors this would have included most of the citizen generation.]
Step 3. The pass and permit system for "military reservations." [This would result, according to Gullion, in excluding citizens of Japanese extraction, "without raising too many legal questions."]
Step 4. Resettlement. [Neither Gullion nor anyone else, as we shall see, had worked this out in any detail. According to the Provost Marshal General, it was "merely an idea and not an essential part of the plan."][39]

By February 10, however, Gullion and Bendetsen, the latter now back on the West Coast to strengthen General De Witt's resolve, seemed to have convinced McCloy, somehow, that a mass evacuation was necessary, although Secretary Stimson still clung to the idea of creating islands around strategic locations, an idea that the Provost Marshal General's men were sure he had gotten from General Stilwell. Bendetsen insisted that safety "islands" would not prevent sabotage: "if they wanted to sabotage that area, they could set the outside area on fire. They could still cut water lines and power lines." According to Bendetsen he had been over that ground twice with McCloy, who seemed to agree, and who had

---

[39] Memo, Gullion to McCloy, February 5, 1942; letter, Gullion to McCloy, February 6, 1942, Assistant Secretary of War, Record Group 107, National Archives.

told Bendetsen that he would call him back after he had had another talk with the Secretary.[40]

The next day, February 11, 1942, was the real day of decision as far as the Japanese Americans were concerned. Sometime in the early afternoon, Secretary Stimson telephoned Franklin Roosevelt at the White House. Shortly after that call, McCloy phoned Bendetsen at the Presidio to tell him the good news. According to McCloy:

> . . . we talked to the President and the President, in substance, says go ahead and do anything you think necessary . . . if it involves citizens, we will take care of them too. He says there will probably be some repercussions, but it has got to be dictated by military necessity, but as he puts it, "Be as reasonable as you can."

McCloy went on to say that he thought the President would sign an executive order giving the Army the authority to evacuate. He also indicated there was at least some residual reluctance on the part of Secretary Stimson, who wanted to make a start in Los Angeles, concentrating on areas around the big bomber plants. McCloy indicated that he thought he could convince the Secretary that the limited plan was not practicable. In his conversation with McCloy, Bendetsen had talked about evacuating some 61,000 people, but in talking to Gullion about an hour later, he spoke of evacuating approximately 101,000 people.[41]

By February 11 the Provost Marshal's men had the situation all their own way. Assistant Secretary McCloy, who had been "pretty much against" their view just a week before, had been converted, and through him, Secretary Stimson and the President, although the latter probably did not take too much persuading. Bendetsen was again in San Francisco, and helping General De Witt draft what the Western Defense commander called "the plan that Mr. McCloy wanted me to submit." Although, in retrospect, it seems clear that the struggle for mass evacuation was over by then, not all the participants knew it yet.

Among those in the dark were the staff at General Headquarters, particularly General Mark Clark who had been assigned to make the official military report on the advisability of mass evacuation. Early on February 12 he called De Witt, and when told that an evacuation, to include citizens of Japanese descent, was in the works, he expressed disbelief. His own official memorandum, completed at about that time, had reached

---

[40] Telephone conversation, Gullion and Bendetsen, February 10, 1942, Provost Marshal General, Record Group 389, National Archives.

[41] Conn, "Japanese Evacuation from the West Coast," pp. 131–32; telephone conversations, McCloy and Bendetsen, Bendetsen and Gullion, February 11, 1942, Stetson Conn, "Notes."

opposite conclusions, and deserves quoting at length, because it alone represents official military thinking on the subject.

General Clark's report concluded:

I cannot agree with the wisdom of such a mass exodus for the following reasons:

(a) We will never have a perfect defense against sabotage except at the expense of other equally important efforts. The situation with regards to protecting establishments from sabotage is analogous to protecting them from air attack by antiaircraft and barrage balloons. We will never have enough of these means to fully protect these establishments. Why, then, should we make great sacrifices in other efforts in order to make them secure from sabotage?

(b) We must weigh the advantages and disadvantages of such a wholesale solution to this problem. We must not permit our entire offensive effort to be sabotaged in an effort to protect all establishments from ground sabotage.

5. I recommend the following approach to this problem:

(a) Ascertain and designate the critical installations to be protected in each area and list them according to their importance.

(b) Make up our minds as to what means are available for such protection and apply that protection as far as it will go to the most critical objectives, leaving the ones of lesser importance for future consideration, or lesser protection.

(c) Select the most critical ones to be protected and delimit the essential areas around them for their protection.

(d) Eject all enemy aliens from those areas and permit entrance of others by pass only.

(e) Only such installations as can be physically protected in that manner should be included in this category. For example, it is practicable to do this in the case of the Boeing Plant, Bremerton Navy Yard and many other similar vital installations. In other words we are biting off a little at a time in the solution of the problem.

(f) Civilian police should be used to the maximum in effecting this protection.

(g) Federal Bureau of Investigation should be greatly augmented in counter-subversive activity.

(h) Raids should be used freely and frequently.

(i) Ring leaders and suspects should be interned liberally.

(j) This alien group should be made to understand through publicity that the first overt act on their part will bring a wave of counter-measures which will make the historical efforts of the vigilantes look puny in comparison.

6. It is estimated that to evacuate large numbers of this group will require one soldier to 4 or 5 aliens. This would require between 10,000 and 15,000 soldiers to guard the group during their internment, to say nothing of the continuing burden of protecting the installations. I feel that this problem must be attacked in a sensible manner. We must admit that we are taking some chances just as we take other chances in war. We must determine what are our really critical installations, give them thorough protection and leave the others to incidental means in the hope that we will not lose too many of them—and above all keep our eye on the ball—that is, the creating and training of an offensive army.[42]

Here was truly "stern military necessity." The General Staff officer, who probably reflected Marshall's real view, would have moved very few Japanese, not because he was a defender of civil liberty, or even understood what the probabilities for sabotage really were, but because, it did not seem to him, on balance, that the "protection" which total evacuation would provide was worth its cost in military manpower and energy. But military views, as we have seen, were not the determinants of policy; political views were. The real architects of policy were the lawyers in uniform, Gullion and Bendetsen. Their most highly placed supporters, McCloy and Stimson, were two Republican, Wall Street lawyers.

Very late in the game, and often after the fact, a very few New Dealers tried to influence the President to take a more consistently democratic approach to the Japanese. On February 3 Archibald MacLeish, then Director of the Office of Facts and Figures, a predecessor of the Office of War Information, wrote one of Roosevelt's confidential secretaries suggesting that the President might want to try to hold down passions on the West Coast. His office, he said, was "trying to keep down the pressure out there." He enclosed, for the President, a statement of Woodrow Wilson's that he thought might be useful. During the other world war, Wilson had said, in a statement highly appropriate to the West Coast situation:

> . . . I can never accept any man as a champion of liberty either for ourselves or for the world who does not reverence and obey the laws of our beloved land, whose laws we ourselves have made. He has adopted the standards of the enemies of his country, whom he affects to despise.

Getting no response from the White House, MacLeish tried the Army six days later. "Dear Jack," the libertarian poet wrote McCloy, "In my opinion

---

[42] Mark W. Clark Memo, General Headquarters, n.d. but ca. February 12, 1942, Stetson Conn, "Notes."

great care should be taken not to reach a grave decision in the present situation on the representations of officials and pressure groups alone. The decision may have far-reaching effects."[43]

MacLeish's efforts were, of course, fruitless. Much more influential was the authoritarian voice of America's chief pundit, Walter Lippmann. Writing from San Francisco in a column published on February 12, the usually detached observer who has so often been on the unpopular side of issues, was, in this instance, merely an extension of the mass West Coast mind. In an essay entitled "The Fifth Column on the Coast," Lippmann wrote:

> . . . the Pacific Coast is in imminent danger of a combined attack from within and without. . . . It is a fact that the Japanese navy has been reconnoitering the coast more or less continuously. . . . There is an assumption [in Washington] that a citizen may not be interfered with unless he has committed an overt act. . . . The Pacific Coast is officially a combat zone: Some part of it may at any moment be a battlefield. And nobody ought to be on a battlefield who has no good reason for being there. There is plenty of room elsewhere for him to exercise his rights.

The pundit's thinkpiece drew a lot of notice. Westbrook Pegler, delighted at finding a respectable man urging what he had long urged, chortled:

> Do you get what he says? This is a high-grade fellow with a heavy sense of responsibility. . . . The Japanese in California should be under armed guard to the last man and woman right now [even Pegler didn't like to talk about children]—and to hell with habeas corpus until the danger is over. . . . If it isn't true, we can take it out on Lippmann, but on his reputation I will bet it is all true.

In the War Department, Marshall sent a copy of Lippmann's column to Stimson, and Stimson sent it to McCloy, and it was undoubtedly read in the White House.[44] It was read in the Justice Department too. Long-suffering Attorney General Francis Biddle, former law clerk to Justice Holmes, civil libertarian and New Dealer, was finally stirred to

---

[43] Letters, MacLeish to Grace Tully, February 3, 1942, President's Personal File 1820, Franklin D. Roosevelt Library, Hyde Park; MacLeish to McCloy, February 9, 1942, Assistant Secretary of War, Record Group 107, National Archives.

[44] Lippmann column and memo slips in Secretary of War, Record Group 107, National Archives; Pegler's column, Washington *Post*, February 15, 1942, as cited in *Congressional Record*, February 17, 1942, pp. 568–69.

respond by Lippmann's column. In his memoirs, published in 1962, deeply regretting the whole affair, Biddle wrote:

> . . . if, instead of dealing almost exclusively with McCloy and Bendetsen, I had urged [Stimson] to resist the pressure of his subordinates, the result might have been different. But I was new to the Cabinet, and disinclined to insist on my view to an elder statesman whose wisdom and integrity I greatly respected.[45]

What Biddle did not reveal, however, was that he himself had given Stimson a kind of green light. In a letter written on February 12, the Attorney General voiced his distaste for the proposed evacuation, particularly of citizens, but assured Stimson that

> I have no doubt that the Army can legally, at any time, evacuate all persons in a specified territory if such action is deemed essential from a military point of view. . . . No legal problem arises when Japanese citizens are evacuated, but American citizens of Japanese origin could not, in my opinion, be singled out of an area and evacuated with the other Japanese.

Then Biddle, Philadelphia lawyer that he was, told Stimson how he thought it could be done.

> However, the result might be accomplished by evacuating all persons in the area and then licensing back those whom the military authorities thought were not objectionable from a military point of view.[46]

Five days later, on February 17, Biddle addressed a memorandum to the President, a memorandum that was, in effect, a last-gasp effort to stop the mass evacuation that was being planned. Biddle apparently was unaware that Roosevelt had given Stimson and McCloy the go-ahead signal almost a week before. The Attorney General opened with a statement about the various West Coast pressure groups and congressmen who were urging the evacuation. He then singled out Lippmann and Pegler, and argued that their concern about imminent invasion and sabotage was not borne out by the facts. Biddle then maintained, rather curiously, that "there [was] no dispute between the War, Navy and Justice Departments," and warned that the evacuation of 93,000 Japanese in California would

---

[45] Francis B. Biddle, *In Brief Authority* (New York: Doubleday, 1962), p. 226.
[46] Letter, Biddle to Stimson, February 12, 1942, Secretary of War, Record Group 107, National Archives.

disrupt agriculture, require thousands of troops, tie up transportation, and raise very difficult questions of resettlement. Then, in an apparent approval of evacuation, Biddle wrote, "If complete confusion and lowering of morale is to be avoided, so large a job must be done after careful planning."

Then, in a parting blast, directed specifically at Lippmann, Biddle attacked columnists acting as "Armchair Strategists and Junior G-Men," suggested that they were essentially "shouting FIRE! in a crowded theater," and warned that if race riots occurred, Lippmann and the others would bear a heavy responsibility.[47]

But Biddle could have directed his attack much closer to home. Not only his Cabinet colleagues but some of his subordinates were doing more than shouting. Three days before the Attorney General's letter, Tom C. Clark, of his staff, assured a Los Angeles press conference that the federal government would soon evacuate over 200,000 enemy aliens and their children, including all American-born Japanese, from areas in California vital to national defense.[48]

On February 13, the Pacific Coast Congressional delegation forwarded to the President a recommendation for evacuation that was fully in line with what Stimson and McCloy were proposing. They recommended, unanimously:

> the immediate evacuation of all persons of Japanese lineage and all others, aliens and citizens alike, whose presence shall be deemed dangerous or inimical to the defense of the United States from all strategic areas . . . such areas [should] be enlarged as expeditiously as possible until they shall encompass the entire strategic areas of the states of California, Oregon and Washington, and the Territory of Alaska.[49]

Finally, on Thursday, February 19, 1942, a day that should live in infamy, Franklin D. Roosevelt signed an Executive Order that gave the Army, through the Secretary of War, the authority that Gullion and Bendetsen had sought so long. Using as justification a military necessity for "the successful prosecution of the war," the President empowered the military to designate "military areas" from which "any or all persons may be excluded" and to provide for such persons "transportation, food, shelter, and other accommodations as may be necessary . . . until other arrangements are made." The words Japanese or Japanese Americans never

---

[47] Letter, Biddle to Franklin D. Roosevelt, February 17, 1942, Franklin D. Roosevelt Library, Hyde Park.

[48] Los Angeles *Times*, February 15, 1942.

[49] "Recommendations" in Assistant Secretary of War, Record Group 107, National Archives.

even appear in the order; but it was they, and they alone, who felt its sting.[50]

The myth of military necessity was used as a fig leaf for a particular variant of American racism. On the very day that the President signed the order, a conference at General Headquarters heard and approved an opposite opinion. Army Intelligence reported, officially, that it believed "mass evacuation unnecessary." In this instance, at least, the military mind was superior to the political: the soldiers who opposed the evacuation were right and the politicians who proposed it were wrong. But, why did it happen?

Two major theories have been propounded by scholars which ought to be examined. Almost as the evacuation was taking place, administrators and faculty at the University of California at Berkeley took steps to set up a scholarly study of the relocation in all its aspects. With generous foundation support and with the cooperation of some of the federal officials most responsible for the decision (for example, John J. McCloy), the "Japanese American Evacuation and Resettlement Study" was set up under the directorship of Dorothy Swaine Thomas, then a University of California Professor of Rural Sociology and a skilled demographer. Her staff included a broad spectrum of social scientists, but curiously did not include either professional historians or archivists. Professor Thomas' own volumes did not seek to determine responsibility for the evacuation, but two volumes that flowed out of the project did: Morton Grodzins, *Americans Betrayed* (Chicago, 1949) and Jacobus tenBroek, Edward N. Barnhart, and Floyd Matson, *Prejudice, War, and the Constitution* (Berkeley and Los Angeles, 1954). Grodzins felt that the major cause of the evacuation was the pressure exerted by special interest groups within California and on the Pacific Coast generally. The "western group," he wrote, "was successful in having a program molded to its own immediate advantage made national policy." Professors tenBroek, Barnhart, and Matson vigorously disputed the Grodzins thesis: for them, the responsibility was General De Witt's, and, they argued, his decision was based essentially on his "military estimate of the situation."[51]

Five years later a professional historian, Stetson Conn, then a civilian historian for the Department of the Army and later the Army's Chief of Military History, published an authoritative account of what really happened, as far as the military was concerned. He found in the contemporary

---

[50] Executive Order No. 9066, February 19, 1942, in *House Report No. 2124*, 77th Cong., 2d Sess., pp. 314–15.

[51] For a good summary, see Chapter IV, "Two Theories of Responsibility," pp. 185–210, in Jacobus tenBroek, Edward N. Barnhart, and Floyd W. Matson, *Prejudice, War, and the Constitution* (Berkeley and Los Angeles: University of California Press, 1954).

evidence "little support for the argument that military necessity required a mass evacuation" and pointed, accurately, to the machinations of Gullion and Bendetsen and their success in bending the civilian heads of the War Department to their will.

The question that remains to be answered is why the recommendation of Stimson and McCloy was accepted by the nation. Grodzins' pressure groups were, of course, important, but even more important than the peculiar racism of a region was the general racist character of American society. The decision to evacuate the Japanese was popular, not only in California and the West, but in the entire nation, although only on the West Coast was it a major issue in early 1942.

The leader of the nation, was, in the final analysis, responsible. It was Franklin Roosevelt, who in one short telephone call, passed the decision-making power to two men who had never been elected to any office, saying only, with the politician's charm and equivocation: "Be as reasonable as you can." Why did he agree? Probably for two reasons: in the first place, it was expedient; in the second place, Roosevelt himself harbored deeply felt anti-Japanese prejudices.

As to expediency, it is important to remember what the war news was like in early 1942. It was a very bad time for the military fortunes of the United States and its allies. The Japanese had landed on the island of Singapore on February 8, on New Britain on the 9th, and were advancing rapidly in Burma. Roosevelt was concerned, first of all with winning the war, and secondly with unity at home, so that he, unlike his former chief, Woodrow Wilson, could win the peace with the advice and consent of the Senate. He could read the Congressional signs well and knew that cracking down on the Japanese Americans would be popular both on the Hill and in the country generally. And the last thing he wanted was a rift with establishment Republicans like Stimson and McCloy; New Dealers like Biddle and MacLeish could be counted on not to rock the boat.

But, in addition, Franklin Roosevelt was himself convinced that Japanese, alien and citizen, were dangerous to American security. He, along with several members of his Cabinet and circle of advisers, persistently pushed for mass internment of the Hawaiian Japanese Americans long after the military had wisely rejected such a policy. And there was a kind of rationale for such a policy. If Japanese were a threat to security in California, where they represented fewer than 2 percent of the population, certainly in wartorn Hawaii, where they were more than a third of the population, they should have constituted a real menace. But it is one thing to incarcerate a tiny element of the population, as was done on the West Coast, and quite another to put away a sizable fraction of the whole. Apart from the sheer size of the problem, relatively and absolutely, there was the question of the disruption that such a mass evacuation would cause in the local economy. Referring to Oahu alone, Lieutenant General Delos C. Emmons, the Army commander there, pointed out to the War Department in January 1942 that Japanese provided the bulk of the main island's skilled labor force and were indispensable unless replaced by an equivalent labor force from the mainland. In addition, the logistical problems of internment in the islands were so great that Emmons recommended that any evacuation and relocation be to the mainland.

At the Cabinet level, however, different views were held. On February 27, for example, Navy Secretary Knox, the most vocal Japanophobe in the Cabinet, suggested rounding up all the Japanese on Oahu and putting them under Army guard on the neighboring island of Molokai, better known as a leper colony. Stimson concurred as to the danger, but insisted that if they were to be moved they be sent to the states. (The shipping situation, for all practical purposes, made this impossible.) The President, according to Stimson, clearly favored Knox's plan.[52] The President and his Navy Secretary continued to press for this policy well into 1942, but eventually were forestalled by a strongly worded joint recommendation to the contrary signed by both Chief of Staff Marshall and Chief of Naval Operations Admiral Ernest J. King.[53] In other words, real rather than imaginary military necessity governed in Hawaii. Although Hawaii was the first real theater of war, fewer than 2000 of the territory's 150,000 Japanese were ever deprived of their liberty.

---

[52] Conn, "The Hawaiian Defenses After Pearl Harbor," pp. 207–10.

[53] See, for example, letter, Knox to Franklin D. Roosevelt, October 17, 1942, copy in Secretary of War, Record Group 107, National Archives; and Franklin D. Roosevelt, autograph memo to Stimson and Marshall, November 2, 1942, Secretary of War, Record Group 107, National Archives. The King-Marshall memo, July 15, 1942, is in President's Secretary File, Franklin D. Roosevelt Library, Hyde Park.

4

THE ROUNDUP

Although, as we have seen, the decision for mass evacuation was made in mid-February, neither the Provost Marshal General's office nor the Western Defense Command, despite their long preoccupation with the idea of a "Jap-free" West Coast, was prepared to act quickly. While they laid and relaid their plans, the Congress of the United States helped prepare and crystallize public opinion. Scattered debates in Congress in mid-February made it clear that no voices of protest would be raised in that body against mass evacuation; in fact, the prevailing sentiment was that the federal authorities were not moving quickly enough. But even more important was a series of hearings held up and down the West Coast by a Congressional committee headed by Representative John H. Tolan of California, which had originally been established to investigate "National Defense Migration." These hearings, held in late February and early March in San Francisco, Portland, Seattle, and Los Angeles, are important, not because of any policy decisions that emanated from them—policy was already largely determined —but because they provide a valuable cross section of West

Coast opinion from both the Caucasian and Japanese American communities.[1]

The overwhelming majority of the witnesses supported, unequivocally, the necessity of getting all Japanese, alien and citizen, off the Coast. Some, however, like San Francisco Mayor Angelo J. Rossi, were very much concerned about the rights of aliens, if they were of German or Italian origin. The problems of German and Italian aliens, he insisted, "should be considered separately from those of the Japanese." West Coast civilian leaders were well aware of General De Witt's intention to move all enemy aliens out of California, and most of them resisted the idea. The most touching (and irrelevant) plea came from San Francisco Attorney Chauncey Tramutolo. With an obvious assist from the Chairman (Tolan: "Tell us about the DiMaggios"), the lawyer indicated how terrible it would be if the parents of famous athletes were evacuated just because they had failed to take out citizenship papers.

> Neither of the DiMaggio seniors is a citizen. They have reared nine children . . . eight of whom were born in the United States. . . . Three of the boys are outstanding persons in the sports world. Joe, who is with the Yanks, was leading hitter [in] 1939 and 1940. . . . Dominic is with the Boston Red Sox and . . . Vincent is with the Pittsburgh team. . . . To evacuate [people like the DiMaggios] would . . . present . . . a serious situation. Many of the people affected by the existing order have boys and girls in the armed forces. . . . I believe that it would be destructive and have a tendency to lower morale . . . if information should reach those in the armed forces that their relatives have been ordered to move out of this area because unfortunately they are not citizens.

This and similar testimony made it very clear that although West Coast opinion was overwhelmingly in favor of mass incarceration of the Japanese, most of those who discussed the matter insisted that doctrines of "racial guilt" should not be applied to Europeans. For Europeans, guilt was individual; for Asians, it was collective. Ironically, no testimony better demonstrates this dual standard than that of Earl Warren, who would later become a champion of the oppressed. But in 1942 Warren was in the grip of precisely those kinds of conspiratorial notions that would be used to attack him and his works in the 1950s and 60s. Warren, already a declared candidate for the governorship, had local law enforcement officials prepare

---

[1] The testimony cited below may be found in U.S. Congress, House, Select Committee Investigating National Defense Migration, *Hearings*, 77th Cong., 2d Sess., Parts 29, 30, and 31 (Washington, 1942).

maps which showed, county by county, property held by Japanese in California. According to the California Attorney General:

> An inspection of these maps shows a disturbing situation. It shows that along the coast from Marin County [north of San Francisco] to the Mexican border virtually every important strategic location and installation has one or more Japanese in its immediate vicinity. . . . Undoubtedly, the presence of many of these persons in their present locations is mere coincidence, but it would seem equally beyond doubt that the presence of others is not coincidence. . . . It will interest you to know that some of our airplane factories in this state are entirely surrounded by Japanese. . . .

It was also true, though Warren did not mention it, that the Japanese had been in most of these areas long before there were any aircraft factories, but this fact was easy to ignore. Warren believed that there was an "Invisible Deadline for Sabotage" that threatened the entire state and the war effort. In a formula that probably came from General De Witt, Warren pushed the conspiracy theory about as far as it would go.

> Unfortunately [many] are of the opinion that because we have had no sabotage and no fifth column activities in this State . . . that means that none have been planned for us. But I take the view that this is the most ominous sign in our whole situation. It convinces me more than perhaps any other factor that the sabotage that we are to get, the fifth column activities that we are to get, are timed just like Pearl Harbor was timed and just like the invasion of France, and of Denmark, and of Norway, and all of those other countries.
>
> I believe that we are just being lulled into a false sense of security and that the only reason we haven't had disaster in California is because it has been timed for a different date. . . . Our day of reckoning is bound to come in that regard.

The future expounder of the Constitution believed, in 1942, that in wartime "every citizen must give up some of his rights." Japanese who were American citizens, he felt, were more dangerous than the aliens. After all, he pointed out, there were twice as many of them and most of the Issei were over fifty-five years of age. The Attorney General admitted that there were some "loyal ones" among the Nisei, but he insisted that "by and large there is more potential danger" from the Nisei than from the Issei. Questioned about the legality of the proposed evacuation, Warren agreed that it was "absolutely constitutional." Warren also presented a number of statements from California law enforcement officials demonstrating that most of them not only went along with his views, but that some went well beyond them. The District Attorney of San Luis Obispo County, for example, felt that

> the best way would be to take every Japanese alien in the United States and in the possessions . . . and send them to Japan or find means of getting them there. . . . We should have as our objective the complete alienation from the United States soil of every single Japanese alien.

Officials in the city of Madera complained that "it is impossible for the police . . . to tell which Japanese are dangerous and which are not. . . . [Therefore] the only safe procedure would be to take up all the Japanese and intern them." The Chief of Police of Culver City argued that the "Nishi be interned along with the Ishi [sic]" because as American citizens "they should be pleased to submit to internment rather than place the security of our Nation in jeopardy. It of course stands to reason that if they should object to such treatment, they could not be looked upon as being true and loyal Americans." The Western Growers Protective Association, an organization of white produce farmers, insisted that its members had special knowledge of the situation because of long association with Japanese. They felt that "no individual alien Japanese, or . . . American citizen of Japanese parentage, can be judged as to his loyalty solely by past experience."

Some of the witnesses, apparently a party to the Olson-Clark scheme of resettlement within California, supported that solution. A Monterey County agriculturalist testified:

> I feel that . . . we are entitled to kill our own snake. [If put in supervised camps in California] they might be taken out to work . . . in the morning, and be brought back at night. Their labor could be utilized, and I think that that would, perhaps, be as good a solution of this problem as any you might offer.

The County Supervisors Association of California, blunter than most, forwarded a resolution urging that all Japanese and their descendants be placed in a "concentration camp under the supervision of the federal government," a position supported by the city council of Portland, Oregon. The mayor there felt that "50 percent or more of the second generation are loyal: but I do not think anyone is in a position to ferret out the 50 percent." The mayor of Seattle, Washington, had an even higher estimate of the loyalty of Japanese Americans; of 8000 Japanese, he testified, "7,900 probably are above question but the other 100 would burn this town down and let Japanese planes come in and bring on something that would dwarf Pearl Harbor." The Executive Secretary of the left-wing Washington Commonwealth Federation, while denying any prejudice and denouncing "racism," agreed that citizen and noncitizen alike should be moved.

There was some, but not much, dissent from the establishment. Most impressive, perhaps, was the testimony of the conservative Republican mayor of Tacoma, Washington, Harry P. Cain, who insisted that guilt was individual, not collective. He argued that local authorities could differentiate between the loyal and the disloyal. He thought that

> a man's background, regardless of who he is, very generally has much to do with what he is going to do. If born in this country; if a Christian; if employed side by side with others who fill the same classification, for years; if educated in our schools; if a producer now and in the past; if maintained in a position of production—I should think that person could be construed to be a loyal American citizen.

A few other white voices were raised in defense of the Nisei; the most numerous were a group of religious leaders and educators called the Committee on National Security and Fair Play. They, too, argued that guilt was individual and that

> since the Nisei are full-fledged American citizens by virtue of birth and upbringing in this country, certainly they should be given not less consideration than German and Italian aliens, sympathetic as we are with those among them who are thoroughly loyal to democratic ideals.

But by far the strongest statements in support of the Japanese Americans came from A. L. Wirin, counsel for the Southern California Branch of the American Civil Liberties Union, and Louis Goldblatt, Secretary of the State CIO. Wirin insisted that even during wartime,

> there must be a point beyond which there may be no abridgement of civil liberties and we feel that whatever the emergency, that persons must be judged, so long as we have a Bill of Rights, because of what they do as persons. . . . We feel that treating persons, because they are members of a race, constitutes illegal discrimination, which is forbidden by the fourteenth amendment whether we are at war or peace.

Goldblatt, in a position diametrically opposed to most of California's labor leaders, maintained that "the second generation of Japanese in this Nation should not be distinguished from the second generation of any other nationality," and tried, without success, to read to the committee the inscription on the Statue of Liberty. More typical of the left-wing attitude was the line taken by the *People's World*, the West Coast Communist daily. Restrictions upon the liberty of Japanese were "unfortunate, but vital," and by late February General De Witt's plans were termed "a sensible program." These sentiments were echoed by the Los Angeles *Doho*, a leftist Japanese newspaper that backed the evacuation in even stronger terms than the Japanese American Citizens League (JACL), saying that "this is no time to holler that our civil liberties and constitutional rights are being denied us," while on the national scene party-lining Congressman Vito Marcantonio of New York gave tacit support to the evacuation by repeating the canard that the disaster at Pearl Harbor was made possible by "the Japanese fifth column."[2] Many liberals, however, perhaps despairing of doing anything much for the Japanese, concentrated their energies on getting fair treatment for refugees, largely German Jews, who were legally German aliens. The distinguished author Thomas Mann, for example, while making an eloquent plea for anti-Nazi refugees, insisted that "it is not my business to talk about the Japanese problem," and even Carey McWilliams, who would later become the chief journalistic champion of the Japanese Americans, devoted most of his prepared testimony to protecting the rights of European-born aliens, who were not really in much danger of mistreatment.

But the confusion among white liberals was nothing compared with the confusion that existed among Japanese American leaders. As a group they had desperately tried to be more American than the Americans, yet most Caucasians viewed them only as Japanese. Either course open to them—resistance to the coming evacuation or acceptance of it—was fraught with peril. Most of the leaders of the Japanese American community and especially those associated with the JACL took the second course. As their national secretary, Mike Masaoka, testified early in the Tolan Committee hearings:

> With any policy of evacuation definitely arising from reasons of military necessity and national safety, we are in complete agreement. As American citizens, we cannot and should not take any other stand. But, also, as American citizens believing in the integrity of our

---

[2] *People's World* (San Francisco), January 31, February 2, 10, 14, 20, 28, 1942. Marcantonio in *Congressional Record*, February 25, 1942, p. A708.

citizenship, we feel that any evacuation enforced on grounds violating that integrity should be opposed.

Masaoka and the other JACL leaders stressed that they wanted federal responsibility for the evacuation. They understood that if they opposed the evacuation, it would merely add to the disloyal stereotype that already existed. It is easier to criticize this accommodationist policy than to construct viable alternatives for a responsible leadership to adopt. Masaoka and the others deliberately chose to cooperate with their oppressors in the obvious hope that by cooperating they would both mitigate the present circumstances and perhaps have a lien on better treatment later. In addition, there was the whole poisonous California climate of opinion which seemed a threat to them all. As Tokie Slocum, a veteran of World War I and a member of both the American Legion and the Veterans of Foreign Wars, put it:

> The very fact and very proof of [the loyalty of the majority of the Japanese Americans] is [that] you don't hear a holler going up when your Commander-in-Chief, through General De Witt says, "Evacuate." Everybody is willing. . . . They want to know where to go and how to go, really. Because when they get there they don't want to be another football, another California problem, and be kicked all over the place again.

Although these views were representative of the majority of the articulate Japanese American community, there were dissenters. James Omura, a worker in the flower industry in San Francisco who published a magazine on the side, felt that the JACL was all wrong.

> . . . I am opposed to mass evacuation of American-born Japanese. It is my honest belief that such an action would not solve the question of Nisei loyalty. If any such action is taken I believe that we would be only procrastinating on the question of loyalty, that we are afraid to deal with it, and at this, our first opportunity, we are trying to strip the Nisei of their opportunity to prove their loyalty.

This, then, was the crux of the Japanese American dilemma: how could they prove their loyalty. For the vast majority of Nisei, at least, loyalty was demonstrated by submissiveness to authority. The government said go, and they went, cooperating, organizing, submitting. This submission, this lack of resistance to oppression, had several consequences. In the long run, perhaps, it proved a viable tactic. In the short run, however, it produced, as we shall see, bitterness and fratricide within the Japanese American community.

* * *

While the civilians were talking, the Army was trying to coordinate its divergent views. De Witt did not bother to send witnesses to the Tolan Committee: McCloy had cautioned him that if he appeared at the hearings he should "not give Mr. Tolan the impression that the coast is just on the verge of a 'mass' evacuation." De Witt was now saying that he was opposed to a mass—that is, immediate—evacuation, that he wanted it to be a gradual process. He was also determined to evacuate all the Japanese and all the German and Italian aliens. He was, he told Gullion, "opposed to any preferential treatment to any alien irrespective of race." His plan was to "take the Japs first, then maybe the Germans and then last the Italians."[3]

By late February, however, the War Department was determined to go ahead with mass evacuation, even though General De Witt was temporarily against "a mass movement."Bendetsen took the blame, admitting, in a memorandum to Stimson, that he had "misunderstood" General De Witt's plan. Although the War Department, and later in the courts the Justice Department, would always argue that "stern military necessity" dictated by the "man on the spot" triggered the evacuation orders, it is now quite clear that it was the politicians and lawyer-bureaucrats in uniform who, in the final analysis, made the crucial decisions and having made them adhered to them even though the man on the ground was willing to temporize.

The matter of evacuating German and Italian aliens—no one even thought of doing anything to citizens of German or Italian descent—from the West Coast, and even from the East Coast where Lieutenant General Hugh A. Drum, De Witt's counterpart, suggested such a move, was contemplated and discussed within the Army for some time. As late as March 28, McCloy wrote the Chief of Army Field Forces:

> As the war progresses it may become necessary to move aliens inland from the East and South Coasts in a manner similar to the way we are now moving Japs along the West Coast. Would it not be well to have the Eastern and Southern Defense Commanders send an officer to the West Coast to study the method used out there for

---

[3] Memorandum, McCloy to De Witt, February 18, 1942, Record Group 107, National Archives; Conn, "Japanese Evacuation from the West Coast," p. 134 in Stetson Conn, Rose C. Engleman, and Byron Fairchild, *The United States Army in World War II: The Western Hemisphere: Guarding the United States and Its Outposts* (Washington: Government Printing Office, 1964).

evacuation and to plan for similar action in their own areas. This will save a lot of time and avoid confusion and criticism if we are ever called on to remove aliens from other areas.[4]

Almost two weeks later, orders were cut sending such officers. At about that time, however, rumors about the evacuation of Germans and Italians from the East Coast leaked out, and the question was discussed in the Cabinet. Attorney General Biddle wrote a much stronger memo in their defense than he ever had for the Japanese.[5] More important, such a move would have had serious political consequences; the German and Italian ethnic vote was significant. Franklin Roosevelt asked questions and wrote memos making it clear that there should be no mass movement of Germans and Italians.[6] By May 15 McCloy could write Stimson, who was not always aware of what his subordinates did, that no such thing had been planned by the War Department.

These reports of an intended mass evacuation have been persistent, but they have all come from other sources than General Drum or the War Department. We have persistently notified . . . everyone who has consulted us that we intend *no* mass evacuations on the East Coast. . . .[7]

McCloy also reported that De Witt still wanted to evacuate German and possibly Italian aliens, but that he, McCloy, personally thought that none but Japanese should be evacuated "unless there is some outbreak of fifth column activity in the future." On May 20 the word went out to De Witt: "For the present" no evacuation of Germans and Italians. In addition, any statement made about them had to be cleared with McCloy before issuance.[8] Happily, the DiMaggios and those like them were spared the horrors of an uprooting.

Allen Gullion, the Provost Marshal General, had probably been the original inspiration for Drum's plan. Gullion continued to see the evacua-

---

[4] Memorandum, McCloy to General Joseph T. McNarney, March 28, 1942, Record Group 107, National Archives.

[5] Memorandum, General Dwight D. Eisenhower to The Adjutant General, April 8, 1942, Record Group 407, National Archives; Memorandum, Biddle to Franklin D. Roosevelt, April 9, 1942, Record Group 107, National Archives.

[6] Memorandum, Franklin D. Roosevelt to Stimson, April 14, May 5, 1942, Record Group 107, National Archives.

[7] Memorandum, McCloy to Stimson, May 15, 1942, Record Group 107, National Archives.

[8] Memorandum, Colonel Ralph Tate to The Adjutant General, May 20, 1942, Record Group 107, National Archives. This item was sent to De Witt by McCloy, May 20, 1942.

tion, even if limited to Japanese rather than all enemy aliens, as an opportunity to build an empire. As late as March 22 he was planning on small camps administered by military police and other troops under his command. Gullion assumed that there would be about 3000 inmates per camp and that only males over fourteen years of age—about 46,000 persons —would be permanently interned from the Pacific Coast plus another 40,000 from Hawaii. He estimated that it would take about 750 men to guard and administer each camp; at this rate it would have taken about 35,000 military personnel—nearly three combat divisions—to guard the Japanese Americans eventually evacuated from the West Coast.[9] This was precisely the kind of manpower drain that General Marshall and the other planners at General Headquarters feared, and, for this reason, at a Cabinet meeting held on February 27 Stimson, supported by Biddle, insisted that a civilian agency be set up to handle the evacuation. A young official of the Department of Agriculture, Milton S. Eisenhower, was selected to head the new agency, and in early March, after what he called "a day and a half of grilling" by Budget Director Harold Smith, he agreed to take the job.[10] Only on March 18, almost a month after the executive order authorizing the evacuation, was another executive order issued establishing the new agency, the War Relocation Authority (WRA), which would actually be responsible for the relocation centers and later for getting the Japanese Americans back into American life. The actual moving out of the Japanese was thus delayed because no arrangements had been made to take care of them. The Provost Marshal General's efforts, after mid-February, were meaningless; none of the sixteen possible sites he suggested in his March 22 memo was ever used. In mid-March a General Staff officer reported on his return from an inspection trip to the Pacific Coast that "it was noted that there was no definite organization for handling . . . the evacuation of enemy aliens."[11]

Although he was not organized, General De Witt was issuing proclamations. On March 2 came Public Proclamation No. 1.[12] This divided Washington, Oregon, California, and Arizona into two military areas, numbered 1 and 2. Military Area No. 1 was further divided into a "prohibited zone"—essentially the Coast and a strip along the Mexican border

[9] Memorandum, Gullion to Chief, Administrative Services, Service of Supply, March 22, 1942, Record Group 107, National Archives.

[10] Letter, Milton S. Eisenhower to Claude Wickard, April 1, 1942, Record Group 16, National Archives.

[11] Memorandum, Lieutenant Colonel I. K. Evans to General Lutes, March 10, 1942, Record Group 107, National Archives.

[12] This and other early documents cited below are found most conveniently in U.S. Congress, *House Report No. 2124*, 77th Cong., 2d Sess., pp. 293–351 (Washington, 1942).

—and a larger "restricted zone" contiguous to it. In addition ninety-eight other limited and presumably strategic areas—military installations, power plants, and so forth—were also labeled prohibited. No one was ordered to move by this proclamation—there was no place to put anyone—but it was made clear that it was aimed at "Japanese, German or Italian" aliens and "any person of Japanese Ancestry." An accompanying press release predicted the eventual exclusion of all persons of Japanese ancestry from Military Area No. 1 and all prohibited areas. It was also specifically stated in the proclamation that "the description of Military Area No. 2 as such does not contemplate any prohibition, regulation or restriction." In other words Japanese were encouraged to move from the coastal zone—which included the cities where most of them lived—to inland, rural California or even farther into the interior. There was little likelihood of any mass, voluntary evacuation, and Bendetsen, if not De Witt, had the intelligence to realize it. In the first place, the government made no serious attempt to prepare public opinion for the coming of the Japanese—and protests from interior states against what they called "dumping" of California's Japs had been endemic since mid-February—and provided practically no assistance to those who might have moved. Most of the Japanese Americans did not have the resources to make such a move (remember, Issei assets had been frozen) and, by this time, almost three months after Pearl Harbor, probably did not have the will to do so either. Several thousand, however (the estimates range from 2000 to 9000), somewhat like dust bowl migrants in reverse, did voluntarily try to "relocate" themselves. Many of these quickly returned when faced with local hostility in the interior. As an official government report later described it:

> Those who attempted to cross into the interior states ran into all kinds of trouble. Some were turned back by armed posses [sic] at the border of Nevada; others were clapped into jail and held overnight by panicky local peace officers; nearly all had difficulty in buying gasoline; many were greeted by "No Japs Wanted" signs on the main streets of interior communities; and a few were threatened, or felt that they were threatened, with possibilities of mob violence.[13]

Many, if not most, of these internal refugees returned to California, and their stories must have dissuaded most of the others who might have tried. Within California there was less hostility, but those who managed to resettle within the Golden State, innocently trusting the word of a

---

[13] U.S. Department of the Interior, War Relocation Authority, WRA: A Story of Human Conservation (Washington, 1946), p. 26.

lieutenant general of the United States Army, were later sent to the same camps as were those who stayed put. For those who asked for federal assistance, practically none was available: the federal Bureau of Public Assistance helped only 118 Japanese families to move—at a cost of less than $100 per family—and put 7 of those in places where the Army got them anyway.[14]

Public Proclamation No. 2, issued March 16, affected few Japanese; it set up four more military areas covering the states of Idaho, Montana, Nevada, and Utah and listed 933 additional prohibited zones. Actually De Witt planned eventually to round up all the Japanese in these states "so there won't be any Japanese in the Western Defense Command" (this would have shocked the JACL, which moved its headquarters to presumably safe Salt Lake City in late February), but the War Department would not let him. Public Proclamation No. 3, however, affected the daily lives of Japanese Americans, and created, for them alone, the closest thing to a police state ever seen in the United States. It instituted, effective March 27, throughout Military Area No. 1 and all prohibited areas, an 8 P.M. to 6 A.M. curfew for all enemy aliens (but not generally enforced or susceptible of enforcement against white people) and "persons of Japanese ancestry" and provided that "at all other times all such persons shall only be at their place of residence or employment or travelling between those places or within a distance of not more than five miles from their place of residence." They could continue to move out of the military area if they did so within noncurfew hours. The day that this went into effect, however, De Witt issued Public Proclamation No. 4, dated March 27 and effective at midnight, March 29, which forbade all Japanese, alien and citizen, to leave Military Area No. 1, where most of them still lived.

None of these orders, however, forced anyone to move or took anyone into custody. On March 24, in a kind of rehearsal for mass evacuation, De Witt had issued a "Civilian Exclusion Order," ominously designated No. 1. This order, it should be noted, followed by three days the enactment of Public Law No. 503, which made it a criminal offense for anyone excluded from a military area to remain there. Thus, though the evacuation was initiated by a mere executive order, it was not carried out by the Army until after Congress had approved. This order affected only a few hundred Japanese families, who lived on Bainbridge Island, in Puget Sound, near Seattle. These were not the first Japanese to be forced to move by the military; that dubious honor fell to the Japanese, largely fishermen and their families, who had been forced to leave Terminal Island, San Pedro,

---

[14] "Report of Bureau of Public Assistance in Connection with the WCCA Program," June 3, 1942, Record Group 107, National Archives.

California, by the Navy the previous month. The Navy's action was as capricious as the Army's: On February 14 the Navy had put up notices saying that all Japanese on Terminal Island—about 500 families lived there —would have to leave by March 14. As it was a strategic location within the Port of Los Angeles, there was some justification for the move, which resembled a condemnation procedure. But, without warning on the afternoon of February 25 new notices were put up saying that all Japanese must be off the island by midnight, February 27. As Bill Hosokawa describes it:

> Near panic swept the community, particularly where the family head was in custody. Word spread quickly and human vultures in the guise of used-furniture dealers descended on the island. They drove up and down the streets in trucks offering $5 for a nearly new washing machine, $10 for refrigerators. . . . And the Japanese, angry but helpless, sold their dearly purchased possessions because they didn't know what to do . . . and because they sensed the need in the uncertain time ahead for all the cash they could squirrel away.[15]

But the Terminal Islanders had been allowed to move essentially where they wished—most stayed in Los Angeles County and thus had to move again—so their misfortune is not a true analogue for the evacuation that came.

The Bainbridge Island move was administered by Karl R. Bendetsen. He had been promoted to full colonel, transferred to De Witt's staff and made director of the Wartime Civil Control Administration (WCCA), which De Witt had set up on March 11 to handle the Army's part of the evacuation. Tom Clark was loaned to WCCA by the Justice Department to coordinate the activities of civilian agencies helping the Army. It was thus the dress rehearsal for the larger move. A set of "Instructions to All Japanese Living on Bainbridge Island" forbade them to move except to an "approved destination" outside Military Area No. 1 and set up a reception center for them. The government was willing to store some possessions "at the sole risk of the owner" and was willing to allow the evacuees to take only "that which can be carried by the family or the individual" if it was bedding, toilet articles, clothing, and "sufficient knives, forks, spoons, plates, bowls and cups for each member of the family." The fifty-four Japanese families on Bainbridge Island had just six days to get ready, and then were moved to an Assembly Center at the Puyallup (Washington) Fairgrounds. And so it went, all up and down the Coast.

---

[15] Bill Hosokawa, *Nisei: The Quiet Americans* (New York: Morrow, 1969), pp. 310–11.

With the dress rehearsal a success, 107 other performances were held, as Bendetsen and his staff systematically divided the West Coast into 108 areas for exclusion purposes, with roughly 1000 Japanese in each area. Orders were posted in each locality, setting up a central receiving and information point—usually a public building—to inform the evacuees what to do, what they could take, and when to report. Interpreters were provided and often friendly Caucasians, usually religious groups like the Friends, did what they could to ease the pain. One such volunteer, Thomas Bodine of Seattle, wrote movingly of what he had seen and felt.

Only 1000 Seattle Japanese remain to be evacuated. For the last four or five days they have been leaving by the hundreds at 9 in the morning (assembling at 7 and 7:30 and at 2 in the afternoon). . . . This afternoon the first trainload of Japanese from the White River Valley farming country left for Pinedale California. I was down to see them off, and my heart split wider than it has for any of the others at the time of departure. No Pullmans this time. . . . Just old ratty coaches for a 2 day 2 night trip to California. . . . The roofs of the coaches were covered with bird dung . . . the windows were like a car windshield on a misty day. . . . The Japanese were their cheerful selves: stoicism is a wonderful thing for circumstances like these. Think of what these people have been doing: The past week standing in line, first to register, then for physical exams. The last frantic arrangements, selling, storing, dispensing with precious possessions, leaving pets and gardens behind, then the last night, most of them up until 4 and 5 AM packing, getting everything ready for the early morning departure, everything neatly labelled and properly boxed. Then for a few hours sleep on the hard floors of a home empty of furniture, no beds or mattresses; these sold or stored. Then up at six or so and get the children ready, dress in your best clothes, come down in the pouring rain of a cold dreary day, stand in line and mill around in the confusion of departure for an hour and a half, then load into the busses and at last we're off. And all with a smile . . . and pretending it's a lark. "California, here we come." . . .

One morning I watched a dark black negro fellow drive a Japanese family up in a fine new Plymouth. He helped them unload and then stood next to them on the sidewalk and in his beautiful deep throaty voice said, "Well, m'am, I'll be saying goodbye. You know that if there's ever anything I can do for you whether it be something big or something small, I'm here to do it." And he shook her hand and then turned to the husband and slapped him on the back: "Goodbye now and good luck." And then down on his hands and knees for a final farewell to the three little kids (I couldn't catch the words he used).[16]

As Bodine indicates, the Japanese Americans complied docilely, obeying almost without complaint the bureaucratic regulations that were destroying their lives. By June 5 all of Military Area No. 1 was evacuated: by August 7 supposedly safe Military Area No. 2 was "Jap-free."

But before this could happen the WCCA had to decide where to put over 100,000 people, for it was soon decided that there would be temporary Assembly Centers on the West Coast and permanent or semipermanent camps somewhere in the interior. As early as March 5, after weeks of discussion, Tom Clark had gotten reluctant approval from Los Angeles officialdom to use Los Angeles-owned land in the Owens Valley for what he called "a concentration or registration center." The reluctance stemmed from the fact that the Owens Valley was the source of much of Los Angeles' water and the local officials, already jittery over an imaginary air raid during which antiaircraft batteries all over the county fired at nothing, feared that the water supply might be poisoned but were assured that the Japanese would be kept under heavy guard. At about the same time Clark was instrumental in getting permission from the Interior Department to use a more logical site—the Colorado River Indian Reservation in Arizona. Interior agreed, but Secretary Harold L. Ickes insisted that there must be some kind of positive program. "If it is to be a program merely of keeping them under guard in concentration camps, we are not interested."[17]

These two initial sites became, as Manzanar and Poston, both Assembly Centers and Relocation Centers. The first to inhabit them were volunteers, largely JACLers and their families, who went to Manzanar from Los Angeles on March 21–22. But Manzanar and Poston could accommodate only a fraction of the West Coast Japanese. Bendetsen and his associates eventually decided to convert existing structures on the West Coast for use as Assembly Centers and let the WRA worry about permanent camps. It was probably more than the housing shortage that inspired them to select sites that had been intended to house livestock. (There were, for example, college dormitories soon to be vacated.) In any event, race tracks like Santa Anita and Tanforan (the evacuees—men,

---

[16] Letter, Thomas Bodine, May 11, 1942, Conrad-Duveneck Collection, Hoover Institution Archives, Palo Alto, Calif.

[17] Telephone conversation, Tom C. Clark and Corrington Gill, March 5, 1942, Record Group 107, National Archives; letter, John Collier, Commissioner of Indian Affairs to A. L. Walker, n.d. but ca. March 5, 1942, Record Group 107, National Archives.

women, and children—went into the stables), fairgrounds like the one at Puyallup the Bainbridge Islanders went to, and livestock exhibition centers were hastily converted to something approximating human habitations.

Although the Army always boasted that, under the circumstances, conditions in the Assembly Centers were ideal, the contrary is true. An official report of the United States Public Health Service, for example, concluded that sanitation was bad. That "so few epidemics have occurred from insanitary conditions has been due to the heroic efforts of the management of the centers, the County Health Departments and the Japanese Medical staffs."[18] And the Army's own reports, from a food consultant and a Quartermaster Corps officer, indicated serious deficiencies.

> The kitchens are not up to Army standards of cleanliness. . . . [In a hospital] there are no cribs for the children. While [we were] there one child had a rather bad fall. . . . The only [foods] for little children were bread and milk. No high chairs for the children and they seemed uncomfortable and unhappy. . . . The dishes looked bad . . . gray and cracked. . . . Dishwashing not very satisfactory due to an insufficiency of hot water. . . . Soup plates being used instead of plates, which means that the food all runs together and looks untidy and unappetizing.[19]

Evacuees had other complaints. As one woman wrote from the Merced, California, center to a friendly Caucasian:

> . . . the only thing I really don't like are the lavatories. It's not very sanitary and has caused a great deal of constipation in camp for both men and women. The toilets are one big row of seats, that is, one straight board with holes out about a foot apart with no partitions at all and all the toilets flush together . . . about every five minutes. The younger girls couldn't go to them at first until they couldn't stand it any longer, which is really bad for them.[20]

Different evacuees, of course, reacted differently. The older folk, particularly those from rural areas, were able to adjust more readily at first than the younger, urban people. For some, particularly Issei women,

---

[18] U.S. Public Health Service, District No. 5, San Francisco, "Report of Activities in the Japanese Evacuation from the West Coast," June 2, 1942.

[19] Surveys of Assembly Centers (July, 1942) by Mary I. Barber, Food Consultant, and 1st Lieutenant J. W. Brearly, Quartermaster Corps, Record Group 107, National Archives.

[20] Letter, ———— to Grace Nichols, June, 1942, Conrad-Duveneck Collection, Hoover Institution Archives.

the relocation was the first "break" in a life of almost unremitting toil. Others resented all Japanese being lumped together. A University of California graduate wrote from Tanforan to a university official:

> At a place like this there are all classes of people—a cross section of every type and many who are not of the most desirable type. With all respects to the farm folks, I must say they are simple folk living in all their plainness and contentment.

But more serious than the discomforts, than the social awkwardness, than even the soldiers and the barbed wire that surrounded the evacuated people, was the demoralization and the effect on loyalty. As one Nisei leader wrote to Los Angeles Supervisor John Anson Ford:

> Many of the Isseis are now saying, "You see, we were right; no matter what you say you are not going to be accepted as full fledged Americans."[21]

---

[21] Letter, ———— to John Anson Ford, May 8, 1942, Box 64, John Anson Ford Mss., Huntington Library, San Marino, Calif.

5

EVACUATION, THE AMERICAN WAY

Milton S. Eisenhower, who had reluctantly agreed to head the War Relocation Authority (WRA) in mid-March and thus became the first director of concentration camps in American history, quickly found the assignment not at all to his liking. Nothing in his experience had taught him anything about his job or his prisoners. Born in Abilene, Kansas, in 1899, he took a B.S. in journalism at Kansas State College in 1924, having worked as city editor of his hometown newspaper before graduation. He taught journalism at his alma mater for a year, served two years as vice-consul in Edinburgh, Scotland, and in 1926 joined the Department of Agriculture, where he remained for sixteen years, most of them as the departments' director of information. Yet he quickly understood, as almost no one else connected with the evacuation did, that it was wrong. On April 1 he wrote privately to his old boss, Agriculture Secretary Claude Wickard: "I feel most deeply that when the war is over and we consider calmly this unprecedented migration of 120,000 people, we as Americans are going to regret the avoidable injustices that may have been done."[1]

---

[1] Letter, Eisenhower to Wickard, April 1, 1942, "Correspondence of

Despite his lack of sympathy with the program, like a good bureaucrat he tried for a while to make it work and never made his misgivings public. Eisenhower reached San Francisco to work with De Witt, Bendetsen and Tom Clark just as the roundup of Japanese got under way. He had been briefed quickly by Franklin Roosevelt and Assistant Secretary of War McCloy. Apparently he knew only that the evacuation was a "military necessity" approved by the Commander in Chief and ratified by Congress. The line of demarcation between his WRA and the Army-controlled Wartime Civil Control Administration (WCCA) was clear. The Army would round up the Japanese Americans, put them in Assembly Centers, and deliver them to the WRA Relocation Centers when these were ready. The Army would also provide armed guards to keep them in the Relocation Centers. But the centers themselves would be run by the WRA.

Almost as soon as Eisenhower reached California it became apparent that voluntary evacuation would not work, and by the end of March the WRA chief was resigned to incarcerating the Japanese Americans in what he called "sand and cactus" centers. Initially, it was hoped that many, if not most, of the citizens at least, could be resettled rather quickly—that is, released from the camps and sent back to civilian life in a nonmilitary area. But Eisenhower quickly learned that vehement anti-Japanese feeling, racism pure and simple, was not confined to the West Coast. On April 7, in Salt Lake City, the WRA called a closed meeting of governors, attorneys general, and other state and federal officials from ten western states.[2] The purpose of the meeting was to explain the evacuation and relocation program and to arrange for cooperation between the government and the states to which the Japanese were to be sent. What it demonstrated was that the governors, whose views probably were representative of their constituents, would have Japanese in their states only if they were under close guard, and would prefer to have them kept on the Coast.

After some introductory remarks by Tom Clark, Bendetsen made a long presentation. He told the conference that the evacuation was dictated by "military necessity" based on the assumption that while most Japanese (Bendetsen almost never said Japanese Americans) might be loyal under most conditions, they "must be regarded as potential enemies, if put to the test of being present during an invasion by an army of their own race."

---

the Secretary of Agriculture, Foreign Relations, 2–1, Aliens-Refugees," Record Group 16, National Archives. The mechanics and rationale behind Eisenhower's selection are not clear. It may have stemmed from Agriculture's concern over food production. In addition, many in the War Department seem to have been pleased that the job went to "General Eisenhower's brother."

[2] "Report on Meeting, April 7, at Salt Lake City, with Governors, Attorneys General and other State and Federal Officials of 10 Western States," enclosed in Letter, Eisenhower to Wickard, April 1, 1942, cited above.

Nevertheless the Army, according to Bendetsen, was giving the Japanese what he called a "fair shake" and handling the evacuation in "an American way" to prove to the world that "justice and humanity are American characteristics, even in war time." Explaining that voluntary evacuation did not work—but not mentioning *why* it did not work—he told the conference that since the freeze order of March 29 "there has been no infiltration of evacuees from the military zone." Stressing the fact that many Americans were and would be in the hands of the Imperial Japanese Government, and that mistreatment of Japanese here might cause reprisals against "our citizens," Bendetsen urged them not to use terms like "concentration camp."

Eisenhower, whose presentation followed Bendetsen's, also stressed the "international angles." Then he explained that evacuees would do five kinds of work.

1. Public work—reclamation, etc., within the relocation centers.
2. Agriculture within the relocation centers.
3. Manufacturing within the relocation centers.
4. Private employment outside the relocation centers.
5. Self-supporting communities might be established outside the centers (something like the subsistence homesteads of the New Deal).

The WRA chief explained that there would be two wage scales: one for work inside and one for work outside the centers. In the first instance, the wage would not exceed the minimum paid American soldiers ($21 a month—actually the top internal wage was soon set at $19); but in the second, the WRA would see that the evacuees got the prevailing wage. (The purpose of the low "wage" in the camps was to avoid Congressional charges of "coddling," which came anyway. The analogy was ridiculous. All evacuees, regardless of skills, were permanent privates by WRA fiat; in addition, there were no veterans' benefits for evacuees.) Then Eisenhower broached the topic that concerned the governors most: What would happen to the evacuees after the war? He promised that the WRA would not transfer or buy land for the evacuees, but insisted that it could not prevent private transactions. But, and this was a bitter pill for the westerners, WRA's policy would neither encourage the evacuees to become permanent residents of the states to which they were moved nor encourage them to return to the states from which they came. Eisenhower closed his discussion of public policy with what became a standard WRA myth:

> It is not the province of the Authority, other than in the orderly evacuation and relocation of the Japanese, to dictate their lives. They will be encouraged to manage their affairs and their community enterprises to the highest degree.

He ended with a plea for cooperation and suggestions. What he got was denunciation and indignation. It surprised him but it should not have. Most of the governors had expressed their feelings previously to the Tolan Committee in early March and their sentiments had been reported in the press.

Herbert B. Maw of Utah led off for the governors: He was disturbed that the people running the show were not westerners and did not know western conditions. Instead of the presumably wasteful federal program, he proposed that each state be given a quota of Japanese—10,000 or 12,000 for Utah—money to handle them, and the state could guard them and work them efficiently and cheaply. In addition he warned that if the "filtering of Japanese into Utah" did not stop, he could not be held accountable for what might happen to them, as feeling was running high in his state. He criticized the Army and the WRA for being "much too concerned about the constitutional rights of Japanese-American citizens . . .the constitution could be changed."

Chase Clark of Idaho agreed with Maw that the states should handle the Japanese under federal subsidy. His chief concern was that Japanese would acquire land in the state. If the Army could keep them out of California, he felt it could also keep them from buying land. The few hundred Japanese who had come into Idaho during the "voluntary evacuation" period should be rounded up by the Army and kept in some kind of custody.

Nels Smith of Wyoming was worried lest the Japanese overrun his thinly populated state. Wyomingites, he declared, had a dislike for any Orientals and simply would not "stand for being California's dumping ground." He too was concerned about Japanese buying land in his state, and reported telling a delegation of Japanese who came to see him about it that if they bought land "There would be Japs hanging from every pine tree." All Japanese, he insisted, should be kept in "concentration camps," not the reception centers Eisenhower had been talking about. And so it went; almost all expressed a desire that the government guarantee that any Japanese evacuated into their states be deported after the war.

But these political leaders were not the only spokesmen for the intermountain West; a parallel meeting with sugar beet growers from the region, held the same day, produced a different set of views. They had a market for all the sugar beets they could grow and process, but were faced with a severe and worsening labor shortage. To them, the hardworking Japanese were not a threat but a godsend. Preston Ellsworth, president of the Idaho Beet Growers' Association, opposed his governor. "We don't like the Japanese better than anyone else, but we will see that they are well treated." These views were echoed by most of the representatives there. S. J. Boyer, of the Utah Farm Bureau, said that farmers "don't love the Japanese, but we intend to work them, if possible."

The Salt Lake City conference was thus an important nodal point in the development of evacuation policy. Although, as we have seen, the notion that the Japanese Americans would be put into some kind of concentration camp was never far from the minds of nearly all of those in government most concerned with the evacuation, this major premise had not been made explicit in either the executive order setting up the WRA or in the instructions given to Milton Eisenhower. If the active racism of the West Coast was the initial catalyst for the evacuation and the more passive national racist climate the precondition for its acceptance, it was the racism of the intermountain West which was the final determinant of WRA policy.

Before the Salt Lake meeting Eisenhower and his planners had assumed that a minimum of restraint would be necessary and that for many, if not most, of the evacuees, relocation would be a transitional stage leading very quickly to resettlement—as individuals, as families, and as whole communities—within the civilian economy of the interior. After Salt Lake it seemed clear to Eisenhower and other WRA officials that for the majority of the evacuated people close confinement would be necessary. Had there been, in the four months between Pearl Harbor and Salt Lake City, an educational and propaganda campaign conducted by the federal government designed to make resettlement acceptable to the people of the intermountain West, a different result might have ensued. A relocation followed by a quick resettlement was indeed possible, just as a truly voluntary evacuation had been possible; whether or not these possibilities would have worked is, of course, an unanswerable question. They were logical alternatives, but they were never truly attempted. That they were not tried was not so much a failure of imagination but rather a direct result of the preconceptions about nonwhites in general and about Japanese in particular held by most Americans, up to and including the Commander in Chief.

After the conference WRA policy was clear: the relocation camps would be semipermanent establishments, surrounded with barbed wire and guarded by small detachments of military police. Rather than the large guard force envisioned by Gullion, the military manpower involved would be minimal. At Heart Mountain, Wyoming, for example, the guard contingent for about 10,000 evacuees numbered only 3 officers and 124 enlisted men.[3] Two of the ten eventual concentration camps—Manzanar and Poston—had been selected and construction begun under WCCA— that is, essentially military—auspices. The other eight were selected by the

[3] For this and other details about Heart Mountain, I am indebted to my student Douglas W. Nelson, "Heart Mountain: The History of an American Concentration Camp," unpublished M.A. thesis, University of Wyoming, 1970. We have both been guided by T. A. Larson, *Wyoming's War Years, 1941–1945* (Laramie, Wyo.: University of Wyoming, 1954), Chapter XXII, "Heart Mountain."

WRA betweeen April and June. All ten sites can only be called godforsaken. They were in places where nobody had lived before and no one has lived since. The Army insisted that all camps be "at a safe distance" from strategic installations, and the WRA decided that, for a number of reasons, the sites should be on federal property. Three of the eight WRA-selected sites—Tule Lake, California; Minidoka, Idaho; and Heart Mountain, Wyoming—were located on undeveloped federal reclamation projects. Gila River, Arizona, like Poston, was on an Indian reservation. Granada (Amache), in southeastern Colorado, was purchased by the Army for the WRA, and Topaz, the central Utah camp, involved some public domain, some tracts that had reverted to local authority for nonpayment of taxes, and several parcels purchased from private individuals. The two Arkansas centers, Jerome and Rohwer, were on lands originally purchased by Rex Tugwell's Farm Security Administration as future subsistence homesteads for low-income southern farm families. That land originally intended to fulfill the promise of American life for some of its most disadvantaged citizens should, under the stress of war, be used as a place of confinement for other Americans is just one of the smaller ironies of the whole program.

That these areas were still vacant land in 1942, land that the ever-voracious pioneers and developers had either passed by or abandoned, speaks volumes about their attractiveness. The Utah camp, Topaz, ironically called the "Jewel of the Desert" by its inmates, can serve as surrogate

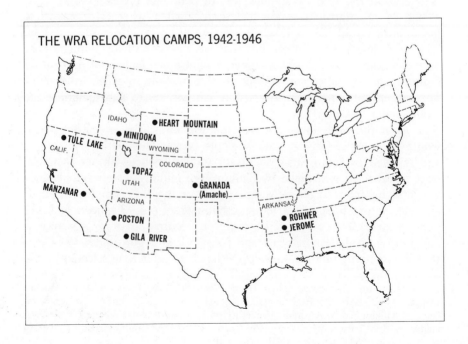

THE WRA RELOCATION CAMPS, 1942-1946

for the rest. As its historian, Leonard Arrington, has written, it is not a very attractive place. The area was first visited by "white" explorers in 1776, who called it the "Valle Solado," or Valley of Salt; its inhospitable alkali-laden soil frustrated completely the efforts of two distinct groups of Mormon pioneers who tried to settle there. A "barren valley" at 4600 feet above sea level, with temperatures ranging from 106° F. in the summer to —30° in the winter, it has an average rainfall between 7 and 8 inches per year. Other climatic characteristics include wind "which keeps up a seldom interrupted whirl of dust" and a "nonabsorbent soil which, after a rain, is a gummy muck, ideal as a breeding ground for mosquitoes." At Topaz, at least, some attempts were made by the WRA to "beautify" the camp. Seventy-five large and 7500 small trees and 10,000 cuttings of shrubs were eventually transplanted, but nearly all died, despite desperately intensive care by the evacuated people, many of whom were experts at horiculture. The Utah camp cost almost $5 million to build (each of the camps produced a small "boom" in its sparsely populated vicinity) and another $5 million annually to operate.[4]

Throughout the spring and summer of 1942 these "sand and cactus" sites were prepared for the evacuated people, who sweltered in the stables and livestock exposition centers of interior California. Even while this "spoilage" was going on—and for many of the Japanese Americans this period of waiting in terribly cramped quarters was the worst time of all— a few Caucasian groups were hard at work to ameliorate somewhat the indiscriminate evacuation. As has been previously noted, small groups of concerned whites, largely church people, did what they could to make the evacuation process less oppressive, and continued to minister to the evacuees in the Assembly Centers. But even more significant, in the final analysis, was the salvage operation mounted by California educators, aimed at getting college-age Nisei out of the camps and back in school where they belonged. The success of this operation was the first significant exception to the policy of mass exclusion and therefore far more important than the relatively small number of evacuees affected might indicate.

Although a number of groups and individuals were involved, the key figure, because of his prestige and influence, was Robert Gordon Sproul, president of the University of California. Sproul (b. 1891), who had headed the university since 1930, was a pillar of the California establishment with a voice that could make itself heard in the highest national circles. Sproul never criticized the evacuation itself. As he wrote to an eastern liberal who had wanted him to help organize and sponsor a protest meeting against the evacuation in the spring of 1942:

---

[4] Leonard J. Arrington, *The Price of Prejudice: The Japanese-American Relocation Center in Utah during World War II* (Logan, Utah: Utah State University, 1962).

I am not in a position to pass judgment upon the evidence which led [to the evacuation]. . . . Neither am I prepared to say that public opinion would have tolerated any other course. . . . I have felt it wise to assume, in the face of an accomplished fact, that evacuation from the military zone on the Pacific Coast is a necessary evil. . . .[5]

He was, however, willing to do everything he could to mitigate that necessary evil, and his efforts to get the college-age Nisei out of the camps and into colleges and universities was doubly motivated. As an educator he naturally favored continued education. In addition, he felt strongly that the treatment of the Nisei was a matter of real significance. As he explained it to the president of the University of Minnesota:

It is my belief that the efforts that we expend now will be repaid a thousandfold in the attitude of citizens of Japanese ancestry in years to come. We look forward to a new and better world. . . . The world may look to us for leadership. Certainly our handling of this serious minority group problem will be looked upon as evidence of our intentions and a proof of the ideals to which we hold.

Sproul worked closely with the Student Relocation Council (later the National Japanese Student Relocation Council) organized at a meeting at the YMCA at the University of California on March 21, 1942. The vast majority of West Coast educators shared Sproul's concern, but even within his own faculty some nativist feeling was expressed. Even before the evacuation took place, a professor of chemistry at Berkeley wrote Sproul that he was "embarrassed in conducting my classes by the presence therein of Japanese and possibly German and Italian students" and a Chinese-born history lecturer at the University of California, Los Angeles, testified before a state senate committee that Japanese Americans were potentially dangerous and that "he was glad to note that steps are being taken for the removal of Japanese." More serious resistance came from the University of Southern California, which for a while refused to issue transcripts to students who had been evacuated. (Without transcripts, entrance into other universities was of course impossible.) The dean of the dental school there, for a time supported by University of Southern California President Rufus B. vonKleinsmid, argued that "issuing a transcript would constitute aid to a person who was the equivalent of a prisoner

---

[5] This and the materials that follow are from the President's Files, University of California Archives, Bancroft Library. I am indebted to the university archivist, Jim Kantor, for calling this material to my attention.

of war and that such aid would be considered as assisting him in evasion of government regulations." But these were distinctly minority voices within the California educational establishment; outside California, however, where Nisei students were almost unknown, the initial reaction from some of the best-known American universities was far from favorable.

Princeton, for example, was initially "not willing to receive American-born Japanese students even though they may be in good standing and not under suspicion." This attitude, Princeton felt, was backed up "by good reasoning." Other institutions used the excuse that because war-oriented research was being conducted on campus, enrollment of Japanese American students was inadvisable. Massachusetts Institute of Technology, for example, while sympathizing with "the humanitarian purpose" of continuing the education of Japanese Americans, adopted "a settled policy for the duration of the war not to accept any students of Japanese ancestry, whether citizens or not." Similarly, Indiana University decided that it would be "unwise" to accept Japanese students "in view of the present uncertain military status of the southern Indiana geographical zone. . . ." Other schools insisted on some kind of security clearance from the federal government. Duke wanted "unquestionable certification" of each individual, while the University of Denver added FBI approval to its entrance requirements for Japanese Americans.

Some schools, like the state universities of Utah, Colorado, Wyoming, and Nebraska and private institutions like Washington University of St. Louis, expressed almost immediate willingness to admit such students. In general, private and religious institutions were more willing to take Nisei students than were the public institutions.

But the mere fact that they might be accepted by schools outside the two West Coast military areas was not enough; it was necessary to get the Army (if they were still in Assembly Centers) or the WRA (if they were in camps) to adopt a policy that made it possible for the Nisei students to get out. The possibility of allowing college students to be released from custody had been broached at a San Francisco planning conference held by the WCCA and WRA as early as April 11. Late that month Governor Culbert Olson of California wrote to President Roosevelt about it. The letter, which may have been drafted by Robert Gordon Sproul, did not quarrel with the evacuation or "ask for any alteration" of the military orders. It did argue that

> unless some special action is taken, the education of those who might become influential leaders of the loyal American born Japanese will abruptly be closed. Such a result would be injurious not only to them, but to the nation, since well-trained leadership for such persons will be needed after the present war.

Olson went on to ask that qualified students be allowed to continue their education in such institutions as would accept them.[6] The White House sent this letter to U.S. Commissioner of Education John W. Studebaker for the preparation of a reply. There was obviously a debate within the administration over the proposal. According to Monroe Deutsch, Provost of the Berkeley campus and perhaps the most zealous advocate of the Nisei students in the academic community, White House adviser Harry L. Hopkins, for one, had urged the President to "give Japanese-Americans a chance to leave reception centers and live normal lives." Soon Assistant War Secretary McCloy became convinced that continuing the education of the Nisei was a desirable step, and Milton Eisenhower established a committee, headed by Clarence E. Pickett, executive secretary of the American Friends Service Committee, the national Quaker social service organization, to advise the WRA and prepare a plan to get the Nisei students back in school. On May 18 Roosevelt answered Olson, accepting the draft prepared by the Office of Education and thus giving approval to this first significant relaxation of the policy of mass confinement. Before September, the President promised, "qualified American-born Japanese students will be enabled to continue their education in inland institutions," and he assured the governor that Eisenhower and his "Japanese Relocation Authority" [sic] would come up with a plan "which will meet with your entire approval."[7]

Eventually some 4300 students went from Assembly Centers and camps to college. The federal government never gave financial support to these students, as the West Coast educators and Olson had requested, although the WRA did eventually subsidize travel from camp to campus. The majority of the students were aided by private philanthropy, most of it organized by various Christian groups. In general, their reception in the academic community was good; the students themselves were delighted, but felt a special responsibility to be "good." As one wrote to Provost Deutsch from the University of Colorado: "It was a thrill to become accustomed to feeling 'free.' . . . I think most of us realize our most important mission of being 'good-will ambassadors,' and to show other Americans that we are also loyal Americans."

Often, there was community hostility to the position taken by university administrators. At the University of Nebraska, American Legion pressure induced the regents to stop admitting the evacuees, even though the Nisei students tried to cut down their "high social visibility." As one of them explained, the negative reaction had come even though "all of us have tried to avoid being seen in conspicuous groups and have tried to

---

[6] Letter, Olson to FDR, April 25, 1942, Franklin D. Roosevelt Library, Hyde Park.
[7] FDR to Olson, May 18, 1942, Franklin D. Roosevelt Library, Hyde Park.

spread out as much as possible." Two more serious incidents involving community prejudice occurred in the spring and fall of 1942.

The first occurred at Park College, Missouri, and became known as the "Battle of Parksville." It involved a community effort to exclude seven Nisei students who had been accepted by the college. After a two-and-a-half hour meeting the college governing board braved local hostility and let the students stay "because their loyalty is unquestioned." That fall there was the "Retreat from Moscow" (Idaho), when six Nisei were refused admission to the state university after having been initially accepted. Local citizens caused so much furor that two of the girls were kept in jail under "protective custody." Later, Nisei students were accepted at the University of Idaho. There were other less spectacular incidents but, in general, the Nisei students were well received and performed excellently.[8]

Temporary release from custody was also gained by some who volunteered to do agricultural work. Persistent requests from labor-starved sugar beet producers and a suggestion from the White House finally got an initial group of fifteen evacuees temporarily released from the Portland Assembly Center on May 21 to pull beets in eastern Oregon. Eventually, during 1942 alone, some 10,000 evacuees did seasonal agricultural work while on leave from Assembly Centers and later from Relocation Centers. They encountered, of course, animosity and insult, and sometimes ran into situations that the WRA officially described as "momentarily ominous," but apparently none suffered serious bodily harm. At least they were out of camp and getting more than $19 a month.[9]

The contribution of the evacuees to the economy and the war effort was considerable. Leonard Arrington, the historian of the western beet sugar industry, has written of the experience of one large company with evacuee labor. Thanks largely to this labor the Utah-Idaho Sugar Company, one of the largest producers in the intermountain West, was able to increase its production from 72,000 acres in 1941 to 89,000 acres in 1942. Of the 10,000 Japanese workers on leave from Assembly Centers and Relocation Centers, the company was able to hire some 3500, who, according to Arrington, "were among the most industrious and intelligent workmen who ever labored in the region. One family of five, the Sakates of Delta, Utah, thinned 131 acres in the spring of 1942 and, in association with two other Nisei, topped, loaded and delivered 1,020 tons of beets during the period October 9 to November 10, 1942." Altogether the evacuated people employed by this one company alone saved enough beets to make almost 100 million pounds of sugar, in itself a significant contribution to the war

---

[8] Robert W. O'Brien, *The College Nisei* (Palo Alto, Calif.: Pacific Books, 1949), tells the story of the National Japanese American Student Relocation Council.

[9] War Relocation Authority, *WRA: A Story of Human Conservation* (Washington, 1946), pp. 31 ff.

effort.[10] But most of the evacuees just stayed in Assembly Centers until the time came for them to be shipped off, like so many cattle, to the Relocation Centers.

But while this transfer was just beginning, the WRA chief, Milton Eisenhower, resigned. In his letter to the President, dated June 18, 1942, exactly three months after his appointment, Eisenhower summarized what had been accomplished, expressed his dissatisfaction with some aspects of the program, but did not condemn the evacuation outright. According to Eisenhower, "public attitudes have exerted a strong influence in shaping the program and charting its direction. In a democracy this is unquestionably sound and proper."

Yet at the same time he offered the President his "considered judgment" that the "great majority" of the evacuees possessed an "essential Americanism." He felt that from 80 to 85 percent of the Nisei were "loyal," that perhaps 50 percent of the Issei were "passively loyal," but that "a large portion of the Kibei (American citizens educated in Japan) feel a strong cultural attachment to Japan" and recommended that those "who prefer the Japanese way of life" be repatriated to Japan. But if most were "loyal," whatever that means, and, if anything, Eisenhower's estimate of Japanese American "loyalty" was too conservative, it followed logically that mass evacuation was wrong. But Eisenhower, whatever he may have felt, pointedly refused to say this and accepted the decision as given. He never told the President what he told his friend Claude Wickard: that the evacuation was a mistake that would be regretted after the war. By the stern standards of the Nuremberg Tribunal then, Eisenhower, who acquiesced in an atrocity and who helped to execute it, was as guilty as Gullion, Bendetsen, De Witt, McCloy, Stimson, Roosevelt, and all the other prime architects of policy. And if we use Eisenhower's criterion of the primacy of "public attitudes," the American people and their endemic racism must share some of the guilt; although, surely, leaders are always more culpable than followers.

But Eisenhower did at least try to ameliorate the conditions of the evacuation, and one shudders to think what it might have been like had not Eisenhower and others at the top of the WRA bureaucracy been essentially on the liberal side of the American ideological spectrum. The resigning director argued against the low wage policy and suggested a substantial increase, but only if "public attitudes" permitted. He wanted light manufacturing to be set up in the camps and protested unsuccessfully the view of the business-oriented War Production Board that no work should be done in the camps that was competitive with American industry. And

---

[10] Leonard J. Arrington, *Beet Sugar in the West* (Seattle: University of Washington Press, 1966), pp. 142–643.

most important of all he suggested, as Archibald MacLeish had done four months earlier, that the President issue "a strong public statement" on behalf of the Nisei and went on to recommend that the White House begin to plan for a special postwar program of rehabilitation for the Japanese Americans.[11]

These recommendations were almost totally ignored; Eisenhower's letter made so little impression on Roosevelt (if, in fact, he ever read it) that nearly a year later, when a WRA policy matter was raised by Interior Secretary Ickes, the President and his staff thought Eisenhower was still running the WRA. The wage policy remained unchanged, and as long as they were kept in camps the Japanese Americans were relegated to stoop labor. Even more serious, no plans at all were made by the administration for the eventual return of the evacuated people to civilian life. Roosevelt had a war to win, and until others began to raise questions about the concentration camps and the people in them, the matter was settled. The new WRA director, Dillon S. Myer, a fifty-year-old Agriculture Department administrator who had been tapped for the job by Eisenhower, saw the President only once, after he had been on the job a year.[12] Policy would change, as we shall see, but not because the White House wanted it that way.

---

[11] Letter, Eisenhower to FDR, June 18, 1942, President's Personal File 4849, Franklin D. Roosevelt Library, Hyde Park.

[12] Dillon S. Myer, *Uprooted Americans: The Japanese Americans and the War Relocation Authority during World War II* (Tucson: University of Arizona Press, 1971), p. 95.

6
A QUESTION OF LOYALTY

Eight months after Pearl Harbor, on August 7, 1942, all the West Coast Japanese Americans had been rounded up, one way or another, and were either in Wartime Civil Control Administration (WCCA) Assembly Centers or War Relocation Authority (WRA) camps. By November 3 the transfer to WRA was complete; altogether 119,803 men, women, and children were confined behind barbed wire. Almost six thousand new American citizens would be born in the concentration camps and some eleven hundred were sent in from the Hawaiian Islands. The rest—112,704 people —were West Coast Japanese. Of these, almost two-thirds— 64.9 percent—were American-born, most of them under 21 and 77.4 percent under 25. Their foreign-born parents presented a quite different demographic profile. More than half of them—57.2 percent—were over 50. The camps, then, were primarily places of confinement for the young and the old, and since young adults of the second generation were, in the main, the first to be released, the unnatural age distribution within these artificial communities became more and more disparate as time went by.[1]

_____
[1] Data from U.S. Department of the Interior, War Relocation Author-

Life in these places was not generally brutal; there were no torture chambers, firing squads, or gas ovens waiting for the evacuated people. The American concentration camps should not be compared, in that sense, to Auschwitz or Vorkuta. They were, in fact, much more like a century-old American institution, the Indian reservation, than like the institutions that flourished in totalitarian Europe. They were, however, places of confinement ringed with barbed wire and armed sentries. Despite WRA propaganda about community control, there was an unbridgeable gap between the Caucasian custodians and their Oriental charges; even the mess halls were segregated by race. Although some of the staff, particularly those in the upper echelons of the WRA, disapproved of the racist policy that brought the camps into being, the majority of the camp personnel, recruited from the local labor force, shared the contempt of the general population for "Japs."

Concerning the WRA staff, Alexander Leighton, who served at Poston, has written that they could be divided into two categories: the "people-minded" and the "stereotype-minded." While the former group—clearly a minority—looked upon the evacuees as human beings and tried to treat them accordingly, the latter group saw them as members of an inferior, enemy race and not under any circumstances to be trusted. Leighton felt that many of the latter almost automatically transferred attitudes held about Negroes to the evacuees. As a WRA report put it, many staff members developed "fear, suspicion and hatred" toward their charges and some identified them "with the Japanese enemy in the Pacific."[2]

Most of the existing literature about the camps stresses the cooperation and compliance of the inmates, thus perpetuating the basic line of both the WRA and the JACL. Like most successful myths, this one contains elements of truth. There was little spectacular, violent resistance; no desperate attempts to escape; even sustained mass civil disobedience rarely occurred. But from the very beginning of their confinement, the evacuated people were in conflict, both with their keepers and with each other. These conflicts started even before the evacuation began, grew in the Assembly Centers, and were intensified in the concentration camps; their effects are still felt in the contemporary Japanese American community as the questioning and often angry members of the third, or Sansei, generation—many of whom began their lives behind barbed wire or in exile—question

---

ity, WRA: A Story of Human Conservation (Washington, 1946), pp. 196, 198. The age data are based on a January 1, 1943, census when camp population was 110,240.

[2] Alexander H. Leighton, The Governing of Men (Princeton, N.J.: Princeton University Press, 1946, pp. 81–89; Edward H. Spicer et al., Impounded People (Tucson: University of Arizona Press, 1969), p. 133.

the relative compliance of most of their parents a quarter century ago.[3]

Although resignation rather than resistance was the more common response of the internees, resistance, both active and passive, did occur and was more frequent and significant than is generally realized. The first major outbreak occurred at Santa Anita racetrack—the most crowded of the Assembly Centers—on August 4, 1942. According to the official Army report:

> a routine search for various articles of contraband was started immediately after the morning meal. A few of the [civilian] security police became over-zealous in their manner of approach to evacuees. . . . Added to this was an Order from the Center Manager to pick up, without advance notice, electric hot plates which had previously been allowed. . . . [Evacuee] complaints, based to a certain extent on solid ground grew in the intervening four or five hours to rumors of all kinds of violations on the part of the police. . . . Two mobs and one crowd of women evacuees formed. One evacuee who had long been suspected by the disorderly elements among the population of giving information to the police was set upon and severely beaten though not seriously injured. The interior security police were harassed but none were injured.[4]

Military police were called in and the disturbance was quickly quelled. The contraband in question was largely reading matter and phonograph records in Japanese, the mere possession of which was deemed to be "subversive." It was typical of the behavior of evacuees under stress that the brunt of their animus was felt by a fellow internee. Very quickly those who cooperated or seemed to cooperate too willingly with the authorities earned the name of "*inu*" (informers, but literally "dogs"). Almost all of these were of the Nisei generation, and many of them were leaders of the JACL.

The most effective early opposition to the JACL and its deliberate policy of collaboration came not from the older generation but from the Kibei, American-born Japanese who had been sent back to Japan for education or employment. The older Issei generation seemed to feel powerless: they were, after all, enemy aliens, and treatment of them was generally in accord with the Geneva Convention. The partly Americanized Kibei, who were, whatever their loyalties, American citizens, led what

---

[3] For contemporary reactions of the Sansei generation, see, for example, *gidra: The News Magazine of the Asian American Community*, Los Angeles, Vol. II, No. 4, April, 1970.

[4] United States War Department, *Final Report: Japanese Evacuation from the West Coast* (Washington, 1943), pp. 218–19.

might be called the "right-wing" opposition among the evacuee population. Some of them, and many Issei as well, were undoubtedly rooting for Imperial Japan. The bulk of the early active conflict within the internee population was between the Nisei and the Kibei, with the former blaming the latter for everything that went wrong. When, for example, a distinguished artist and University of California professor was brutally assaulted by an unknown assailant, the incident was characterized by JACL-oriented inmates as a "typical Kibei attack from the rear with a lead pipe."[5]

Sometimes these "Kibei" attacks received great support from the camp populations; one of them led to the most serious outbreak of violence in the entire evacuation, the Manzanar riot of December 6, 1942. The previous evening Fred Tayama, a restaurant owner who had been a leading JACL official, was attacked by an unknown group and beaten seriously enough to require hospitalization. Although he could not positively identify his attackers, the WRA authorities arrested several Kibei malcontents for the assault. The chief of these was Harry Ueno, whose major demonstrable offense had been an attempt to organize a Kitchen Workers' Union. He not only agitated for better working conditions but also accused WRA officials of appropriating sugar and meat intended for the evacuees, thus accentuating the food anxieties that are usually prevalent among imprisoned people.

Ueno's arrest sparked a mass demonstration led not by a Kibei but by Joe Kurihara, a Hawaiian Nisei who was the most effective anti WRA-JACL agitator in the camp. A veteran of the United States Army who had been wounded in World War I, Kurihara was understandably embittered by his imprisonment, although another ex-doughboy inmate of Manzanar, Tokataru Slocum, was a staunch defender of the necessity of the evacuation. According to Bill Hosokawa, Kurihara swore, after he was put behind barbed wire, "to become a Jap a hundred per cent and never do another day's work to help this country fight this war." After listening to Kurihara, the demonstrators made two demands:

1. The release of those arrested.
2. An investigation of Manzanar by the Spanish consul (the Spanish government represented Japanese nationals during the war).

Some speakers also urged further violent action against Tayama and other "*inu*" who were suspected, correctly, of having urged the WRA to segregate the Kibei malcontents from the other evacuees, citizen and alien. In the course of this and other meetings, "death lists" and "black lists" of alleged informers were read over loud speakers: almost all of those de-

---

[5] As cited in letter, Monroe Deutsch to John W. Nason, April 27, 1943, President's Files, University of California Archives.

nounced were JACL leaders; many of them held relatively responsible positions under the WRA.

After some fruitless discussions with the Manzanar management, another and more heated mass meeting was held about 6 P.M. More "death lists" were read and the crowd was exhorted to kill Tayama immediately. One group from the mass meeting invaded the hospital to "get" him (he was successfully hidden under a hospital bed) while another element went to the jail, presumably to effect the prisoners' release. Some accounts say that these demonstrators hurled rocks at police, others that their abuse was all verbal; in any event there were no casualties reported among the security forces. The WRA authorities then called in the military police, who pushed the crowd back from the jail but failed to disperse it. The troops then tear-gassed the crowd of several hundred, mostly teen-agers and young men, which scattered in great confusion, but re-formed later. At this juncture the troops, apparently without orders, fired submachine guns, shotguns, and rifles into the unarmed crowd. Two young men were killed and ten other evacuees were treated for gunshot wounds, as was one soldier, apparently hit by a ricocheting army bullet.

Although an official WRA report insists that this crisis "cleared an air that had become heavy with distrust," the opposite is true. Sixteen malcontents were sent to isolation camps in Moab, Utah, and Leupp, Arizona, and 65 of the most prominent JACL leaders were taken into protective custody at an abandoned Civilian Conservation Corps camp in the Mohave Desert. Within the camp a strike took place. Black armbands were distributed, and according to Togo Tanaka, one of the suspected "inu," two-thirds to three-quarters of the inhabitants wore them, some probably under coercion. For about a month no real work activities took place and then Manzanar returned to "normal."[6]

Four months later a trigger-happy military policeman at Topaz was responsible for another death. Camp regulations forbade any alien to approach an outer fence, and when an elderly and obviously harmless Issei man did so and allegedly failed to respond to a command of "Halt!" the sentry shot and killed him in broad daylight. A mass funeral was held and much indignation was expressed, but there was no significant prisoner

---

[6] Descriptions of the Manzanar riot vary. I rely heavily on the account in Dorothy S. Thomas and Richard S. Nishimoto, *The Spoilage* (Berkeley and Los Angeles: University of California Press, 1946), pp. 49–52; but see Allan R. Bosworth, *America's Concentration Camps* (New York: Norton, 1967), pp. 157–62; Spicer et al., *Impounded People*, pp. 135–38; Hosokawa, *Nisei: The Quiet Americans* (New York: Morrow, 1969), pp. 361–62; Audrie Girdner and Anne Loftis, *The Great Betrayal* (New York: Macmillan, 1969), pp. 263–66; and War Relocation Authority, *WRA: A Story of Human Conservation*, pp. 49–51.

violence at Topaz. At all the camps there were, at one time or another, protest demonstrations and "strikes" over this or that inequity, but other serious internal violence was avoided except for the crisis at Tule Lake in late 1943 and early 1944, which will be discussed later.

These outbreaks of violence were obviously not characteristic of camp life, whose salient feature was probably boredom and mild discomfort. Normal family life was obviously impossible. A father complained:

> The worst part of it is not being able to bring up the baby right. He's just eighteen months. . . . Naturally he cries some. If you were living alone in your own house, you could let him cry . . . and not spoil him. But here you've got to pay attention to it. You don't feel like letting him bother the people on the other side of the partition. They can hear everything that goes on. You've got to shut him up some way. So you have to fuss around with his crying and pay attention to him. That's not good for the baby.[7]

Not only semiprivate housing, but public feeding created problems for parents. A mother complained:

> My small daughter and I used to eat at a table where two little boys . . . ate with their mothers. They had become so uncontrollable that the mothers had given up, and let them eat as they pleased. . . . They would come running into the mess hall, and the first thing both of them did was to take off their shoes and stockings and jump up and down on the seat. Then they would start yelling for their food. After they were given their food they wouldn't eat it, but just play with it. . . . They would often bring toy automobiles and trains, etc., with them, making noises as they pushed toys in and out of food that was spilled on the table. . . . Now these little boys had older brothers and sisters, and if they had eaten at one table with both parents, things like that couldn't have happened, for the older children would have protested out of pride, and the father probably would have forbidden it.[8]

The children, particularly the teen-agers, had a degree of freedom within the confines of the camp far greater than they would have known on the outside. Among the parents, the authority of the father was greatly reduced; not only did he have less control over his children, but he also often lost his traditional role as provider. If he was an alien, his citizen

---

[7] Spicer et al., *Impounded People*, p. 105.
[8] *Ibid.*

children were in a superior legal position to him. If his wife worked, she brought in the same meager wage as he did.

There were, however, some positive aspects of camp life, as Harry Kitano has pointed out in his sociological study *Japanese Americans: The Evolution of a Subculture*. For the first time, Japanese Americans were able to play all the social roles, not just those traditionally reserved for minority group members. Those in school became student body leaders, captains of athletic teams, and editors of yearbooks. Those with teacher training could teach; positions of some authority and community leadership were filled by others. And for some of the older people there was for the first time in their adult lives a time for leisure.[9]

But the camps, it must be emphasized, were not static places. There were constant changes in basic regulations, changes that removed many of the most active and dynamic individuals from the camps, in one way or another, leaving a population that was more and more the very young and the very old and therefore progressively more passive. We have already seen how this occurred at Manzanar, when almost a hundred of the most dynamic leaders, both pro- and anti-administration, were withdrawn from the main camp population. This process was continued, not by internal crises, but by external changes in WRA and Army regulations that enabled many of those who wished to do so to leave the camps: these changes involved resettlement in the interior of the country, the opportunity to enter military service, and, finally, segregation of the militant right-wing opposition in the camp for "malcontents" at Tule Lake.

As we have seen, even as the evacuation and relocation began, two significant groups of Japanese Americans were allowed to leave reception centers and relocation camps: the college students who left permanently and the farm workers who left temporarily. On October 1, 1942, new WRA "leave clearance procedures" went into effect which eventually enabled many of the Nisei to reenter civilian life. Essentially, these leave procedures involved a loyalty check, a WRA determination of the candidates' prospects for self-support outside the center, and the general receptiveness of the community where they proposed to resettle. During 1943 some 17,000 evacuees were allowed to leave and reenter civilian life. The great majority of these were Nisei between 18 and 30. The increasing shortage of skilled and semiskilled civilian labor undoubtedly facilitated their absorption into the economy with, all things considered, a minimum of friction. Chicago, in particular, became the favorite city for relocatees, with many others being attracted to Denver and Salt Lake City. The WRA helped by setting up local resettlement committees of volunteers from

---

[9] Harry H. L. Kitano, *Japanese Americans: Evolution of a Subculture* (Englewood Cliffs, N.J.: Prentice-Hall, 1969), pp. 34–39.

civic and religious groups in the receiving communities which cooperated with field offices set up by the WRA. For those willing and able to relocate, the experience was usually rewarding. As a University of California graduate wrote Robert Gordon Sproul from Chicago:

> Hundreds of Japanese Americans are employed in occupations which were denied to them on the Pacific Coast. They have, for the first time, found occupational outlets, and I do feel for that reason a great many of them will not return to the Pacific Coast. As you well know a great many Japanese Americans graduated from institutions of higher learning but were pigeon-holed into narrow employment channels because the doors were closed to them in California. Now that they have found that they can express themselves, I do feel that a great many of them are quite happy, despite what they have undergone.[10]

Another Californian found Chicago harsh: "I still can't get used to the dirtyness, smoke, soot in this city," he wrote four days after arriving, "but it sure is good to be free again."[11]

The decision to allow "leaves" still left the question of loyalty unsettled in the minds of many within the WRA, and, when it became known outside the centers that some "Japs" were being turned loose, all kinds of protests were made. General De Witt's Western Defense Command made a sweeping "segregation" proposal at the end of 1942 which would have taken many if not most of the evacuated people from the essentially civilian control of the WRA and put them back under military auspices. Earlier a similar but less drastic proposal had been made to the WRA by an Office of Naval Intelligence "expert," Lieutenant Commander K. D. Ringle. Ringle assumed that "disloyalty" was more likely to be found among Issei and especially Kibei, whom, he felt, should be considered guilty until proven innocent, although he admitted that this was "a reversal of the commonly accepted legal procedure." All those who could not "prove" their loyalty, were to be segregated into separate camps.[12] The great attraction of this for WRA administrators was that it would presumably make the camps easier to administer and that it would also give them a "club" to use against those "loyals" who might be inclined to protest some future policy or administrative decision. In addition, others felt, it would be easier to convince the American public of the loyalty of

---

[10] Letter, B. Y. to Robert Gordon Sproul, October 9, 1944, President's Files, University of California Archives.

[11] Letter, H. Y. to Monroe Deutsch, *ca.* May 15, 1943, President's Files, University of California Archives.

[12] Hosokawa, *Nisei*, pp. 362–363.

the "unsegregated" Japanese Americans and thus facilitate the resettlement program. Although both of these proposals were rejected at the top of the WRA—each clearly had some initial support within the agency—a strike at Poston in November, the December riot at Manzanar, and an increasing level of protest throughout the camps caused many to reconsider. In addition, the resettlement program was going slowly: in January 1943, for example, only 3.9 per thousand left the camps.

At the same time, press and Congressional criticism of the WRA intensified. Most serious was an "investigation" staged by Senator A. B. (Happy) Chandler, a Kentucky Democrat who headed a Special Subcommittee of the Senate Committee on Military Affairs. After a "quickie" investigation that included a junket to the camps, Chandler told the press that disloyal evacuees were ready to commit "almost any act for their Emperor" and that, in some camps "as many as 60 per cent" were disloyal.

In the meantime, the United States Army had decided that it needed Japanese American manpower. WRA officials were summoned to a meeting in Assistant Secretary of War John J. McCloy's office in mid-January 1943. Director Dillon S. Myer and his associates were informed that the Army had decided to recruit an all-Nisei combat team of about 5000 men drawn from both the Hawaiian Islands and the Relocation Centers. Obviously, only "loyal" Japanese Americans would volunteer or be acceptable for such a unit, and the Army directed that the loyalty of the Nisei males of military age be determined by a questionnaire. The WRA leaped at this opportunity, although it had been pushing a different proposal to the same general end. It had wanted young men of military age subjected to the same selective service rules that applied to the general population (Japanese Americans had been put into a nondraftable 4–C category shortly after Pearl Harbor). Had this option been followed, a segregated, all-Japanese unit would have been almost impossible.

The WRA quickly adapted the Army's proposal to its own purposes. Instead of administering the loyalty questionnaire to male Nisei over seventeen years of age, the agency decided to determine administratively the loyalty of all internees over seventeen, regardless of sex or nationality. National publicity was given to the decision. On January 28, 1943, War Secretary Stimson announced the decision to form an all-Nisei combat team. Three days later, President Roosevelt issued a public statement praising the decision. In a letter drafted by the WRA and Office of War Information Director Elmer Davis, the President said:

> No loyal citizen of the United States should be denied the demo-
> cratic right to exercise the responsibilities of citizenship, regardless
> of his ancestry. The principle on which this country was founded
> and by which it has always been governed is that Americanism is a

matter of the mind and the heart; Americanism is not, and never was, a matter of race or ancestry. A good American is one who is loyal to this country and to our creed of liberty and democracy. Every loyal American citizen should be given the opportunity to serve this country wherever his skills will make the greatest contribution— whether it be in the ranks of the armed forces, war production, agriculture, government service, or other work essential to the war effort.[13]

This statement was widely publicized within the camps; but if the President's message was true, many of the evacuated people must have asked, why are we in concentration camps?

The resulting questionnaire was singularly inappropriate. First distributed on February 10, 1943, it was headed "Application for Leave Clearance." Many of the Issei, particularly the more elderly, had no desire to leave the camps, so the very title created confusion. The public announcement of the Japanese American combat team had already created all kinds of rumors in the camps, and, it must be remembered, the inmates had little reason to trust the United States government. But the most serious problems were created by questions 27 and 28 on the questionnaire, which had originally been intended for Nisei of military age.

No. 27. Are you willing to serve in the armed forces of the United States on combat duty, wherever ordered?

No. 28. Will you swear unqualified allegiance to the United States of America and faithfully defend the United States from any or all attack by foreign or domestic forces, and forswear any form of allegiance or obedience to the Japanese emperor, to any other foreign government, power or organization?

What aged Issei or women of any age were to make of question 27 is hard to say. But even worse was question 28. For the Issei, who were by law ineligible because of race to become United States citizens, it was asking them voluntarily to assume stateless status, and, in addition, a violation of the Geneva Convention governing the treatment of enemy aliens. Eventually, the question was rewritten for Issei to read:

No. 28. Will you swear to abide by the laws of the United States and to take no action which would in any way interfere with the war effort of the United States?

---

[13] As cited by Hosokawa, *ibid.*, pp. 365–367.

This, of course, was a more proper question which many Issei were able to answer affirmatively, but great confusion had already been caused. For the Nisei, both questions created problems. Some contended that question 28 was a trap and that to forswear allegiance to Japan was to confess that such allegiance had once existed. Many answered question 27 conditionally, saying things like: "Yes, if my rights as citizen are restored," or "No, not unless the government recognizes my right to live anywhere in the United States." Some simply answered "No-No" out of understandable resentment over their treatment and others refused to fill out the forms at all. On the other hand, the JACLers viewed the questionnaire and the opportunity to volunteer as a way to redeem their questioned loyalty. As a former University of California student who volunteered wrote to Monroe Deutsch, it was "a hard decision. . . . I know that this will be the only way that my family can resettle in Berkeley without prejudice and persecution."[14]

Out of the nearly 78,000 inmates who were eligible to register almost 75,000 eventually filled out the questionnaires. Approximately 6700 of the registrants answered "No" to question 28; nearly 2000 qualified their answers in one way or another, and thus were set down in the government's books as "disloyal"; and a few hundred simply left the question blank. The overwhelming majority—more than 65,000—answered "Yes" to question 28. More than 1200 Nisei volunteered for combat aud about two-thirds of them were eventually accepted for military service.

An analysis of the answers by camp shows clearly that internal local conditions modified the results. At five camps everyone registered; at four others a total of only 36 individuals—10 aliens and 26 citizens—refused to register; but at Tule Lake almost a third of the camp population 3218 people (1360 citizens and 1856 aliens) refused.[15] Dorothy Swaine Thomas and Richard S. Nishimoto, who studied Tule Lake, concluded that administrative blunders were largely responsible for the high degree of non-registration and disloyalty at Tule Lake, but to this almost surely must be added the factor of effective leadership among the "disloyals." Hosokawa argues that coercion by militant disloyals was also a factor.[16]

Although originally designed as a method of getting volunteers for an Army program, the loyalty questionnaires were eventually used by the WRA as a basis for separating the "loyal" from the "disloyal" and shipping the latter to Tule Lake, which became a segregation center for "disloyals," with "loyal" inmates shipped out to other camps and segregants moved in.

---

[14] Letter, K. O. to Monroe Deutsch, March 15, 1943, President's Files, University of California Archives.

[15] Data from U.S. Department of the Interior, War Relocation Authority, WRA: A Story of Human Conservation, pp. 199–200.

[16] Thomas and Nishimoto, The Spoilage, pp. 82–83, and Hosokawa, Nisei, p. 365.

Apart from the spurious nature of the loyalty determination, other factors entered into the decision of individuals to go to Tule Lake or remain there. Family loyalties, the desire to remain where they were, and often sheer resentment and disillusionment were as significant as "loyalty" or "disloyalty."

An Issei man, aged 41, later said:

> He didn't register because of the rumor that those who registered would be forced to leave [Tule Lake] and he had no place to go.[17]

Two young brothers, aged 20 and 23, from Venice, California:

> We'd like to sit in Tule Lake for a while. We don't want to relocate. The discrimination is too bad. I see letters from the people on the outside. There are fellows in Chicago who want to come back [to camp] but who are not allowed in.[18]

A young Nisei mother, who asked for repatriation to Japan explained:

> I have American citizenship. It's no good, so what's the use? . . . I feel that we're not wanted in this country any longer. Before the evacuation I had thought that we were Americans, but our features are against us. . . . I found out about being an American. It's too late for me, but at least [in Japan] I can bring up my children so that they won't have to face the same kind of trouble I've experienced.[19]

Eventually, more than 18,000 Japanese Americans were segregated at Tule Lake; almost a third of these were family members of segregants rather than segregants themselves. Another third were "Old Tuleans," many of whom just simply did not want to move. One such Issei pointed out that

> Tuleans who are staying are often doing so because they didn't want to move. Those who are coming in here are among the worst because they wouldn't bother to pack and come here unless they were fairly bad.[20]

Conversely, JACL types at the other centers welcomed the segregation. As one wrote from Topaz:

---

[17] Thomas and Nishimoto, *The Spoilage*, pp. 88–90.
[18] Thomas and Nishimoto, *The Spoilage*, p. 93.
[19] Thomas and Nishimoto, *The Spoilage*, pp. 95–96.
[20] Thomas and Nishimoto, *The Spoilage*, p. 111.

the disloyal ones have been segregated and sent to Tule Lake. As a result the place is very peaceful now with the radical element gone. [It] certainly was a good idea . . .something they should have done a long time ago.[21]

Predictably, Tule Lake became a trouble spot and was turned over to the Army for a time and placed under martial law. Even there some inmates were accused by others of being "*inu*," and several serious beatings and one murder occurred. During the period of Army control one evacuee was shot and killed by a sentry, who, although exonerated by both civilian and military courts, seems to have overreacted. Within Tule Lake, a strong minority movement for what was called "resegregation" grew up. Its proponents, strongly pro-Japanese and desirous of returning to Japan, objected to the presence of a majority, who, despite their presumably "disloyal" status, had no such orientation or desire. Eventually more than a third of those at Tule Lake formally applied for repatriation to Japan after the war; of the 7222 persons who did so, almost 65 percent were American-born.

The renunciation of American citizenship, usually a very difficult thing, was made easier by an act of Congress, the so-called Denationalization Act of 1944. Francis Biddle's Justice Department supported this dubious act on the assumption that 300 to 1000 citizens might avail themselves of its provisions. The reasons, as later explained by Edward J. Ennis, the department's expert on the Japanese, were

1. A fear that the courts might eventually declare continued detention of American citizens unconstitutional, and Justice wanted some way to hold on to "disloyals."
2. The fear that militant disloyals, released, might be dangerous.
3. That the bill would induce militant disloyals to renounce their citizenship, and that they then could be detained.[22]

Actually, like the "No" answer on question 28, statements made about repatriation and citizenship renunciation were motivated by many factors. Chief, of course, was the fact that the incarcerated people were subject to all kinds of pressures, real and imaginary. Statements gathered by the University of California's Japanese American Evacuation and Resettlement Project make this abundantly clear. For many in Tule Lake and to a lesser degree in the other camps, the fear of being thrust back,

---

[21] Letter, T. K. to Monroe Deutsch, October 17, 1943, President's Files, University of California Archives.
[22] Thomas and Nishimoto, *The Spoilage*, pp. 355–56.

virtually penniless, into a hostile, wartime atmosphere was frightening. Many, as we have seen, went to or stayed at Tule Lake because it seemed to offer a kind of refuge in an otherwise stormy world. As one Nisei girl put it:

> Are they going to kick us out? What good will that do, when we don't want to get out? My mother said that segregation was a dirty trick, bringing us here with so much trouble and now it doesn't mean a thing. We hope that by renouncing citizenship, we will be allowed to stay here, but we are not sure.[23]

As it turned out, renunciation was not enough; even before the war was over, many renunciants were, as they would put it, turned out of Tule Lake as the WRA liquidated the camps in 1945–1946. And surely no sadder commentary on what America seemed to be to some of her citizens can be made than the fact that thousands of her people preferred a Tule Lake to freedom.

But trouble and reluctance to leave were not confined to Tule Lake. Protests and resistance to resettlement characterized the history of the other nine camps even after the "disloyals" had been segregated. Heart Mountain, Wyoming, often classified as a "happy camp," is a good case in point.[24] From the very beginning there had been conflict and organized resistance there.[25] In October and November 1942, protests and demonstrations occurred over the erection of the standard barbed wire fence surrounding the camp, which had not yet been erected when the evacuees began to arrive in August. The fence and other guard facilities were denounced in a petition signed by half the adults in the camp as "devoid of all humanitarian principles . . . an insult to any free human being." The fence, of course, stayed, but other, more pragmatic protests continued.

Despite concerted efforts by the camp administration to avoid conflict (the project director, Guy Robertson, later wrote that it was necessary "to avoid too much leisure" so that the evacuees wouldn't have time to organize and agitate), it consistently took place, often over the work details necessary for the housekeeping chores incidental to running a "city" of ten thousand people. Always in the background of these disputes

---

[23] Thomas and Nishimoto, *The Spoilage*, p. 338.

[24] Girdner and Loftis, *The Great Betrayal*, p. 247.

[25] For the data on resistance at Heart Mountain I draw on the work of my student, Douglas W. Nelson, "Heart Mountain: The History of an American Concentration Camp," unpublished M.A. thesis, University of Wyoming, 1970. Some or all of this should soon find its way into print. Except for the work of Thomas and Nishimoto on Tule Lake it is, by far, the most detailed and sophisticated study of an individual camp.

was the bitter resentment of the token wage scale, $12 to $19 a month, which governed all evacuee employment. In early November, which can be bitterly cold in Wyoming, the work crews assigned to unloading and delivering coal to the barracks walked off the job, demanding higher wages and the issuance of work clothes and gloves. The administration successfully resisted the strike, and, aided by the desperate need for coal and the antistrike position taken by the evacuee-run newspaper, the *Heart Mountain Sentinel*, volunteers from the camp broke the strike. That same month two other groups protested. One strike occurred at the hospital, which, in all the camps, was a focal point of trouble. The crux of the problem was that evacuee doctors, nurses, and technicians received lower pay and had to play subordinate roles vis-à-vis Caucasian staff members doing the same work who were often less qualified than their Japanese American counterparts. This protest was broken by sterner means; the three alleged ringleaders were shipped off to the detention center at Leupp, Arizona. At about the same time a strike of the evacuee internal security police was more successful. Aimed primarily at their Caucasian chief, it ended with his resignation. The evacuees organized a kind of labor council, called the Fair Practices Committee, which the administration recognized, but labor trouble continued.

Discontent also continued over the restrictions enforced by the military police. In December a mass arrest of thirty-two inmates occurred for a violation of security. The culprits, formally taken into custody by the United States Army, were sledding on a hill just outside the camp; none of them was over eleven years old. Although they were released the same day, this callous treatment of their children understandably inflamed many of the Japanese Americans and sparked a general protest against the whole theory and practice of the evacuation. This protest, like most of the others, came to nothing, but it did highlight a growing division among the impounded people at Heart Mountain, a division between those who insisted on the immediate restoration of their rights—what one might call the "left opposition"—and those who took the JACL-WRA line of accommodation to "military necessity." I use the term left opposition not to denote persons with a Marxist viewpoint—what few Japanese American Marxists there were took a position of all-out support for the war—but to differentiate them from what I call the "right opposition," those who for one reason or another rejected American and professed Japanese ideals. The camp paper, edited by JACLer Bill Hosokawa, reacted typically to the "left" protest by assuring the Heart Mountaineers that Director Dillon Myer's WRA was doing "everything possible" under the circumstances. This view was clearly not representative; during late 1942 and early 1943 a majority of adults at the Wyoming camp publicly expressed their opposition to some aspect of WRA policy, although concerted, sustained opposition was always a minority phenomenon.

Also apparent at Heart Mountain was a growing alienation between children and parents, as the natural "generation gap" was exacerbated by incarceration. Children seemed to resent their inherited characteristics— what they often called the "Japanese face"—which had landed them behind barbed wire, while parents often sneered at the value of the highly prized American citizenship of the Nisei generation. One girl's poem, written in confinement, illuminates this tension.

> Father, you have wronged me grievously
> I know not why you punish me
> For sins not done or reasons known
> You have caused me misery
> But through this all I look on you
> As child would look on parents true
> With tenderness commingling in
> The anguishment and bitter tears;
> My heart still beats with loyalty
> For you are my father
> I know no other.[26]

But it was the registration and segregation crisis of 1943 which most clearly demonstrated the degree of opposition at Heart Mountain, as it did in the supposedly less happy camps. The most effective ally of the minority dissidents was the almost total distrust that most inmates felt for the WRA, and eventually, for its JACL allies. As Project Director Guy Robertson later reported:

> There were factions who refused to believe in anything inaugurated by the administration. . . . The administration were *inu* . . . and the evacuees who cooperated were called worse. . . . They considered the WRA as the government, making no distinction between the different sections of the government . . . they caused a great deal of difficulty.[27]

Robertson's general estimate is undoubtedly correct, but the tangible results at Heart Mountain suggest strongly that his "factions" probably better represented the majority view than did the accommodationist JACL.

The unreality of the administration's expectations is nowhere better demonstrated than in the registration-segregation crisis, sparked by the issuance of the Army-WRA "Leave Clearance" questionnaires in February

---

[26] *Heart Mountain Sentinel*, May 15, 1943.
[27] "Project Director's Final Report" (Heart Mountain), War Relocation Authority Collection, Bancroft Library.

1943. Despite official statements that "we are not trying to force any person to relocate who does not desire to do so," many in the camp felt: "It's a trick. Sign that application for leave and they'll throw you out to starve."[28] Massive administration pressure, including the palpably false statement that filling out the questionnaire was "compulsory," plus the already referred to modification of question 28 for aliens, secured almost total compliance among the Issei. Among the citizen population, however, these tactics were less successful. The left opposition organized the Heart Mountain Congress of American Citizens, which was explicitly anti-WRA, and insisted that "the JACL is not truly representative of the citizens . . . [and] should be willing to step aside if Niseidom cannot get together under its banner."[29] The leader of this left opposition, Frank T. Inouye, argued that

> we must demand that our name be cleared; and have it read to the world that there had never been a justification for our evacuation, and that we are fighting, not to redeem ourselves or to clear our names, but for what we have always believed in.[30]

An informal boycott of registration by most Nisei lasted until the end of February. Concessions by the Army, which said it would accept conditional answers to questions 27 and 28, and pressure from the WRA and the *Heart Mountain Sentinel*, were, for a time unavailing. Dillon Myer wired Project Director Robertson to assure the evacuees that the WRA would "continue to defend . . . citizenship rights," and the evacuee's paper, while conceding that some of the objectives of the militants were "understandable," insisted that there was "too much at stake to brood over the injustices of the past" and warned the dissidents "to cooperate . . . for their own sakes if nothing else." Inouye answered for the left opposition with a retort that what Heart Mountain really needed was an "open press which will not only realize the possibilities of Nisei concerted action, but which will also dare to publish the truth." At the same time, the opposition to registration slackened, and by the end of March every Nisei had filled out a questionnaire. Of some 3800 Nisei registrants, 126 refused to answer question 28, 104 gave qualified answers, and 278

---

[28] "Community Analyst's Report on Registration at Heart Mountain, No. 1" (Forrest LaViolette, April, 1943), War Relocation Authority Collection, Bancroft Library.

[29] Executive Council of Heart Mountain Citizens Congress to the Citizens in Nine Other Relocation Centers, February 14, 1943, War Relocation Authority Collection, Bancroft Library.

[30] *Heart Mountain Sentinel*, February 13, 1943. For Inouye's current views, see a two-part interview with him, Honolulu *Star-Bulletin*, March 2-3, 1971.

answered "No." In other words one of seven Nisei at Heart Mountain refused to cooperate.[31]

But that does not tell the whole story of resistance; many of the Nisei who eventually answered "Yes-Yes" on the loyalty questionnaires were merely beating a strategic retreat: opposition would now center first on the voluntary combat team and eventually on the draft. Initially, the WRA had expected perhaps as many as 2000 volunteers from Heart Mountain alone; as the opposition to the whole program began to develop, its sights were lowered accordingly and it was estimated that there would be 3600 volunteers from all ten camps or about 360 from each. As we have seen, that figure was far too high; only some 1200 volunteered at that time. But even on this diminished scale, the Heart Mountain participation was disproportionately small and indicative of the effectiveness of the left opposition and the unrepresentative character of the JACL leadership. Only 38 young men in Heart Mountain volunteered, and half of these failed their physicals.

This resistance was maintained in the face of both concessions and pressure. War Secretary Stimson sent a telegram to Heart Mountain arguing that "the formation of an American-Japanese combat team composed entirely of volunteers will help tremendously to convince those who oppose the American-Japanese." Later, Project Director Robertson, implying that the resistance was the responsibility of the older, alien generation, wrote an open letter to the Issei leaders in which he claimed that it was their responsibility, not his, "to see that Heart Mountain maintain at least a comparable position with the other centers" in volunteering for the combat team. He also argued that a "life-long stigma will be borne by their children who fail to assume their responsibility in a democratic government." The argument was too much even for the usually docile Issei leadership, who insisted that it was absurd to think that camp inmates, and especially camp inmates who were enemy aliens, could possibly be held responsible for the success or failure of a program initiated by the same government which had put them behind barbed wire.[32]

The whole loyalty-registration-combat team fiasco adversely affected everyone concerned with Heart Mountain, keeper and prisoner alike. Among the staff, there was, according to an official WRA report:

> An intensification of caste feeling, based on belief in moral superiority and lack of understanding of evacuee position. Manifest in such statements as "It's about time we got hard boiled." "A Jap's a Jap.

---

[31] *Heart Mountain Sentinel*, February 20, 29, 1943.

[32] *Heart Mountain Sentinel*, February 29, March 6, 13, 1943; Letters, Guy Robertson to Dillon Myer, March 9, 1943, and Block Chairmen to Guy Robertson, n.d., War Relocation Authority Collection, Bancroft Library.

This proves it." "They don't appreciate what we do for them." "Might as well drop this sentimental attitude and be realistic." Etc.[33]

As for the impounded people, a WRA community analyst observed that the "sense of injustice deepened. . . . Bitterness over loss of citizenship increased [and] cynicism and spiritual discouragement" grew.[34] This disillusionment can be measured quite tangibly in the data about those at Heart Mountain who applied for repatriation or expatriation to Japan. Up to the start of the loyalty-registration crisis only 42 Heart Mountain people had requested to go to Japan. In February alone, triggered by the issuance of the questionnaires, 50 additional people made this request, followed by 314 more requests in March. By August 1943 the total number of such requests at Heart Mountain had grown to 800, about 8 percent of the camp population. A majority of these were individuals who had answered "Yes-Yes" to questions 27 and 28.

An even larger number was affected by the segregation program, the outgrowth of the loyalty check which began in July 1943. The *Sentinel*, following the JACL-WRA line, commented that "loyal residents . . . will welcome [the] decision as a necessary and overdue measure" and argued that it was "one step toward the larger objective of restoring full rights for those unquestionably loyal."[35] By the end of September, 903 people were shipped to Tule Lake from the Wyoming camp: 352 adult aliens, 309 adult citizens, and 242 children. The following month their places were taken by approximately 1000 "loyal" evacuees from Tule Lake. But unlike the situation at Tule Lake and, to a lesser degree at Manzanar, where pro-Japanese government and anti-American statements and slogans abounded, there were no such activities at Heart Mountain. Douglas W. Nelson, from whose perceptive account of Heart Mountain most of the foregoing was drawn, has written:

> . . . it is significant that in all the material I have seen concerning Heart Mountain from its beginning to the time of segregation, there is *not one* expression of or reference to pro-Japanese or anti-American sentiment.[36]

One of the major inarticulate premises behind the segregation of "disloyals" at Tule Lake, an assumption shared by WRA administrators and "loyal" JACLers alike, was that with "troublemakers" removed, the

---

[33] "Report on Registration," n.d. but *ca.* March 15, 1943, War Relocation Authority Collection, Bancroft Library.

[34] *Ibid.*

[35] *Heart Mountain Sentinel*, July 17, 1943.

[36] Douglas W. Nelson, "Heart Mountain . . .", p. 128.

camps would become more placid and that resistance and protest would all but cease. At Heart Mountain such was not the case; there was more tangible protest, and protest of greater consequence, after segregation than before. As it turned out, almost all the key leaders of what I have called the "left opposition" remained at Heart Mountain after segregation because they had either answered "Yes-Yes" to the crucial questions or had so qualified their answers that they were not "eligible" for segregation.

One such leader was Kiyoshi Okamoto. Born in Hawaii in the 1920s, he was educated in Los Angeles and became a construction engineer, thus breaking out of the employment ghetto that restricted most of his contemporaries.[37] He had never been to Japan and could not speak Japanese. He had been a principal supporter of the antiregistration and antivolunteer movement among the Nisei, but it was only after the segregation crisis that his leadership became outstanding. As Okamoto explained it later, he became increasingly disturbed, in the fall of 1943, by what he considered "un-American practices" at Heart Mountain. These included specific incidents involving acts of brutality and discrimination by Caucasian staff members, the denial of free speech, the substandard living and working conditions of the evacuees, and a growing awareness, by him, of the general injustice of the whole evacuation. In November 1943 he formed what he called a "Fair Play Committee of One" and began to agitate and speak to his fellow prisoners about doing something to clarify the legal status of the incarcerated Nisei, paralleling, as we shall see, arguments that were being made in the federal courts. Soon he was running "open forums" in the camp, and he attracted a number of followers who eventually formed what they called the Fair Play Committee. (This had no connection whatsoever with the Fair Play Committee that had been organized by Caucasian educational and religious leaders in California in 1941.)

Although it had considerable support, the Fair Play Committee would not have had much impact had not the Army changed the rules again. On January 20, 1944, War Secretary Stimson announced that because of the fine record of Nisei volunteers normal selective service procedures would again be applied to Japanese Americans, both inside and outside the camps. (Actually, the fact that there were not enough volunteers from the camps was equally a factor.) The WRA and the JACL had long urged such a step, and of course it had been an issue raised during the loyalty-registration crisis. The *Sentinel*, now under the editorship of Haruo Omura but still following the JACL line, hailed Stimson's announcement

---

[37] This and other material on the "left opposition" drawn from the records of *U.S.* v *Okamoto et al.*, Case Nos. 3076–3082, 10th U.S. Circuit Court of Appeals, Denver Federal Records Center. I am indebted to Delbert Bishop and Robert Svenningsen of the Center staff for their assistance.

as "the most significant development in returning Japanese Americans to full civic status," but it soon had to admit that "to say that the War Department's announcement . . . brought joy to the hearts of all draft-age men would be misleading and inaccurate." Nevertheless the *Sentinel* urged Heart Mountaineers to avoid another "senseless" round of "endless questions" and "picayune issues."[38]

By mid-February the Fair Play Committee members had allies outside the camp: Samuel Menin, a Denver attorney, was advising them about their legal rights, and James Omura, who had been one of the few Japanese Americans to take an anti-JACL line at the Tolan Committee hearings before the evacuation and was now resettled in Denver, opened the columns of the Denver *Rocky Shimpo*, of which he was English language editor, to the Fair Play Committee. In addition, with funds raised from a $2 membership fee, the Committee purchased a mimeograph machine and began to distribute its own bulletin within Heart Mountain. The Committee members were warned both by camp authorities and local selective service officials against counseling draft resistance. The evacuee dissidents contended that they were merely advising Nisei to get a clarification of their rights, and an FBI investigation in February could find no indictable behavior. At the end of February the first seventeen Heart Mountain inductees reported for their draft physicals, and WRA officials thought the crisis was over, predicting that at most perhaps two or three individuals might refuse preinduction physicals.[39]

As a counterweight to the Fair Play Committee, the evacuee community council, perhaps at the instigation of the WRA circulated a petition to President Roosevelt accepting the draft but mildly protesting other aspects of government policy. Opposed by the Fair Play Committee, the petition was viewed as a test of strength. Only slightly over a third of the adult inmates signed, much to the disappointment of the Heart Mountain administration. Shortly after the test of strength, the first tangible results of the Fair Play Committee's agitation appeared: in the first weeks of March twelve Nisei refused to board the bus to take their selective service physicals, and an increasing number of potential draftees were promising to do likewise.

At this juncture the *Heart Mountain Sentinel* launched a full-scale attack on the Committee, and the *Rocky Shimpo* retaliated with a blast at the camp paper. According to the *Sentinel*:

> During the last week, in the hidden recesses of boiler rooms and latrines, behind closed doors and under the protection of darkness, leaders of the Fair Play Committee have fired with fanatical zeal

---

[38] *Heart Mountain Sentinel*, January 22, 29, 1944.
[39] Memorandum, A. T. Hansen to M. O. Anderson, Assistant Project Director, March 10, 1944, War Relocation Authority Collection, Bancroft Library.

the weaker members and departed from their mimeographed statements which are purposely toned down for public consumption.[40]

The *Rocky Shimpo* counterblast insisted that the *Sentinel* staff had

> purchased a seat in the great gallery of bigots, racist demagogues,
> autocrats, and fascist-minded. . . . It has deserted justice, fair play,
> equal rights and all that are revered in our constitution and in the
> government of our United States.[41]

Naturally the question of loyalty came up. The *Sentinel* suggested that
the leading spirits, at least, of the Fair Play Committee had answered
questions 27 and 28 untruthfully, thus implying that they should be sent
to Tule Lake, while the Committee leadership insisted that the real
disloyalty to American democracy and its traditions was the "patriotism
equals submission" formula of the *Sentinel* and the JACL.

The *Sentinel* couched some of its arguments in pragmatic terms in-
sisting that "fighting against issues that are beyond our control . . . is a
waste of time and space." The real fallacy of the resisters' case was,
according to the *Sentinel*:

> the contention that a restriction of our rights means a loss of those
> rights. We don't lose any rights unless the constitution itself is
> changed. . . . If the Supreme Court rules evacuation was constitu-
> tional, then we will not have been deprived of any rights.[42]

Whatever the merits of the debate, many Heart Mountain draft
eligibles were won to the militant's position. By the end of March 1944, 54
of the 315 evacuees ordered to report for physicals had failed to do so.
Late that month the Fair Play Committee, broadening its attack, began
to agitate for a general strike at Heart Mountain. Predictably, the WRA
reacted. The project director was informed from Washington that a re-
examination of the papers of Fair Play Committee leader Kiyoshi Okamoto had discovered evidence of disloyalty; he was quickly taken into
custody and shipped off to Tule Lake. Okamoto's "transfer" angered his
fellow protestants; Isamu Horino, also a Fair Play Committee leader, in
order to dramatize the lack of freedom, publicly announced his intention
of leaving Heart Mountain and tried in broad daylight to walk out the
main gate. Naturally, the military police stopped him, and, with this overt
evidence of "disloyalty," the administration soon shipped him off to
Tule Lake.

---

[40] *Heart Mountain Sentinel*, March 18, 1944.
[41] *Rocky Shimpo*, March 20, 1944.
[42] *Heart Mountain Sentinel*, April 1, 1944.

The third leader of the Fair Play Committee, 27-year-old Paul T. Nakadate, committed no overt act; he was subjected to a long interrogation by the project director about his loyalty. Nakadate felt that "democracy is sharing of equal responsibilities and sharing of equal rights." Since he felt that his treatment had been unequal, he could no longer say whether he would serve in the United States Army (he had not yet been called). These and similar answers failed to satisfy the project director and with the approval of Washington, Nakadate, too, was shipped off to Tule Lake.[43] But the administration was not just after leaders. At Robertson's urging, a reluctant U.S. attorney caused the arrest, in late March and early April, of all 54 evacuees who had refused induction. This effectively broke the back of Fair Play Committee resistance within Heart Mountain. But its outside voice needed to be silenced as well.

On April 1, 1944, Project Director Robertson wrote to WRA Director Dillon Myer, arguing that Omura's editorials in the Rocky Shimpo bordered on "sedition" and asked for an investigation of the newspaper, whose assets were administered by the Alien Property Custodian, its original owners having been Issei and thus enemy aliens. The following week, in what can hardly have been a coincidence, the Sentinel attacked Omura as "the number one menace to the post-war assimilation of the Nisei," insisted that he was "responsible for wrecking the lives" of the draft evaders, and charged that he was "prostituting the privileges of freedom of the press to advocate an un-American stand." By the end of April federal officials had seized Omura's records and correspondence, and the Alien Property Custodian fired him and his staff. The Heart Mountain resistance was all but dead; only if its exponents could be vindicated in the courts would it stay alive.[44]

Before his transfer to Tule Lake, Okamoto had written to the American Civil Liberties Union asking for help in testing the constitutionality of drafting citizens who were behind barbed wire. In mid-April, American Civil Liberties Union Director Roger Baldwin, in a public letter, disassociated himself and his organization from the Fair Play Committee fight. The dissidents had, Baldwin admitted, "a strong moral case," but, he insisted, "no legal case at all." He admonished Okamoto that "men who counsel others to resist military service are not within their rights and must expect severe treatment." What caused Baldwin to release his letter publicly is not clear, but a letter from Project Director Robertson to Dillon Myer implies that the JACL's Salt Lake City headquarters may have requested him to do so. In any event, the major spokesman for civil

---

[43] "Leave Clearance Hearing: Paul Takeo Nakadate," March 30, 1944, War Relocation Authority Collection, Bancroft Library.

[44] Letter, Guy Robertson to D. S. Myer, April 1, 1944, War Relocation Authority Collection, Bancroft Library; Heart Mountain Sentinel, April 8, 1944; Rocky Shimpo, April 12, 1944.

liberties in the United States had supported the JACL line, whose adherents were jubilant: ACLU TAKES ISSUE WITH OKAMOTO was the *Sentinel* headline. Letters from Nisei in the Army were printed to buttress the accommodationist position, and the Army Air Force arranged it so that Sergeant Ben Kuroki, the first Japanese American war hero, could visit Heart Mountain. The visit, according to Project Director Robertson, had "a very good effect on the general morale of the people."[45]

On May 10, 1944, a federal grand jury in Cheyenne indicted the draft resisters, whose number had grown to 63. They were tried the next month in the largest mass trial for draft resistance in our history. The defense, by attorney Menin, argued that the defendants violated the draft orders only to clarify their ambiguous draft status and that no felonious intent was involved. The court was not impressed. Federal District Judge T. Blake Kennedy found all 63 guilty and sentenced them to three years' imprisonment and, in a memorandum, questioned their loyalty: "If they are truly loyal American citizens they should . . . embrace the opportunity to discharge the duties [of citizenship] by offering themselves in the cause of our National Defense."

An appeal filed by their attorney, which also argued that the defendants had been deprived of liberty without due process of law, was rejected in March 1945 by the Tenth Circuit Court of Appeals in Denver, and the Supreme Court refused *certiorari*.[46]

In the meantime, however, other charges were brought against the Heart Mountain resisters and one of their allies. The same federal grand jury that had indicted the draft resisters had also brought in an indictment against seven members of the Fair Play Committee's executive council (including Okamoto and Nakadate, who had been sent to Tule Lake) and editor James Omura for unlawful conspiracy to counsel, aid, and abet violations of the draft. The indictments were kept secret by federal authorities until after the initial conviction of the draft violators themselves. A few days after the first convictions, the *Sentinel*, perhaps in on the secret, argued that those who encouraged the draft resisters not to report "deserve penitentiary sentences even more than those convicted." On July 21, 1944, the indictments were made public and the eight defendants arrested.

The seven evacuee defendants were represented by Abraham Lincoln Wirin, a Southern California ACLU attorney whose views about the evacuation and other matters were often more libertarian than those of

---

[45] Letters, Guy Robertson to D. S. Myer, April 8, 17, and 29, 1944, War Relocation Authority Collection, Bancroft Library; *Heart Mountain Sentinel*, April 22, 29, 1944.

[46] Criminal Court Docket, *U.S. v. Fujii et al., Case* Nos. 4928, 4931–4992, U.S. District Court, Cheyenne, Wyoming, Denver Federal Records Center; *U.S. v. Fujii et al.* (1945) 128 F. 2nd, Fed. Rep., 298–300; an account of the trial appears in the *Wyoming Eagle* (Cheyenne), June 12–20, 1944.

the national body; Omura was represented by a Denver attorney, Sidney Jacobs. Jacobs unsuccessfully tried to get a separate trial for Omura on the grounds that he had never seen the other defendants (he had corresponded with some of them) before they appeared in court together. Wirin, using an argument that probably would have been successful two decades later, tried to get the case dismissed on the grounds that evacuees were systematically excluded from jury duty. The government contended that the Fair Play Committee was a conspiracy against the selective service system in particular and the war effort in general. Editor Omura was found innocent, but all seven of the evacuees were found guilty and sentenced to terms of four and two years' imprisonment.

After the verdict, Nisei war hero Ben Kuroki, who had been a government witness, told the press:

> These men are fascists in my estimation and no good to any country. They have torn down [what] all the rest of us have tried to do. I hope that these members of the Fair Play Committee won't form the opinion of America concerning all Japanese-Americans.[47]

Attorney Wirin filed an appeal contending that there was insufficient evidence and that the judge's instructions to the jury were improper. More than a year later the Tenth Circuit Court of Appeals, in a 2–1 decision, upheld Wirin's second contention while rejecting the first, and the defendants were free.[48] But even while this was going on, resistance to the draft was continuing at Heart Mountain, although on a reduced scale. Between the summer of 1944 and the closing of the camp in November 1945, 22 more men were indicted and convicted for draft resistance, bringing the total of such convictions at Heart Mountain to 85.[49] To put draft resistance into numerical perspective, more than 700 Heart Mountain men did board the bus for their draft physicals, and 385 were inducted; of these 11 were killed and 52 wounded. Nor was the Heart Mountain case an isolated one; similar figures for both draft resistance and compliance can be tabulated for the other regular camps.[50] This account of the "loyal" Japanese American resistance—what I

---

[47] *Wyoming State Tribune* (Cheyenne), November 3, 1944.

[48] *U.S. v. Okamoto et al.*, Case No. 4930, U.S. District Court, Cheyenne, Wyoming, and *U.S. v. Okamoto et al.*, Case Nos. 3076–3082, 10th U.S. Circuit Court of Appeals, Denver Federal Records Center; *Heart Mountain Sentinel*, July 1, 1944; *Wyoming State Tribune* (Cheyenne), November 3, 1944.

[49] *U.S. v. Eta et al.*, *U.S. v. Nozawa et al.*, U.S. District Court, Cheyenne, Wyoming, Case Nos. 5050–5068, 5132–5134, Denver Federal Records Center.

[50] For statistics on draft resistance, by camp, see War Relocation Authority, *The Evacuated People*, p. 126.

have called the "left opposition"—is highly significant. It calls into question the stereotype of the Japanese American victim of oppression during World War II who met his fate with stoic resignation and responded only with superpatriotism. This stereotype, like most, has some basis in reality. Many Japanese Americans, conforming to the JACL line, honestly felt that the only way they could ever win a place for themselves in America was by being better Americans than most. Whether or not this kind of passive submission is the proper way for free men to respond to injustice and racism, is, of course, a matter of opinion. But it is important to note that not all 'loyal" Japanese Americans submitted; the resistance of the Heart Mountain Fair Play Committee and of other individuals and groups in the other camps, has been almost totally ignored and in some instances deliberately suppressed by chroniclers of the Japanese Americans. The JACL-WRA view has dominated the writing of the evacuation's postwar history, thereby nicely illustrating E. H. Carr's dictum that history is written by the winners. The authors of these works have in some cases been ignorant of the nature and scope of the "left opposition"; others, more knowledgeable, have either consciously underplayed it or suppressed it completely, hoping thereby, in their view at least, to manage and improve the image of an oppressed people. There are those, however, who will find more heroism in resistance than in patient resignation.

7

THE COURT APPROVES

In addition to the opposition which took the form of protest and civil disobedience, a more orthodox but equally futile opposition was testing the legality of the evacuation in the federal courts. It was an opposition that the federal government had anticipated, and there were those within it, like Provost Marshal General Gullion, who had serious doubts about the constitutionality of evacuating and incarcerating citizens without the declaration of martial law. Much more common, however, was the view taken by California Attorney General Earl Warren, who argued that the entire war emergency was a kind of clear and present danger which, in effect, nullified the constitutional rights of citizens, like the Nisei, who might be presumed, somehow, to be a threat to the nation. At an early stage of the evacuation, General De Witt even went so far as to order subordinate commanders within the Western Defense Command to disregard court orders, including writs of habeas corpus, unless his headquarters authorized them to obey such directives.[1] Within the camps the court cases were

---

[1] Directive, General De Witt to Commanding Generals, All Sectors, WDC . . . , August 22, 1942, Record Group 394, National Archives.

followed closely, and the decline of faith in America and its institutions is not unrelated to the sorry performance of the federal judiciary.

The first test case was decided in Seattle Federal District Court on April 13, 1942, even before the evacuation began. The challenger was Mary Asaba Ventura, a Nisei resident of Seattle who was married to a citizen of the Philippines. Her protest was against the curfew, her attorneys alleging for her that she was a loyal and devoted citizen who had been unreasonably threatened with military punishment at a time when the state and federal courts were open, no rebellion or state of invasion existed, and martial law had not been declared. Two days after the petition for habeas corpus, Federal District Judge Lloyd Llewellyn Black read his verbal opinion.

> Her complaint is, to say the least, very premature. She wishes to be relieved of an imprisonment before any such occurs. . . . The question here should be viewed with common sense. . . . These are critical days. To strain some technical right of petitioning wife to defeat the military needs in this vital area during this extraordinary time could mean that perhaps the "constitution, laws, institutions" of this country to which her petition alleges she is "loyal and devoted" would be for a time destroyed here on Puget Sound.

After suggesting that modern implements and techniques of war had made the Constitution obsolete anyway, Judge Black raised the question of dual citizenship, which Mrs. Ventura had specifically denied:

> How many in this court room doubt that in Tokyo they consider all of Japanese ancestry though born in the United States to be citizens or subjects of the Japanese Imperial Government? How many here believe that if our enemies should manage to send a suicide squadron of parachutists to Puget Sound that the Enemy High Command would not hope for assistance from many such American-born Japanese?

If Mrs. Ventura were really loyal, Judge Black concluded, she would be glad to conform to the precautions directed by higher authority.[2] Black's opinion was a little raw, even for the western judiciary, not often given to subtlety, but it must be noted that he had cut his legal teeth prosecuting members of the Industrial Workers of the World during World War I.

More than a year later, in June 1943, the Supreme Court of the

---

[2] I quote from the stenographic record furnished De Witt by Black in Record Group 394, National Archives. The case is reported in 44 *F Supp* 520, filed April 15, 1942.

United States ruled on the same question. The case involved Gordon Kiyoshi Hirabayashi, a Nisei who was a senior at the University of Washington. He deliberately refused to follow General De Witt's orders and was convicted in federal court under the Act of Congress of March 21, 1942, which made it a misdemeanor to violate the orders of a military commander in a designated military area. He was convicted on two separate counts—curfew violation and failing to report for evacuation—and sentenced to three months' imprisonment on each count, the sentences to run concurrently. The contention of Hirabayashi and his attorneys was that, to be constitutional, General De Witt's curfew and exclusion orders should have applied to all United States citizens or none.

The decision was rendered by the same judge who had refused to grant Mrs. Ventura's petition five months earlier. Although somewhat more restrained in *Hirabayashi* he did wave the flag a little.

> It must not for an instant be forgotten that since Pearl Harbor we have been engaged in a total war with enemies unbelievably treacherous and wholly ruthless . . . civilization itself is at stake in this global conflict.[3]

An appeal of the 1942 conviction eventually reached the Supreme Court in May 1943, and the decision was announced on June 21. The Court unanimously upheld the conviction, but behind that façade of unanimity there was much disagreement among the justices. The majority opinion was written by Chief Justice Harlan Fiske Stone, who, his biographer tells us, was pushed by one of the "war hawks" on the Court to sanction "shrinking judicial review of the war powers almost to the vanishing point."[4] The issue, for Stone, was the war power of the American government which he defined as "the power to wage war successfully." His opinion ranged erratically over the history of Japanese in the United States and focused on the following:

1. "Espionage by persons in sympathy with the Japanese had been found to have been particularly effective in the surprise attack on Pearl Harbor."

---

[3] 46 *F Supp* 657 (September 15, 1942). Another early case involved Lincoln Seiichi Kanai, born in Hawaii and described by a Federal District judge as a "full blooded Japanese." He did not report for evacuation, remained at large, and resettled himself in Milwaukee, Wisconsin, where, in July, 1942, he was hailed before a federal commissioner and ordered sent back to California for proper relocation. He applied for a writ of habeas corpus, which was denied. See *Ex parte Lincoln Seiichi Kanai*, 46 *F Supp* 286 (July 29, 1942).

[4] Alpheus Thomas Mason, *Harlan Fiske Stone: Pillar of the Law* (New York: Viking, 1956), p. 675.

2. Japanese were concentrated on the Pacific Coast, most of them around the three large cities of Los Angeles, Seattle, and Portland.

3. The discrimination suffered by Japanese in the United States (Stone cites denial of naturalization, exclusion, alien land laws, miscegenation statutes, and restriction of employment) has intensified the solidarity of the Japanese and inhibited their assimilation.

4. Young Japanese have been sent to Japanese language schools, which "are generally believed" to be nationalistic, and some 10,000 American-born Japanese have been sent to Japan for schooling.

5. The Japanese Government recognizes dual citizenship for many American-born Japanese which might have an influence on the loyalty of some persons of Japanese descent.

6. The most influential members of the Japanese American community are aliens who have been under the influence of Japanese consular officials in this country.[5]

Because of these factors, according to the Chief Justice, Congress and the President could "reasonably have concluded" that all of the circumstances worked toward "the continued attachment of members of this group to Japan and Japanese institutions." Obviously this was racism, and Stone went on to point out that, in his view, racism was not totally barred by the Constitution.

> Because racial discriminations are in most circumstances irrelevant and therefore prohibited, it by no means follows that, in dealing with the perils of war, Congress and the Executive are wholly prevented from taking into account those facts . . . which may in fact place citizens of one ancestry in a different category. . . .
>
> The adoption by Government, in the crisis of war and of threatened invasion, of measures for the public safety, based upon the recognition of facts and circumstances which indicate that a group of one national extraction may menace that safety more than others, is not wholly beyond the limits of the Constitution. . . . [The] facts, and the inferences which could be rationally drawn from them, support the judgment of the military commander. . . .

---

[5] 320 US 81 (1943). The legal literature on the Japanese American cases, as they are called, is vast. I have relied heavily on the analysis in Milton R. Konvitz, *The Alien and the Asiatic in American Law* (Ithaca, N.Y.: Cornell University Press, 1946) and sometimes paraphrase his summaries of complex arguments. Other particularly useful general summaries include: Eugene V. Rostow, "The Japanese-American Cases—A Disaster," *Yale Law Journal*, June, 1945; and Nanette Dembitz, "Racial Discrimination and the Military Judgment: The Supreme Court's Korematsu and Endo Decisions," *Columbia Law Review*, March, 1945.

After all this justification, Stone chose to decide the question on as narrow grounds as possible even though some of the justices, according to Stone's biographer, wanted the opinion "written in such a way as to suggest that all avenues of legal relief were foreclosed to the Japanese evacuees." Justice Hugo L. Black, on the other hand, stated in judicial conference that "I want it done on [the] narrowest possible points" and, generally, Black's approach prevailed.[6] Stone refused to consider the question of failure to report for evacuation and ruled only on the curfew violation. Since the sentences were concurrent, he neither reversed nor sustained the other sentence.

Three separate concurring opinions were filed. Justice William O. Douglas was disturbed by Stone's doctrine of collective ancestral guilt. In a private note he wrote the Chief Justice that the reasoning in the opinion "implies or is susceptible to the inference that the Japs who are citizens cannot be trusted because we have treated them so badly." His concurrence, designed largely to leave the door open for future judicial review of the matter, went to some lengths in an attempt to justify the military. The Court, he argued, had to trust the military.

> We must credit the military with as much good faith . . . as we would any other public official. . . . The point is that we cannot sit in judgment of the military requirements of that hour. . . .
> The military [should not] be required to wait until espionage or sabotage becomes effective before it moves.

Having put forward this curious doctrine—for effect, substitute in Douglas' opinion "police" for his "military," and "murder or robbery" for his "espionage or sabotage"—Douglas then denied the racism that Stone had avowed. In language more appropriate to a dissent, Douglas insisted:

> We are dealing here with a problem of loyalty not assimilation. Loyalty is a matter of mind and of heart not of race. . . . Moreover, guilt is personal under our constitutional system. Detention for reasonable cause is one thing. Detention for ancestry is another. . . .
> We need go no further here than to deny the individual the right to defy the law. [Hirabayashi had deliberately made a test case and had so informed the FBI in advance. For a libertarian like Douglas to call this traditional method of testing the constitutionality

---

[6] Black quoted from Justice Murphy's conference notes as cited by Sidney Fine, "Mr. Justice Murphy and the Hirabayashi Case," *Pacific Historical Review*, May, 1964, p. 201; Douglas from Mason, *Harlan Fiske Stone*, pp. 673–74.

of a statute or an action defiance is incredible.] It is sufficient to say that he cannot test in that way the validity of the orders as applied to him.

A second concurrence, by Justice Wiley B. Rutledge, insisted that even in wartime there were some limits on a general's authority.

> The officer of course must have wide discretion. . . . But it does not follow that there may not be bounds beyond which he cannot go and, if he oversteps them, that the courts may not have power to protect the civilian citizen.

The third concurrence, by Justice Frank Murphy, is a strange document indeed which puzzled many observers of the Court at the time. We now know, thanks to research in Murphy's papers by Professors Sidney Fine and J. Woodford Howard, that Murphy originally wrote it as a dissent but changed it to a concurrence under pressure from his colleagues, particularly Felix Frankfurter.[7] Murphy's motives were dictated by his almost reflexive patriotism and the desire to maintain national unity. Nevertheless, his concurrence was a powerful document that assailed many of the premises of the majority opinion. Originally Murphy found the statute "unconstitutional in its broad aspects" and the action taken under it "defective." His opinion, of course, did not say this, but it came close:

> The broad provisions of the Bill of Rights . . . are [not] suspended by the mere existence of a state of war. . . . Distinctions based on color and ancestry are utterly inconsistent with our traditions and ideals. . . .
>
> Today is the first time, so far as I am aware, that we have sustained a substantial restriction of the personal liberty of citizens of the United States based on the accident of race or ancestry. . . . It bears a melancholy resemblance to the treatment accorded to members of the Jewish race in Germany. . . . This goes to the very brink of constitutional power. [As originally written, Murphy had this going "*over* the brink of constitutional power."]

---

[7] Sidney Fine, "Mr. Justice Murphy and the Hirabayashi Case," *Pacific Historical Review*, May, 1964, p. 201; and J. Woodford Howard, Jr., *Mr. Justice Murphy: A Political Biography* (Princeton, N.J.: Princeton University Press, 1968). pp. 300 ff. The latter has some of the basic facts about *Hirabayashi* wrong. Frankfurter was still alive when Fine published, and is quoted but not identified; Woodford names him. Since Frankfurter informally advised "Jack" McCloy about restrictions on aliens—chiefly to get better treatment for German Jewish refugees who were technically enemy aliens—there are those who would argue that he should have disqualified himself in any case involving the War Department alien program. See several Frankfurter-McCloy letters in Record Group 107, National Archives.

In the concluding paragraphs of his curious concurrence Murphy served public notice that the issue of the relocation was not yet settled.

> In voting for affirmance of the judgment I do not wish to be understood as intimating that the military authorities in time of war are subject to no restraints whatsoever, or that they are free to impose any restrictions they may choose on the rights and liberties of individual citizens or groups of citizens in those places which may be designated as "military areas." While this Court sits, it has the inescapable duty of seeing that the mandates of the Constitution are obeyed. That duty exists in time of war as well as in time of peace, and in its performance we must not forget that few indeed have been the invasions upon essential liberties which have not been accompanied by pleas of urgent necessity advanced in good faith by responsible men. . . .
>
> Nor do I mean to intimate that citizens of a particular racial group whose freedom may be curtailed within an area threatened with attack should be generally prevented from leaving the area and going at large to other areas that are not in danger of attack and where special precautions are not needed. Their status as citizens, though subject to requirements of national security and military necessity, should be at all times accorded the fullest consideration and respect. When the danger is past, the restrictions imposed on them should be promptly removed and their freedom of action fully restored.

Hirabayashi was decided in the spring of 1943, when the war in the Pacific could still be deemed in doubt;[8] the Court's limited ruling on the

---

[8] A companion case, involving Minoru Yasui, was disposed of in an opinion by Stone the same day as *Hirabayashi*. Yasui, native-born, graduated from the University of Oregon, took a law degree there, and was admitted to the Oregon bar. He was a 2nd Lieutenant in the United States Army reserve. Shortly after graduation, in 1939, he was employed by the Consulate General of Japan in Chicago, during which time he was registered as an agent of a foreign government. Immediately after Pearl Harbor he resigned, returned to Oregon, and volunteered for active duty. He was, of course, not accepted. He deliberately violated the curfew by walking into a police station late at night. He was tried in Oregon Federal District Court by Judge James Alger Fee, who found that De Witt's orders "were void as respects citizens" and therefore unconstitutional. Nevertheless Judge Fee found Yasui guilty and sentenced him to a year in prison, because the court concluded that by working for the Japanese government Yasui, who, like all Nisei, was eligible for dual citizenship, had chosen "allegiance to the Emperor of Japan" and was therefore not a citizen of the United States, despite his birth, reserve commission, and admission to the Oregon bar. When the case came before the Supreme Court, the government did not press the revocation of citizenship, which Stone therefore did not rule on; he did reverse Fee on the constitutionality of

rights of Japanese citizens in wartime was not modified for a year and a half. Finally, a week before Christmas 1944, three years after Pearl Harbor, the high court decided, in a most unsatisfactory way, the legality of the evacuation. It did so in two distinct cases which were handed down on the same day. By this time, of course, any Japanese threat to the United States was inconceivable, although most authorities expected that the Pacific war would last for years.

The first, and narrower case, involved Fred Korematsu, California-born and a graduate of an Oakland high school.[9] The issue at stake, as argued in the American Civil Liberties Union brief *amicus curiae*, was "whether or not a citizen of the United States may, because he is of Japanese ancestry, be confined in barbed-wire stockades euphemistically termed Assembly Centers or Relocation Centers—actually concentration camps." Justice Hugo Black wrote the majority opinion for a Court divided 6 to 3 which upheld Korematsu's conviction for failure to report for evacuation, thus sustaining the constitutionality of the evacuation.

Black's argument was essentially that "the gravest imminent danger to the public safety" existing in the spring of 1942 justified the actions taken. He recited a number of reasons:

1. The presence of an indefinite number of disloyal persons of Japanese ancestry.
2. Because of the impossibility of determining loyalty of individuals quickly, temporary exclusion of the whole group was deemed by appropriate authorities a military necessity.
3. Subsequent to exclusion many refused to swear unqualified allegiance and others requested repatriation or expatriation.
4. In wartime citizenship carries heavier burdens than in time of peace.

Black, like Douglas in *Hirabayashi*, insisted that prejudice and racism had nothing to do with either the evacuation or his sanctification of it.

Our task would be simple, our duty clear, were this a case involving the imprisonment of a loyal citizen in a concentration camp because of racial prejudice. Regardless of the true nature of the assembly and relocation centers—and we deem it unjustifiable to call them concentration camps with all the ugly connotations that term implies—we

---

De Witt's orders as applied to citizens. When the case returned to Fee, he struck the ruling about Yasui's citizenship from the judgment. See 48 *F Supp* 40, 320 *US* 115, and 51 *F Supp* 234 (July 14, 1943).

[9] *Korematsu* v. *U.S.*, 323 *US* 214 (December 18, 1944).

are dealing specifically with nothing but an exclusion order. To cast this case into outlines of racial prejudice, without reference to the real military dangers which were presented, merely confuses the issue. Korematsu was not excluded from the Military Area because of hostility to him or his race.

Black was careful in limiting the scope of the decision, noting that "we uphold the exclusion order as of the time it was made and when the petitioner violated it." In other words, an exclusion order that was, somehow, constitutional in the spring of 1942 might not be constitutional later. In case anyone missed the distinction, Black also referred to *Endo,* which the Court would hand down the same day, December 18, 1944:

> *Endo* . . . graphically illustrates the difference between the validity of an order to exclude and the validity of a detention order after exclusion has been effected.

For many, this would be a distinction without a difference. Justice Frankfurter, in a concurrence, tried to disassociate the Court from the judgments involved in exclusion and evacuation.

> To find that the Constitution does not forbid the military measures now complained of does not carry with it approval of that which Congress and the Executive did. That is their business, not ours.

Some of his brethren, however, did not think that the Court could so easily wash its hands of the matter. Roberts, Jackson, and Murphy all dissented. Roberts, whose false report of Japanese American sabotage at Pearl Harbor was a minor factor in the decision for mass evacuation, distinguished sharply between *Hirabayashi,* in which he silently concurred, and *Korematsu*:

> This is not a case of keeping people off the streets at night as was Hirabayashi. . . . It is a case of convicting a citizen . . . for not submitting to imprisonment in a concentration camp solely because of his ancestry. . . .

He denied, vehemently, the majority's contention that there could be a separation between reporting for shipment to an Assembly Center and detention. He saw the cumulative effect of De Witt's several proclamations as

> a cleverly designed trap to accomplish the real purpose of military authority, which was to lock him in a concentration camp.

The majority contention that Korematsu should have submitted to evacuation he found

> a new doctrine of constitutional law that one indicted for disobedience to an unconstitutional statute . . . must obey it . . . and then, and not before, seek, from within prison walls, to test the validity of the law.

Justice Robert Jackson's dissent was somewhat paradoxical. He refused to say whether or not General De Witt's orders were proper; in fact he asserted that there was no way for him to tell whether they were proper or not.

> But even if they were permissible military procedures, I deny that it follows that they are constitutional. If, as the Court holds, it does follow, then we may as well say that any military order will be constitutional and have done with it.

This doctrine of military supremacy was too much for the future prosecutor at Nuremberg; but Jackson would not have estopped the military either.

> My duties as a justice as I see them do not require me to make a military judgment as to whether General De Witt's evacuation and detention program was a military necessity. I do not suggest that the courts should have attempted to interfere with the Army in carrying out its task. But I do not think they may be asked to execute a military expedient that has no place in law under the Constitution. I would reverse the judgment and discharge the prisoner.

But what of the hundred thousand prisoners who had already spent more than two years behind barbed wire? Jackson, who even in hindsight would not have issued a writ to stop their detention, did little more for them than his brethren of the majority.

Murphy's dissent was another matter, and, for anyone concerned with civil liberty, his opinion, belated though it was, clearly takes the honors. Murphy was not content to give the military primacy in determining what was or was not military necessity. He used De Witt's mendacious *Final Report*,[10] the testimony before Congressional committees, and the ACLU brief to weigh the evidence, just as in any other case. His conclusion was

---

[10] For just one example of the suppression of evidence in the *Final Report*, see Conn, "Japanese Evacuation from the West Coast," fn. 74, p. 136.

unambiguous: the exclusion order, made while the state and federal courts were still open, went over "the very brink of constitutional power" and toppled into "the ugly abyss of racism." There had to be, Murphy insisted:

> definite limits to military discretion, especially where martial law has not been declared. Individuals must not be left impoverished of their constitutional rights on a plea of military necessity that has neither substance nor support. Thus, like other claims conflicting with the asserted constitutional rights of the individual, the military claim must subject itself to the judicial process of having its conflicts with other interests reconciled.

General De Witt's orders and proclamations, Murphy found, did not meet any reasonable test.

> Being an obvious racial discrimination, the order deprives all those within its scope of equal protection of the laws as guaranteed by the Fifth Amendment. It further deprives these individuals of their constitutional rights to live and work where they will, to establish a home where they choose and to move about freely. In excommunicating them without benefit of a hearing, this order deprives them of all their constitutional rights to procedural due process. . . . This dangerous practice of protective custody, as proved by recent European history, should have absolutely no standing as an excuse for the deprivation of the rights of minority groups.

Murphy examined in detail the mishmash of charges, some wholly imaginary and others *ex post facto*, quoted some of De Witt's choicer remarks, and concluded:

> A military judgment based upon such racial and sociological considerations is not entitled to the great weight ordinarily given the judgments based upon strictly military considerations. . . . I dissent, therefore, from this legalization of racism. . . . All residents of this nation are kin in some way by blood and culture to a foreign land. Yet they are primarily and necessarily a part of this new and distinct civilization of the United States. They must accordingly be treated at all times as the heirs of the American experiment and as entitled to all the rights and freedoms guaranteed by the Constitution.

After all this, the *Endo* case, handed down the same day, came as a distinct anticlimax.[11] It involved Mitsuye Endo, a native Californian, a

---

[11] *Ex parte Endo*, 323 US 283 (December 18, 1944).

permanent civil servant of the State of California who had a brother serving in the United States armed forces. Like almost all the Japanese Americans, she docilely submitted to De Witt's regulations, but once she reached her camp, Topaz, she sought release on a writ of habeas corpus. The WRA fought the writ, allegedly because she had not gone through the process of leave clearance which was instituted after her petition had originally been filed. The ACLU, in a brief for her, argued that

1. The government was without power to detain a citizen against whom no individual charges had been instituted.
2. Segregation and detention of citizens on the basis of ancestry is patently unconstitutional.
3. Since she was kept behind barbed wire involuntarily and without due process she was entitled to release without complying with WRA regulations.

Justice Douglas wrote the opinion for a unanimous Court. As he had indicated in his *Hirabayashi* concurrence, there were means by which a Japanese American could gain release, and Endo and her attorneys had found them. But the decision did not find the Act of March 21, 1942, unconstitutional. Instead it held, against all the evidence, that, since the act did not mention detention, "the law makers intended to place no greater restraint on the citizen than was clearly and unmistakenly indicated by the language they used." It was, according to Justice Douglas' quaint theory of history, the civilian WRA, not the military, which violated Endo's rights. "Whatever power the War Relocation Authority may have to detain other classes of citizens, it has no authority to subject citizens who are concededly loyal to its leave procedures." After almost three years of detention, deprivation, and demoralization, all the Court could find fault with was an administrative regulation of the WRA.

This was too much for two justices; Murphy and Roberts filed concurrences which agreed with the result—Miss Endo's release—but dissented from the Court's failure to come to grips with the real constitutional issues—the rights of citizens vis-à-vis the military in wartime. Justice Murphy insisted, correctly, that detention of citizens had been envisaged and supported by both the President and Congress, and he found the whole as just "another example of the unconstitutional resort to racism inherent in the entire evacuation program." Roberts, similarly, found it "inadmissible to suggest that some inferior public servant exceeded the authority granted by executive order in this case." His brethren, Roberts rightly felt, had copped out, although they had been

squarely faced with a serious constitutional question—whether [Endo's] detention violated the guarantees of the Bill of Rights . . .

and especially the guaranteee of due process of law. There can be but one answer to that question. An admittedly loyal citizen has been deprived of her liberty for a period of years. Under the Constitution she should be free to come and go as she pleases.

Thus spoke the Roosevelt Court. Its majority consistently refused to inhibit the broad war and police powers of the federal government in the interests of civil liberty, especially when it involved the civil liberties of nonwhites. Even that paladin of personal liberty, Justice Murphy, was curiously color blind; his caustic concurrence in *Hirabayashi* illustrates that blindness. His statement, "Today is the first time . . . that we have sustained a substantial restriction of the personal liberty of citizens of the United States based on the accident of race or ancestry," and his analogies to European persecution and racism show a curious refusal to make a more appropriate analogy—the treatment of the black man in the United States. World War II was fought by Americans for freedom and democracy— Eisenhower would call it a "crusade in Europe"—and yet it was fought with a Jim Crow army, and the separate but equal doctrine was still the law of the land. The United States would remain, until almost a decade later, an officially racist nation. The Roosevelt Court, which made so many important breakthroughs, was incapable of coming to grips with the nation's most pressing dilemma, so it is not surprising that it significantly shortchanged the tiny Japanese American minority.

But the decisions of the Roosevelt Court in the Japanese American cases did not affect only that minority. As Morton Grodzins wrote shortly after the war:

> Japanese Americans were the immediate victims of the evacuation. But larger consequences are carried by the American people as a whole. Their legacy is the lasting one of precedent and constitutional sanctity for a policy of mass incarceration under military auspices. This is the most important result of the process by which the evacuation decision was made. That process betrayed all Americans.[12]

Just one year after Grodzins published these words, the Congress of the United States passed the "Emergency Detention Act of 1950." (It is a component part of the McCarran Act.) This law, still on the books, gives civilians—the Attorney General and the President are specifically mentioned—the statutory right, some would say duty, to set up camps for, as Sec. 101, (14), puts it: "The detention of persons who there is reasonable

---

[12] Morton Grodzins, *Americans Betrayed: Politics and the Japanese Evacuation* (Chicago: University of Chicago Press, 1949), p. 374.

grounds to believe will commit or conspire to commit espionage or sabotage. . . ."[13]

All it takes to put the process into motion is a Presidential proclamation of an "Internal Security Emergency" which may be created, according to the statute, by (1) invasion, (2) declaration of war, (3) insurrection within the United States. Such camps were actually constructed and put into readiness during the early 1950s and are now in mothballs. Quite obviously, the precedents established in the evacuation and detention of the Japanese Americans have been followed rather closely; at least one of the camps (Tule Lake) used for them in the 1940s was prepared for subversives in the 1950s. In 1935 Sinclair Lewis wrote a sensational novel about fascism coming to the United States called *It Can't Happen Here*. As far as one of the chief trappings of fascist regimes is concerned, it has happened here. In addition, we have enabling legislation on the books which makes it much easier for it to happen again, and, even if the law were repealed, any Attorney General has the Supreme Court precedents established in *Hirabayashi* and *Korematsu* to fall back on.

If it does happen again, the cast of characters will certainly be different. Surely it won't strike the Japanese American community; nor do the Chinese Americans have much to fear despite the unpopularity of the People's Republic of China. One of the fringe benefits of continued international tension is an increasing sophistication: World War II taught us that there are "good" and "bad" Germans; the cold war, that there are "good" and "bad" individuals even within enemy Asian countries. Nor is it likely that, in the event that continuing urban insurrections and/or continuing frustrations in Southeast Asia were to give us a superhawk/white backlash president, these "legal" concentration camps would be used to provide a "final solution" for our major domestic race problem. Any foreseeable use of these concentration camps will be for ideological rather than racial enemies of the republic. Yet, should they be used at all, it will be, in the final analysis, merely one more bitter draught from the racist tradition that has long been a central theme of all American history.

---

[13] For a slightly hysterical treatment of this subject, see the pamphlet sponsored by the Citizens Committee for Constitutional Liberty, Charles R. Allen, Jr., *Concentration Camps U.S.A.* (New York, 1966).

8
THE ROAD BACK

Without in any way minimizing the opposition among the evacuated people, it must be emphasized that the majority accepted, at least passively, almost all to which they were subjected. Even if they were not active supporters of the JACL, in general, they followed its line. The JACLers collaborated actively with the government because they were convinced that by cooperating they could most effectively influence both government policy and public opinion and thus make easier their return to a normal life and facilitate their fuller acceptance into American society. Whether or not this collaboration was too high a price to pay is a question still being debated by Japanese Americans, and, it should be noted, debates over accommodation are a continuing argument within most ethnic groups in the United States. Right or wrong, deliberate accommodation was the path chosen by most of the Nisei leadership; what success it had was due largely to their tactical persistence in pursuing it. They did have allies among the Caucasian power structure; some of them, like Elmer Davis and Archibald MacLeish, had tried, early in 1942, to stop or inhibit the evacuation. But New Deal liberals were not the prime policy makers during the war; the military and its civilian bosses were in the saddle. It was the military establishment, in the final analysis, that was responsible for the evacuation; the same military establishment, under pressure from the liberals, eventually was chiefly responsible for its relaxation.

Less than a week after the basic decision to evacuate was made, an intragovernmental group, the Joint Evacuation Board, composed of middle echelon military personnel and their opposite numbers from several executive departments and agencies formally proposed that

> special effort . . . be made to draft or enlist American citizens of Japanese extraction into the armed forces and [employ them] where they can be of service to their country and where they are least likely to fall under suspicion, justified or unjustified.[1]

By May 1942 Assistant Secretary of War McCloy, the key figure in the decision for mass evacuation, had become convinced, after some prodding from Milton Eisenhower, that

> it might be well to use our American citizen Japanese soldiers in an area where they could be employed against the Germans. I believe that we could count on these soldiers to give a good account of themselves.[2]

In mid-July a special general staff board was organized to investigate the possibilities of utilizing the manpower of United States citizens of Japanese ancestry. Its initial erroneous premise was that there would be enough Japanese American manpower for a division—12,000 to 15,000 men. The Western Defense Command was opposed to any real change in the *status quo*, and had even resisted the earlier recruitment of a few linguists by the Army Language School, which De Witt had forced to move from California to Camp Savage, Minnesota. The Language School commandant, Lieutenant Colonel Kai E. Rasmussen, acting on War Department authority in early July 1942, had bypassed De Witt and Bendetsen and sent recruiting teams directly to the Assembly Centers and Relocation Centers. As Bendetsen later described it:

> Col. Rasmussen, from his school in Minnesota, sent a detail in to Manzanar to gather up a few enlistees. Four or five only enlisted at

---

[1] Minutes, Meeting of Joint Evacuation Board, February 25, 1942, Record Group 107, National Archives.

[2] Memo, John J. McCloy to Dwight D. Eisenhower, May 20, 1942, enclosing letter, Milton Eisenhower to McCloy, May 18, 1942, Record Group 107, National Archives.

that time. They came down [from] Manzanar on the train, in company of a non-commissioned officer and an officer. By jove, when they got to Los Angeles, the whole town was in a tail spin for the entire night upon reports of seeing Japanese there. . . . Here is what happened. For example, one Japanese was seen and then a hundred reports would come in on him, and the police think that there were probably a hundred Japanese and their prowler cars were out, and we couldn't get it straightened out until the next morning.[3]

By October 1942 liberals within the administration were pressing for action. Elmer Davis and Milton Eisenhower wrote the President recommending two actions:

1. Two bills in Congress—one aimed at depriving the Nisei of citizenship and the other proposing to "intern" them for the duration of the war—have heightened the feeling that this may be after all a racial war and that, therefore, the evacuees should be looked upon as enemies. A brief public statement from you, in behalf of the loyal American citizens, would be helpful. I think WRA and the Justice Department would concur in this recommendation.

2. Loyal American citizens of Japanese descent should be permitted, after individual test, to enlist in the Army and Navy. It would hardly be fair to evacuate people and then impose normal draft procedures, but voluntary enlistment would help a lot. This matter is of great interest to the OWI. Japanese propaganda to the Philippines, Burma, and elsewhere insists that this is a racial war. We can combat this effectively with counter propaganda only if our deeds permit us to tell the truth. Moreover, as citizens ourselves who believe deeply in the things for which we fight, we cannot help but be disturbed by the insistent public misunderstanding of the Nisei; competent authorities, including Naval Intelligence people, say that fully 85 percent of the Nisei are loyal to this country and that it *is* possible to distinguish the sheep from the goats.[4]

The Davis-Eisenhower proposals were circulated throughout the military. The Army, as we have seen, was already moving in this direction, but the Navy balked. Its top authority on Japanese, Captain Elias Zacharias, who had probably advised Davis on the memorandum, "con-

---

[3] Telephone conversation, Bendetsen and Colonel Scobey, February 17, 1943, Record Group 394, National Archives.

[4] Letter, Elmer Davis to FDR, October 2, 1942, President's Personal File 4849, Franklin D. Roosevelt Library, Hyde Park. Davis specifically associates Milton Eisenhower with the letter.

curred heartily" with Davis.[5] But the Vice Chief of Naval Operations, speaking for the brass, felt "that permitting such enlistments would serve no useful purpose."[6] The civilian head of the Navy agreed. Frank Knox wrote Roosevelt that he did not think the bills had any chance of passage and that therefore no statement was necessary; the Navy, he said, was against allowing citizens of Japanese ancestry to enlist, but he gave no reasons. More important, according to the Navy Secretary, was to do something about the "very large number of Japanese sympathizers, if not actual Japanese agents, still at large in the population of Oahu."[7]

Despite the Navy's opposition, the Army gained approval for its program. General De Witt's headquarters, however, was terribly upset when it discovered that the War Department intended to form a Japanese American combat team (De Witt and Bendetsen favored putting Japanese Americans in labor battalions if they were to be used at all) and protested, with some logic, against the attempt to determine loyalty. As De Witt told his superiors in January 1943:

> I don't see how they can determine the loyalty of a Jap by interrogation. . . . There isn't any such thing as a loyal Japanese. . . . I feel . . . that it is a sign of weakness and an admission of an original mistake.

Bendetsen, the architect of the program, protested similarly:

> The issue is that the War Department is undertaking to determine their loyalty and to be responsible for that determination. It is going to be a little hard for the War Department to explain why when they were in Assembly Centers, under control, satisfying all the then requirements, that if it is possible to determine loyalty, they didn't do it then. And save 80 million dollars worth of Relocation Centers that were built. That's the fundamental point.[8]

Not all concerned commanders felt this way. General Delos Emmons, in Hawaii, was a strong supporter of the combat team. In late January

[5] Zacharias, holograph memorandum, October 15, 1942, President's Personal File 4849, Franklin D. Roosevelt Library, Hyde Park.

[6] Memorandum, Vice Chief of Naval Operations to the Secretary of the Navy, October 15, 1942, President's Personal File 4849, Franklin D. Roosevelt Library, Hyde Park.

[7] Letter, Knox to FDR, October 17, 1942, Record Group 107, National Archives.

[8] Telephone conversations: De Witt and Gullion, January 14, 1943; De Witt and McCloy, January 18, 1943; Bendetsen and Colonel Watson, January 23, 1943; Bendetsen and Colonel Scobey, February 17, 1943, all Record Group 394, National Archives.

1943 the official announcements of the formation of the Japanese American combat units were made, but De Witt's command still tried, by every means possible, to circumscribe the program. De Witt formally filed his objections to the loyalty program.[9] His next line of defense was to try to keep the new Japanese American soldiers out of the Western Defense Command for the duration of the war. McCloy, and the Army brass generally, now felt strongly that "when a man was in the uniform of the U.S. Army, that, unless he was guilty of some offense, that he should have the rights of a citizen to be at large" and that these rights definitely included the privilege of going home on furlough. De Witt lost this battle too; he then tried to sabotage the program by stirring up West Coast opinion.

At an off-the-record news conference in San Francisco on April 14, 1943, De Witt told the press that, although it had not yet been announced officially, Japanese Americans inducted into the service would get seven-day furloughs just like any other soldier.

Q. What is to prevent Japanese from obtaining a uniform and coming around here?
DE WITT. [That is] exactly what I told the War Department. . . . Of course, I don't oppose the orders of my superiors. . . . It is their decision and I am going to carry it out [but] the precedent is bad.

He also told the press that if the Japanese government should find out about the new policy it would afford them a good opportunity "to infiltrate men in uniform."[10]

The War Department apparently did not know of this deliberate insubordination by a general officer, but his testimony, five days later to the same effect before a House Naval Affairs Committee in San Francisco was a matter of public record; shortly thereafter his impending relief was announced, and in September he was moved from the West Coast and made commandant of the Army and Navy Staff College in Washington. His replacement was General Emmons from Hawaii whose views about Japanese Americans were more congruent with those now held by the civilian chiefs of the Army.

Each of the steps designed to ameliorate the lot of the evacuated people, or part of them, produced the expected unfavorable reaction from most Californians and some members of Congress. California newspapers, the state legislators, and the House Committee on Un-American Activities

---

[9] De Witt's formal objections are in a memo to the Chief of Staff, January 27, 1943, Record Group 394, National Archives.
[10] Press Conference transcript, April 14, 1943, Record Group 394, National Archives.

all attacked the WRA for "coddling Japs"; Earl Warren, now governor of California, told his fellow governors in June 1943 that continued release of Japanese Americans would result in a situation in which "no one will be able to tell a saboteur from any other Jap" and he opposed, vehemently, the return of any of the evacuees to California before the end of the war.[11] Stimulated by this high-level activity scores of anti-Japanese groups and committees sprang up throughout California; many of them called for the "deportation" of all Japanese, citizen and alien, at the end of the war.

At about the same time, however, more and more liberals within the administration pressed for better treatment for the Japanese Americans. Chief of these was crusty Harold L. Ickes, Secretary of the Interior. At an early stage of the resettlement program he had employed a couple from a camp to work on his Maryland farm and caused his action to be publicized. In April 1943 he wrote the President:

> Information has come to me from several sources that the situation in at least some of the Japanese internment camps is bad and is becoming worse rapidly. Native-born Japanese who at first accepted with philosophical understanding the decision of their government to round up and take far inland all of the Japanese along the Pacific Coast, regardless of their degree of loyalty, have pretty generally been disappointed with the treatment they have been accorded. Even the minimum plans that had been formulated and announced for them have been disregarded in large measure, or, at least, have not been carried out. The result has been the gradual turning of thousands of well-meaning and loyal Japanese into angry prisoners. I do not think we can regard, as of no official concern, the unnecessary creating of a hostile group right here in our own territory consisting of people who are engendering a bitterness and a hostility that bodes no good for the future. . . . I am unwilling to believe that a better job in general could not have been done. Neither do I believe that we can't do better from here out, especially if we tackle the job in a different spirit and with real determination without further delay.[12]

Another Cabinet officer took a different view. In answer to a query from the President's wife, War Secretary Stimson agreed with Ickes that things had gotten worse in the camps, but found fault with the prisoners rather than with the captors. As he wrote Eleanor Roosevelt:

---

[11] Warren as quoted in Bill Hosokawa, *Nisei: The Quiet Americans* (New York: Morrow, 1969), p. 373.

[12] Letter, Ickes to FDR, April 13, 1943, President's Personal File 4849, Franklin D. Roosevelt Library, Hyde Park.

Unfortunately, a rather marked deterioration in evacuee morale appears to have occurred at the relocation centers. While this is certainly in part the natural result to be expected from confinement, I believe that activities of pro-Axis minorities in each center have been a major factor in promoting unrest and destroying confidence in this country among the evacuees. The War Department has urged on several occasions that the undesirables be segregated out and kept by themselves, but little has yet been accomplished in this direction.[13]

In 1943 the War Department's view prevailed. The disastrous segregation program was adopted, partially to appease those in Congress who wanted the "liberal" WRA abolished and all the impounded people put under strict military control. In July 1943 the Senate adopted a resolution calling for segregation of all those whose loyalty was not established and asked for a full report on conditions in the camps and future plans. The President replied, officially, more than two months later, that segregation was proceeding, that "disloyals" would not be eligible to leave Tule Lake until after the war, and that there would be an appeals procedure "to allow for the correction of mistakes." But he also told the Senate that resettlement would continue.

. . . the War Relocation Authority proposes now to redouble its efforts to accomplish the relocation into normal homes and jobs in communities throughout the United States, but outside the evacuated areas, of those Americans of Japanese ancestry whose loyalty to this country has remained unshaken through the hardships of the evacuation which military necessity made unavoidable. We shall restore to the loyal evacuees the right to return to the evacuated areas as soon as the military situation will make such restoration feasible. Americans of Japanese ancestry, like those of many other ancestries, have shown that they can, and want to, accept our institutions and work loyally with the rest of us, making their own valuable contribution to the national wealth and well-being. In vindication of the very high ideals for which we are fighting this war, it is important for us to maintain a high standard of fair, considerate, and equal treatment for the people of this minority as of all other minorities.[14]

---

[13] Letter, Stimson to Eleanor Roosevelt, May 21, 1943; he expressed similar sentiments in a letter to Dillon Myer, May 10, 1943; both in Record Group 107, National Archives.

[14] Congressional Record, 78th Cong., 1st Sess., pp. 7521–22, September 14, 1943.

However hypocritical it may seem—treatment had been just the opposite of "fair, considerate and equal"—this Presidential statement, coupled with the Army's decision to use Japanese Americans as combat troops, marks a turning point in the history of the relocation as well as of the Japanese Americans. From the time of Pearl Harbor until September 1943 repression was generally intensified; from September 1943 on, although there were many setbacks, a general liberalization took place. One largely unnoticed aspect of this change was an Executive Order of February 16, 1944—just three days short of two years after the order that triggered the mass evacuation—which transferred the WRA to the Department of Interior. Until that time, the War Department, in effect, was the authoritative Cabinet voice which spoke on matters Japanese; after that, Interior Secretary Ickes, and his deputy, Abe Fortas, played that role.

Ickes' voice, loud and sarcastic, was one to be reckoned with. Shortly after he assumed responsibility for the WRA there was a flurry of incidents and public statements protesting Japanese resettlement in the eastern half of the United States. Conservative Republican governors like Walter Edge of New Jersey and John W. Bricker of Ohio led off the criticism and were soon joined by Fiorello La Guardia, the liberal mayor of New York City. All objected, in one way or another, to Japanese being resettled within their bailiwicks. Ickes loosed a blast at all three. The resettled Japanese Americans, he insisted, were citizens of proven loyalty. The three Republicans, according to Ickes, formed "a strange fife and drum corps to be playing the discordant anthem of racial discrimination."[15]

But much more important than the words of Ickes or other members of the growing platoon of public defenders of the Japanese Americans were the actions of those of them who wore the national uniform into battle. The first Nisei to go to war did so without publicity, as translators and intelligence experts with Army and Marine Corps units throughout the Pacific Theater of Operations. From the Aleutians to Burma, from the time of Guadalcanal through the postwar occupation of Japan, several thousand Nisei specialists made telling contributions to American victory in the Pacific.

More significant from the standpoint of the national image of the Japanese Americans was the performance in Europe of two segregated infantry units—the 100th Battalion, composed largely of Hawaiian Nisei, and the 422nd Regimental Combat Team, composed largely of voluntary inductees and draftees from the concentration camps and from the resettled Nisei. Although there were understandable complaints about the segregated nature of the units—the term "Jap Crow" was often heard—the morale and performance of these units, both in training and in battle, were

---

[15] Los Angeles *Times*, April 28, 1944.

absolutely first class. The same cannot be said for the performance of all-black combat units during World War II, and particularly during the Korean War, a performance that was a definite factor in the decision to integrate the armed forces. The difference was, I think, that the first all-Japanese units represented a breakthrough. Their morale and performance are more properly comparable to that of the crack all-black regular regiments formed after the Civil War—the 9th and 10th Cavalry and the 24th and 25th Infantry—whose formation also represented a breakthrough. Had all-Japanese units been formed in the Korean War or sent to Viet Nam, undoubtedly morale and performance would not have been the same. And, it should be noted, when black men were permitted to fly fighter planes during World War II in the 99th Pursuit Squadron and the 332nd Fighter Group, they too, despite complaints about the segregated nature of their outfits, compiled a first-class record.

The Hawaiians of the 100th Battalion, who had left the Islands in June 1942, were first sent to Camp McCoy, Wisconsin, where they stayed until the end of the year. They then went to Camp Shelby, Mississippi, where the 442nd was activated early in 1943. Members of both units were instructed by the War Department to use "White" rather than "Colored" facilities when off post. From the very beginning, the Army, since its prestige was at stake, gave special treatment to the Japanese American units. In May 1943, for example, due to a suggestion from Assistant War Secretary McCloy, the 442nd was given its own band, even though the normal Army table of organization did not authorize a band for a regimental combat team.

Both units were eventually sent to the European theater and fought in Italy under General Mark W. Clark. They fought well. The 100th Battalion went overseas in August 1943 and went into action in the Salerno sector in September. It fought in many of the bloodiest actions in Italy—the Rapido River, Cassino, and the Anzio beachhead—and became a component part of the 442nd when the latter came to Italy in June 1944. The 442nd fought there and in France throughout the rest of the war. In seven major campaigns it suffered almost 10,000 casualties, more than three times its original strength. Some 600 of its soldiers were killed in action or died of wounds later.[16]

Military honors of all kinds were showered upon the Japanese American troops as they became the "most decorated" unit in the Army. Without in any way detracting from the superb performance of these men in combat, the historian must insist that this particular accolade is largely meaningless. The whole system of decorations in the United States Army

---

[16] The fullest account of Japanese American troops in Italy is Thomas D. Murphy, *Ambassadors in Arms* (Honolulu: University of Hawaii Press, 1954).

is farcical, and within larger units they are usually awarded on a quota basis. After his January 1943 announcement that Japanese Americans would be formed into special combat units, War Secretary Stimson's prestige was involved, and constant inquiries about their performance from the Secretary's office made it almost a certainty that the accomplishments of the 100th Battalion and the 442nd would not go unnoticed. Once they began to perform well, that performance was highly publicized. The Army's public relations men, Elmer Davis' Office of War Information, and the WRA's publicity apparatus, all made sure that whatever decorations came their way were well advertised. Yet even while these honors were being showered on the troops and while hundreds of Japanese Americans were making the ultimate patriotic sacrifice, the concentration camps continued to exist, and the Army still insisted that, except for service men on furlough, the presence of any Japanese American on the West Coast was inconsistent with the national safety.

In June 1944 the President wrote to Ickes and the State Department suggesting that any change in the *status quo* of the majority of the evacuated people be gradual. Apparently settling a matter that had come up in the Cabinet, he proposed two methods, not for the sake of military necessity but for "internal quiet." (There was a national election that November.)

(*a*) Seeing, with great discretion, how many Japanese would be acceptable to public opinion in definite localities on the West Coast.

(*b*) Seeking to extend greatly the distribution of other families in many parts of the United States. I have been talking to a number of people from the Coast and they are all in agreement that the Coast would be willing to receive back a portion of the Japanese who were once there—nothing sudden and not in too great quantities at any one time. Also, in talking to people from the Middle West, the East and the South, I am sure that there would be no bitterness if they were distributed—one or two families to each county as a start. Dissemination and distribution constitute a great method of avoiding public outcry.

Why not proceed seriously along the above line—for a while at least?[17]

Shortly after his successful reelection to an unprecedented fourth term, Franklin Roosevelt returned to this theme in a press conference. A knowledgeable reporter asked him:

---

[17] Memorandum, FDR to Acting Secretary of State, The Secretary of the Interior, June 12, 1944, President's Personal File 4849, Franklin D. Roosevelt Library, Hyde Park.

Q. Mr. President, there is a great deal of renewed interest on the Pacific Coast about the matter of allowing the return of those Japanese who were evacuated in 1942. Do you think that the danger of espionage or sabotage has sufficiently diminished so that there can be a relaxation of the restrictions that have been in effect for the last two years?

THE PRESIDENT. In most of the cases. That doesn't mean all of them. And, of course, we have been trying to—I am now talking about Japanese people from Japan who are citizens——

Q. (interjecting). Japanese Americans.

THE PRESIDENT. ——Japanese Americans, I am not talking about the Japanese themselves. A good deal of progress has been made in scattering them through the country, and that is going on almost every day. I have forgotten what the figures are. There are roughly a hundred—a hundred thousand Japanese-origin citizens in this country. And it is felt by a great many lawyers that under the Constitution they can't be kept locked in concentration camps. And a good many of them, as I remember it—you had better check with the Secretary of the Interior on this—somewhere around 20 or 25 percent of all those citizens have replaced themselves, and in a great many parts of the country. And the example I always cite, to take a unit, is the size of the county, whether in the Hudson River Valley or in western "Joe-gia" (Georgia) which we all know, in one of those counties, probably half a dozen or a dozen families could be scattered around on the farms and worked into the community. After all, they are American citizens, and we all know that American citizens have certain privileges. And they wouldn't—what's my favorite word?—discombobolate—(laughter)—the existing population of those counties very much. After all—what?—75 thousand families scattered all around the United States is not going to upset anybody.

Q. (interposing). But, sir, if I may interrupt——

THE PRESIDENT (continuing). And, of course, we are actuated by the—in part by the very wonderful record that the Japanese in that battalion in Italy have been making in the war. It is one of the outstanding battalions we have.

Q. But sir, the discussion on the West Coast is more about the relaxation of the military restrictions in that prohibited area, as to whether they should be allowed in the areas from which they have been excluded. It isn't about allowing them to go elsewhere in the country. I was wondering if you felt that the danger of espionage had sufficiently diminished so that the military restrictions that were passed could be lifted.

THE PRESIDENT. That I couldn't tell you because I don't know.

Q. There hasn't been any difficulty about that general policy question?[18]

Roosevelt did not answer that last question and moved on to another topic. But the reporter was on the right track. There had been great difficulties about just that question—difficulties that had begun as soon as the military began relaxing restrictions on the Japanese Americans.

In April 1943 De Witt, in his testimony to a House Committee, stressed this point:

As far as I am concerned I am not concerned with what they do with the Japanese as a whole just so they are not allowed to return to the West Coast. My superiors know that I consider it unsafe to do so.[19]

In July 1943, when a Senate Resolution of concern over WRA policies necessitated a White House statement, the Western Defense Command tried to have the statement say that no Japanese would return to the Coast for at least the duration of the war. McCloy told Bendetsen that such a statement was impossible and that the Commander in Chief had so ordered. The Assistant Secretary also made it clear that the decision to let Japanese Americans return to the Coast involved "many considerations . . . other than military."[20] The White House statement, given out as coming from Director of War Mobilization James Byrnes, said simply:

There is no present intention to alter [the present restrictions], nor is any relaxation under contemplation. . . . The present restrictions against persons of Japanese ancestry will remain in force as long as the military situation requires.[21]

On September 14 the President himself replied to the Senate. He defended the WRA, described the segregation program, and for the first time publicly defended the loyalty of some Japanese Americans, those "whose loyalty to this country has remained unshaken through the hardships of the evacuation which military necessity made unavoidable."

---

[18] From Press Conference 982, November 21, 1944, Franklin D. Roosevelt Library, Hyde Park. This dispersion proposal is strikingly similar to one made by William Jennings Bryan during the Wilson administration. See Roger Daniels, "William Jennings Bryan and the Japanese," *Southern California Quarterly,* September, 1966.

[19] A transcript of De Witt's testimony is in Record Group 394, National Archives.

[20] Telephone Conversation, McCloy and Bendetsen, July 10, 1943, Record Group 107, National Archives.

[21] The Byrnes statement, July 17, 1943, President's Personal File 4849, Franklin D. Roosevelt Library, Hyde Park.

In January 1944 two groups of West Coast congressmen wrote the White House asking for sterner treatment of the evacuated people. Their statements were triggered by the discovery of atrocities that had been committed by Japanese troops in the Philippines. Among their suggestions were the resignation of Dillon Myer, the transfer of Tule Lake to the Army or to the Department of Justice, expatriation or deportation of any "disloyal" Japanese Americans, resettling many Japanese Americans as far as possible from the West Coast, and keeping all Japanese Americans away from the Coast for the duration.[22]

By May, however, partially because of fear about what the Supreme Court might do, the Army was seriously considering almost total relaxation of the ban. Chief of Staff George C. Marshall made it clear in a memo to McCloy that there were no purely military objections to the return.

I have gone over your memo of May 8 concerning the return of persons of Japanese ancestry to the West Coast. . . . In my opinion the only valid military objection to this move is the one presented by G-1 that the return of these people to the West Coast will result in actions of violence that will react to the disadvantage of American prisoners in the hands of the Japanese. There are, of course, strong political reasons why the Japanese should not be returned to the West Coast before next November, but these do not concern the Army except to the degree that consequent reactions might cause embarrassing incidents.[23]

In other words, the number one soldier of the United States feared only that white racist mob violence might cause trouble, and speculated that a return might cost the administration votes in November.

Even Western Defense Command, under the more enlightened leadership of General Emmons, began to talk about relaxation. It too feared what the Court might do. In a June memorandum the Command's Judge Advocate favored some relaxation:

The increasing possibility of unfavorable action by the courts, which would tend to undermine all authority for military restrictions on civilians, makes it highly advisable as soon as the military situation permits, to initiate an orderly and progressive relaxation of the restriction program.[24]

---

[22] Objections from West Coast congressmen, dated January 23 and 26, 1944, President's Personal File 4894, Franklin D. Roosevelt Library, Hyde Park.

[23] Memorandum, Chief of Staff to McCloy, May 13, 1944, OPD 291.2 (Race)/20, cited from Stetson Conn, "Notes," Office, Chief of Military History, U.S. Army.

[24] Memorandum, Judge Advocate General, Western Defense Command for Commanding General, Western Defense Command, June 5, 1944, OPD 371, Western

By mid-1944, whatever remote possibilities there had been of a Japanese attack on the West Coast were past. Yet the restrictions remained in force until almost the end of the year. Roosevelt was reelected in November, and by December the Court was ready to hand down *Korematsu*, and, more important, *Endo*. After the cases had been argued but before decisions were announced, the easing of exclusion from the West Coast was in the works. I have discovered no evidence that the War Department or the White House knew in advance what the Court would do, but, as O. W. Holmes, Jr., used to say, "there is such a thing as presumptive evidence."

Five days before *Endo* made continued confinement for "loyal" citizens unconstitutional, War Secretary Stimson sent a secret message to the White House in which he admitted that "mass exclusion from the West Coast of persons of Japanese ancestry is no longer a matter of military necessity." There had been no military developments that month; if exclusion was unnecessary in mid-December 1944, it had been unnecessary for some time. He did claim that "face saving" raids from Japan were still possible. Then came the real reason:

> The matter is now the subject of litigation in the Federal Courts and in view of the fact that military necessity no longer requires the continuation of mass exclusion it seems unlikely that it can be continued in effect for any considerable period.[25]

The War Secretary speculated that there might be some trouble from whites, but was confident that

> the common sense and good citizenship of the people of the Coast is such that the inauguration of this program will not be marred by serious incidents or disorders.

Just four days after Stimson's secret memorandum and only one day before the Court handed down *Endo*, Major General Henry C. Pratt, who had just taken over Western Defense Command from General Emmons, publicly announced that total exclusion from the West Coast of loyal Japanese American civilians was terminated, effective January 2, 1945.[26]

Defense Command/9, cited from Stetson Conn, "Notes," Office, Chief of Military History, U.S. Army.

[25] This and the following quotation, Memorandum, Stimson to FDR, December 13, 1944, President's Personal File 4849, Franklin D. Roosevelt Library, Hyde Park.

[26] Pratt's proclamation was announced in the *New York Times*, December 17, 1944.

The West Coast reaction, predictably, was unfavorable. California politicians, in particular, were bitter. Los Angeles District Attorney Fred N. Howser, in a Bill of Rights week speech early in December, called the expected return of the evacuated people "a second attack on Pearl Harbor," while the Los Angeles *Times* labeled the decision "a grave mistake" and argued that the real way for Japanese Americans to show their loyalty was "by seeking homes elsewhere than on the Pacific Coast."

The political leadership of the state, happily, was in responsible hands. Governor Earl Warren, who as late as November 1944 was publicly warning against letting Japanese Americans return because of "the dangers to the war effort from [possible] civil disturbances," immediately urged the people of California to support the Army decision.[27] Even more crucial, in the final analysis, were the efforts of California's Attorney General Robert W. Kenny, a liberal Democrat who would unsuccessfully oppose Warren for the governorship in 1946 and is now a municipal judge in Los Angeles.

Kenny's role in the evacuation was a curious one. Although a strong proponent of racial equality, he did not oppose the evacuation in 1942. Elected attorney general in that year, he filed briefs *amicus curiae* for the state of California (and got the attorneys general of Oregon and Washington to subscribe to them) supporting the government contentions in *Hirabayashi* and *Korematsu*, but not in *Endo*. During and after the war his office prosecuted escheat cases against alien Japanese under the 1920 Alien Land Law more vigorously than any previous attorney general. But he also worked very hard to make the return of the evacuated people as peaceful as possible and used his office's prestige to get local law enforcement agencies to do likewise.

In mid-January 1945 there was a two-day conference in the Palace Hotel in San Francisco aimed at planning for the "orderly and harmonious integration" of the returnees into community life. Called by the Pacific Coast Fair Play Committee, it was attended by representatives of sixteen federal and state agencies and of an even larger number of private agencies. Particularly noteworthy was the attendance and pledged cooperation by representatives of Negro, Filipino, and Korean community organizations, who agreed that "any attempt to make capital for their own racial groups at the expense of the Japanese would be sawing off the limbs on which they themselves sat." This and similar meetings probably contributed significantly to the relative lack of violence that accompanied the return to the West Coast.[28]

---

[27] Los Angeles *Times*, November 19, December 18, 23, 1944.

[28] "Highlights of Conference on Interracial Cooperation," 11 pp., mimeo, in Pacific Coast Committee for American Principles and Fair Play Mss., Bancroft Library.

Some, if not most, urban officials also tried to make the return easier. Mayor Fletcher Bowron, who as late as May 1943 had insisted that Los Angeles wanted none of its "Japs" back and hoped that some method would be found to deprive all of them of their citizenship, staged a public ceremony at city hall in mid-January 1945 to reassure the first relocatees to Los Angeles: "We want you and all other citizens of Japanese ancestry who have relocated here to feel secure in your home. . . ."[29]

In much of rural California, however, particularly in the interior valleys from Imperial County on the Mexican border to Placer County, north and east of Sacramento, local feeling against the returnees was virulent; there was sporadic lawlessness, often abetted by law enforcement officials. One of the Central Valley's congressmen, Representative Alfred Elliott, a Democrat from Tulare, had insisted on the floor of the House in mid-1943 that "the only good Jap is a dead Jap" and prophesied that this would be the fate of "every one of them that is sent back" to California. The threat was overstated; no returnees were killed. But Girdner and Loftis have calculated that of seventy instances of terrorism and nineteen shootings that took place in California in the first six months of 1945, more than 90 percent took place in the Central Valley.[30] In Placer County, for example, a mass meeting was called by a deputy sheriff, who was also commander of the local Veterans of Foreign Wars Post, to protest the return of the evacuated people and circulate a boycott pledge. Some in that county went further. The first Japanese to return to Placer County were the Doi family, who had sons in the armed forces. The night of the boycott meeting, an attempt was made to burn a packing shed on their ranch. Two days later, January 19, 1945, shots were fired into their home and an attempted dynamiting occurred. Good police work, spurred by Attorney General Kenny, discovered the culprits, among whom were two soldiers AWOL from the Army. When brought to trial, after a defense consisting largely of anti-Japanese harangues, a local jury refused to convict and the acquitted terrorists were regarded as local heroes.[31] Anti-Japanese agitation continued strong in Placer County, and later that year the Board of Supervisors illegally voted to deny relief to any alien Japanese.

Similarly, in rural Fresno County, one Levi Multanen of Parlier fired four blasts from a double-barreled shotgun into the farmhouse of Charles Iwasaki, while Iwasaki, his wife, three children, and a grandparent were inside. Happily, the blasts hit no one. The local authorities saw fit to charge Multanen only with "exhibiting" a deadly weapon. This kept the case within the jurisdiction of the local justice of the peace. At his trial the

[29] Los Angeles *Times*, January 15, 1945.

[30] Audrie Girdner and Anne Loftis, *The Great Betrayal* (New York: Macmillan, 1969), pp. 383–406.

[31] For the Doi incidents, see Girdner and Loftis, *The Great Betrayal*, pp. 389–91.

district attorney complimented him for using a shotgun rather than a more deadly deer rifle. The justice of the peace sentenced Multanen to six months in jail, but immediately suspended the sentence because, he said, a jail sentence would only result in more violence.[32]

In urban San Jose, in February 1945, someone threw a brick through the window of a returning Nisei. When he called the police, he reported:

> they said that the next thing they would probably do was shoot bullets into the house so the best thing was to barricade the door with mattresses and the like. They said they couldn't watch the place all the time. We slept in the back without lights for a couple of weeks.[33]

In Orange County, where there seems to have been no violence, the anti-Japanese campaign was more subtle. According to a report of the Western Defense Command, which became actively interested in promoting peaceful resettlement in July 1945, the anti-Japanese campaign went something like this:

> One of the [agitators] goes to call upon a Japanese and tells him how glad he is to see him again. He then asks him how long he plans to remain. When the reply comes that he plans to remain permanently, the visitor shakes his head and says, "Oh, I wouldn't do that. Some of the people here in the county are planning trouble for you Japanese." This is repeated regularly.[34]

Sometimes the harassment took the form of bureaucratic sabotage. In May 1945, when a returning Nisei in Los Angeles applied for a sales tax permit in order to open a grocery, the local office of the State Board of Equalization illegally refused to issue it unless he got a letter of approval from either the general or admiral in command of Los Angeles. As the clerk probably knew, there were no such officials.[35]

Mass meetings against the returning Japanese were held throughout the state, and signs reading "No Japs Wanted" were frequently posted. In Yolo County, according to an investigator for the American Council on Race Relations:

---

[32] For Iwasaki incident, see letter Ernest Besig to Kenny, June 3, 1944, Box 13, Kenny Mss., Bancroft Library.

[33] U.S. Department of the Interior, *People in Motion* (Washington, 1947), p. 106.

[34] Copy of Report, Colonel John A. Geary and Lieutenant Colonel Lyle E. Cook to Commanding General, Western Defense Command, July 21, 1945, Box 36, Kenny Mss., Bancroft Library.

[35] Memorandum, Dick Wylie to Kenny, May 22, 1945, Box 8, Kenny Mss., Bancroft Library.

The Assemblyman, Mr. Lowery, who is a confirmed "Jap hater," has aggravated the situation by making a speaking tour of the county talking to Rotary Clubs, service clubs of all kinds and the Anti-Japanese Leagues which have been organized at Esparto and Winters. . . . He has a Sgt. Lo Bue, discharged veteran of the first Philippine Campaign (World War II) who recites horror stories [about Japanese atrocities there].[36]

In Vacaville, where the local Anti-Japanese League had press support from the Vacaville *Reporter,* about 1500 people signed petitions agreeing to boycott any Japanese who might return. When a local Chinese restaurant owner refused to put a "No Japs Allowed" sign in his window, he was pressured into compliance by the boycotters. Around Vacaville, and elsewhere, there were concerted and sometimes successful attempts to play off other minority groups against the Japanese. In addition to Filipinos and Chinese, the movement tried to play upon the fears of Mexican American farmers and farm workers who, in many cases, had replaced the Japanese Americans in 1942. The American Council of Race Relations investigator reported that the reason Mexican Americans were very anti-Japanese was that they were afraid their economic gains would be destroyed. "Most of them were farm laborers before the Japanese-Americans left. Now they have occupied [*sic*] Japanese farms and have made an excellent living on them."[37]

Trade unionists as well as farmers made mass protests. In Stockton, just as the war ended in August, warehousemen in the International Longshoremen's and Warehousemen's Union walked off the job rather than work with a few newly hired returnees, and their walkout was backed by the local union. The national office of the union, headed by Harry Bridges, eventually had to suspend the recalcitrant local to get the men to work with Japanese.

Hostility was not confined to California. In one of the incidents to receive great national publicity, the Hood River, Oregon, American Legion Post removed the names of all sixteen local Japanese American servicemen from the public honor roll, and American Legion posts from Seattle to Hollywood barred Nisei veterans from membership. Fruit growers, florists, and produce merchants in the Pacific Northwest organized a systematic and effective boycott of returned Japanese growers that eventually drew a desist order from Agriculture Secretary Clinton P. Anderson directed at the Northwest Produce Dealers Association.

[36] Report, Ellen Turner to Lawrence J. Hewes, February 14, 1946, in California Federation for Civic Unity Mss., Bancroft Library.

[37] Report, Ellen Turner to Lawrence J. Hewes, March 26, 1946, in California Federation for Civic Unity Mss., Bancroft Library.

Yet despite these and many other incidents, the West Coast anti-Japanese campaign of 1945–1946 was relatively ineffective; most of the exiles returned and picked up the pieces of their shattered lives successfully. The reasons for this are many and complex. In the first place, the political leadership of California, including many like Earl Warren and Mayor Bowron of Los Angeles who had helped whip up the hysteria that accompanied their expulsion, actively worked to facilitate their return. Federal government policy and propaganda, which for the first time during the war stressed racial tolerance and the accomplishments of minority groups, was certainly a factor. Even the coincidence that San Francisco was the site of the organizing meetings for the United Nations in early 1945 spurred some members of the California establishment to work to avoid incidents that might bring disgrace on the state. In addition, the entire West Coast, particularly its urban centers, was changing. The Pacific War made the West Coast an essential part of what is now called the military-industrial complex, and wartime and postwar growth drew millions of internal migrants to the western cities. In 1944 alone, according to one estimate, more than 1,100,000 people migrated to California; between 1940 and 1950 the net migration to the Pacific Coast was more than 3 million, and the region's population jumped from 9.7 to 14.5 million. Not only did the return of fewer than 100,000 Japanese Americans seem insignificant within this massive migration but there were also much greater numbers of blacks and Mexican Americans among the migrants. The Negro population of California more than tripled during the same period, growing from 124,000 to 462,000. The fact that so many westerners were new westerners and that all of them faced growing ethnic problems certainly made the returnees a less highly visible group. In addition, there is evidence that members of the younger generation of the West Coast, regardless of where they were born, were less prejudiced against Orientals than were their parents. In at least one West Coast high school, in Santa Monica, California, all the class officers resigned in the spring of 1942 and soon-to-be-evacuated Nisei were named in their place.

In the short run, however, even more crucial to the successful reentrance into West Coast society of the evacuated people was the existence of a well-organized and active minority of whites who for one reason or another wanted what they considered justice for the Japanese Americans. Some of these were people who had been involved in the Fair Play Committee which had tried to function in 1941–1942; many were church people—Quakers were particularly prominent—and white liberals working through organizations like the American Council for Race Relations and the California Federation for Civic Unity. These groups cooperated with the WRA and the Western Defense Command and other federal, state, and local agencies that were working for acceptance of the returnees. In

Sierra Madre, in suburban Los Angeles County, the leader of one such group described its efforts:

> Our group was formed in December, 1944, when we heard that a restrictive covenant was being circulated among home owners in Sierra Madre and that a group of 70 had pledged themselves to shoot the first "Jap" to return here. The F.B.I. was immediately notified of this rumor (naturally we do not know their findings); and a meeting of as many liberal-minded Sierra Madreans as could be found on short notice was called at our house. (The meeting was called on Saturday for Sunday.) . . . One Bruce McGill had aroused the public here by taking a full page ad in the Sierra Madre News to rage against the Japanese Americans on the basis that not enough blood was being donated to the Red Cross. [About thirty people signed an answering ad. Our ad] caused some outraged comment on the part of those who "would shoot any Jap" they saw; most people seemed to approve it. When the Nisei returned [some of us] could offer them temporary shelter in [our] homes; others in other ways made them welcome. When the first Nisei couple to marry in California since the war were married in a Sierra Madre church there were 40 Caucasian guests, many uninvited but attending to show their sympathy. . . . When the first Nisei boy was to enroll in the Sierra Madre School, Mr. Booth of the War Relocation Authority came to the school and gave a talk on the [442nd Regimental Combat Team] the day before, through the courtesy of Mr. Korsmeier, then the principal. The little boy was welcomed as one of the fellows, accepted without any discrimination at all. The group met about three times and then decided that the situation in Sierra Madre was sufficiently under control to make further meetings unnecessary.[38]

The problems of small towns like Sierra Madre could be handled by tiny *ad hoc* groups; the return of relatively large numbers of Japanese to growing cities already facing a serious housing shortage required the assistance of government agencies. In the three largest Coast cities—Los Angeles, San Francisco, and Seattle—incoming blacks had settled in what had been the Japanese ghetto, and there was literally no place to put the returnees. What happened in Los Angeles, both the largest city on the Coast and the largest center of Japanese American population, is representative. There were few "incidents" in Los Angeles; John Modell describes what resistance there was to the returnees as "confused opposition

---

[38] Letter, Idella P. Stone to Mrs. Ruth Kingman, November 12, 1946, in California Federation for Civic Unity Mss., Bancroft Library.

in retreat before determined authority" and argues that by 1946 "food prices were more important to Angelenos than the yellow peril." Nothing more violent occurred there than the "decoration" of Linus Pauling's Pasadena garage with a rising sun and the words "Americans Die But We Love Japs—Japs Work Here—Pauling." The Nobel Prize winner had made public statements in favor of the returnees and had hired a Japanese gardener. There was resistance to handling Japanese produce sparked by the Teamster's Union, but it was ended, under WRA pressure, by December 1945.

Mayor Bowron, despite his welcome to the first returnees, feared the consequences of their return. The responsibility for maintaining law and order, he felt, was the federal government's. He wrote the White House, in January 1945, warning of possible vigilante action against the returnees, and argued that if more than 10 per cent of the prewar Japanese population returned, violence would probably result. Many people, apparently including the mayor, were "determined that there must not again be such a large concentration of Japanese population in this area."[39] Although the return was not immediate, by 1950 there were almost exactly as many Japanese in Los Angeles as there had been before Pearl Harbor, but, due to population growth, their incidence in the population was much lower. While some of the returnees, particularly the younger and more aggressive Nisei, were able rather quickly to regain footholds in the the booming postwar economy, many others were, by the end of the war, so scarred by their experiences and in some cases by their years that they became public charges. In January 1946 a Los Angeles supervisor reported that although even during the Depression very few Japanese had been on relief—he estimated the pre-Pearl Harbor county relief load as about 25 Japanese—the postwar relief load was about 4000 and rising. This was costing the county an estimated $1 million annually, and naturally the supervisors insisted that it was a federal responsibility. The federal government, however, was interested in liquidating its Japanese problem, not continuing it. Dillon Myer and the WRA were essentially annoyed that so many of their former charges were still causing them trouble. Many of the returnees were housed in Federal Public Housing Authority trailer camps that had been used as temporary housing for defense plant workers. The WRA chief told the county supervisors in mid-1946, as the WRA was winding up its affairs, that the increased postwar dependence of the Japanese Americans was due to the lack of initiative of many members of the group.

---

[39] John Modell, "The Japanese in Los Angeles: A Study in Growth and Accommodation, 1900–1946," unpublished Ph.D. dissertation, Columbia University, 1969, contains a good account of "Relocation and Its Aftermath," Chapter XI.

Many, . . . after four years of living in barracks in relocation centers, had become institutionalized to that kind of living and were hesitant to leave the group living which was so much like the relocation centers.[40]

He also stated that many of them were essentially content with welfare and intimated that they did not really want to work.

Langdon Post, Regional Director of the Federal Public Housing Authority, held similar social darwinistic views about the returnees. It would be much better, he felt in early 1947, to throw these people on their own responsibility. If they were helped too much, according to Post, they would become passive.

The WRA and other federal groups were the targets of much criticism, in the postwar era, from various "conscience" groups of white liberals. One Quaker official charged that the WRA had "lost sight of its stated objective, that of permanently locating the persons assigned to its charge, and aiding in their integration into normal community life." Similarly, a group of social workers and civic leaders, organized into the Los Angeles Coordinating Committee for Resettlement, charged, correctly in my judgment, that federal policy had not been strong enough to secure effective action in matters of civil liberty, housing, employment, resumption of former businesses, and remuneration for losses suffered in the evacuation.[41]

The WRA went out of business officially on June 30, 1946, although it had been phasing out for a good eighteen months. In its final, self-congratulatory report, it gave itself a collective pat on the back.

> WRA feels, in short, that the obligation of the Federal Government to the evacuees has [except for the problem of compensation for losses] been adequately discharged. Although there can never be full or adequate recompense for the experiences which the evacuated people went through, it is best, we feel, to set these down among the civilian casualties of the war and to build on the present base toward a better and more secure future for people of Japanese descent in this country. The building of that future lies largely in the hands of the still-active groups which have supported the evacuated people throughout the war and, even more importantly, in the hands of the evacuees themselves.[42]

---

[40] This and similar Los Angeles material from Box 64, John Anson Ford Mss., Huntington Library.

[41] *Ibid.*

[42] War Relocation Authority, WRA: *A Story of Human Conservation* (Washington, 1946), pp. 153–54.

A historian's balance sheet is quite different from the WRA's. In the first place, the Japanese Americans were not like the other civilian war casualties; their wounds were inflicted by their own government. Some, as we have seen, renounced that government. A total of 4724 Japanese Americans actually left the United States for Japan, either as expatriates or repatriates. Of these, 1659 were aliens, 1949 were American citizens accompanying repatriating parents, and 1116 were adult Nisei. During the entire war period 5766 American citizens of Japanese ancestry renounced their citizenship. Most of these never went to Japan, and were, for a time, legally regarded as stateless persons resident in the United States. Thanks, however, to court actions initiated in 1945 by San Francisco attorney Wayne Collins, and which dragged out in some cases until 1968, all but a few hundred of these, including many who actually went to Japan, have been able to regain their citizenship. What the federal courts have ruled, with the eventual reluctant consent of the Department of Justice, is that renunciations made behind barbed wire were essentially under duress, and thus of no legal validity.[43]

The WRA hoped, as Roosevelt had, that the relocation would scatter the Japanese. As an official report put it:

> In administrative thinking, resettlement would bring many obvious benefits. Not the least of these was that it would disperse persons of Japanese ancestry throughout the country. . . . [T]he relocation program really had three objectives: to get the evacuees out of the centers, to disperse them, and to integrate them into the communities where they settled.[44]

It seemed to WRA, shortly after the war, that its program of dispersal had significant success, but the postwar demography of the Japanese Americans calls that success into question. In mid-1947, an Interior Department review of resettlement estimated that, whereas before the war 88.5 percent of the Japanese Americans in the continental United States lived on the West Coast, the combination of forced evacuation and resettlement had reduced that figure to about 55 percent. The 1950 census bore out that estimate: although the total number of Japanese Americans had risen from 127,000 to 169,000, the number in all three West Coast states had actually declined, so that only a little more than 58 percent of mainland Japanese Americans lived there. By 1960, however, the same old

---

[43] There are excellent treatments of postwar legal and economic adjustments in Hosokawa, *Nisei*, pp. 435–55, and Girdner and Loftis, *The Great Betrayal*, pp. 428–54.

[44] U.S. Department of the Interior, War Relocation Authority, *Impounded People* (Washington, 1946), p. 218.

tendency to cluster had clearly reasserted itself. Both because of natural increase and renewed immigration from Japan, the Japanese American population grew sharply, from 169,000 to 260,000. On the West Coast, the population grew faster than on the rest of the mainland, so its percentage of Japanese Americans grew significantly, to nearly 69 percent. Evacuation and resettlement did create new permanent centers of Japanese American population—the most striking case is Illinois, where 1940 census takers found only 462 Japanese and those in 1960 found 14,074, most of them around Chicago—but did not achieve anything even approximating the dispersal which WRA administrators and social scientists thought desirable.

Probably the greatest postwar failure of the WRA's resettlement program was in the economic sphere, a failure that both it and the evacuees were aware of. In mid-February 1945 the WRA held an All Center Conference of evacuee leaders in Salt Lake City. The major recommendations of the spokesmen were ignored. They wanted the WRA to stay in business indefinitely and be prepared to accept back into custody those of the evacuated people who could not, for reasons of age, infirmity, or demoralization, make some kind of successful readjustment to life outside the camps. As previously noted, the WRA was disbanding as fast as possible—all the camps but Tule Lake were closed by early March 1946, and even it went out of business on May 5 of that year—and after the war was over, in August 1945, more than a third of the evacuated people still huddled in the camps. Then, as the Department of the Interior put it, "the Government placed the remaining evacuees [about 44,000] under direct compulsion to leave. The evacuees unable to make up their minds, or who refused to leave, were given train fare to the point of the evacuation."

The evacuees at Salt Lake City had also asked for significant financial assistance—a few talked of reparations—in getting started again. Both direct lump sum grants and long-term, low-interest loans—the precise measures the New Deal had used during the Depression—were asked for, but the government was only willing to allow citizen returnees to participate in those programs of economic reconstruction which were available to the general public.[45] Many of these programs were closed to the still alien Issei. Given the general wartime and postwar inflation, even those of the evacuated people who had been able to dispose of their property on decent terms found themselves seriously disadvantaged. Take the case of one Issei farmer from Santa Clara County, California, who told his story to a government interviewer sometime shortly after the war was over.

45 War Relocation Authority, *Community Government in War Relocation Centers* (Washington, 1946), pp. 95–97, contains an account of the Salt Lake City conference.

Before war I had 20 acres in Berryessa. Good land, two good houses, one big. 1942 in camp everybody say sell, sell, sell. Maybe lose all. Lawyer write, he say sell. I sell $650 acre. Now the same land $1500 acre. I lose, I cannot help. All gone. Now I live in hostel. Work like when first come to this country. Pick cherries, pick pears, pick apricots, pick tomatoes. Just like when first come. Pretty soon, maybe one year, maybe two years, find place. Pretty hard now. Now spend $15,000 just for [half as much] land. No good material for house. No get farm machinery. No use look back. Go crazy think about all lost. Have to start all over again like when come from Japan, but faster this time.[46]

Those who did not sell were often worse off. A well-to-do farm family on Vashon Island, Washington, closed up their home and stored their furniture and equipment in it before they were sent off to Minidoka; shortly thereafter the insurance company canceled their coverage, and they could find no carrier willing to take the risk. The two sons who held legal title to the property served with the 442nd in Italy, where one of them was seriously wounded. On the night of February 1, 1945, three Caucasian youths, aged 16, 17, and 22, burned the place to the ground. The three were required by the court to make $1000 restitution apiece—a tiny fraction of the replacement cost—the eldest being allowed by the local judge to join the merchant marine so he could earn the money.[47]

Many other evacuees, particularly those who held only leaseholds on their land or business properties, suffered serious losses. In addition most lost or sacrificed much of their household property, and many were without significant income during the entire period of their confinement. Recognizing this, the Department of the Interior sponsored legislation, as early as 1946, which would have set up an Evacuee Claims Commission, with authority to settle moderate-sized claims—up to $2500—but it failed to win Congressional approval. No act entitling the evacuees to compensation was passed until July 1948, when President Harry S Truman signed the Japanese American Evacuation Claims Act. This act, extended and modified, began seventeen years of litigation, as the last claim was not settled until 1965. Although a conservative estimate by the Federal Reserve Bank of San Francisco put evacuee losses at $400 million, Congress appropriated less than 10 percent of that sum, $38 million, to settle all claims. Claims could only cover "damage to or loss of real or personal property" and could not include such normal economic concerns as good-

---

[46] U.S. Department of the Interior, *People in Motion*, p. 53.

[47] War Relocation Authority, *The Wartime Handling of Evacuee Property* (Washington, 1946), pp. 104–05.

will or anticipated profits or earnings. In all, some 23,000 claims were filed which asked for about $131 million in damages. The Department of Justice, which administered the processing of the claims, moved with agonizing bureaucratic slowness and inefficiency. In all of 1950, for example, only 210 claims were cleared and only 73 people were actually compensated. According to Bill Hosokawa, it cost the government more than $1000 to settle a $450 claim. Some of the Issei claimants died while waiting for their claims to be processed; one 92-year-old accepted a settlement of $2500 for a $75,000 claim because he was sure he would not live long enough to see the matter through the courts. All the claims for losses were settled on the basis of 1942 prices without interest. One economist has pointed out that the losses suffered by the Japanese American community are still being felt. As Kenneth Hansen put it:

> The Nisei are paying the price today in the loss of opportunity and gains which they would have made had [the government] not taken this outrageous action. Losses are still being compounded because of constantly increasing evaluations of often valuable lands they were forced to let go.[48]

For most American businessmen and the economy as a whole, World War II was a time of high profits, the prelude to affluence. Every identifiable socioeconomic group in the United States, save one, profited from the war; for the Japanese Americans, it was a serious economic setback. Although most did not become impoverished, their economic progress was significantly retarded, not only during the war but in the postwar period as well.

Slowly but surely however, their legal and social status improved. Some of the improvement was due merely to the passage of time; every passing year saw the growth of the citizen Nisei and Sansei majority and the corresponding shrinkage of the alien Issei generation. In the immediate postwar years the state of California continued the assault on Issei agricultural property begun during the war under Attorney General Kenny. Between 1944 and 1948 some eighty escheat cases were filed against Issei by the state of California in which the state took land and money worth about a quarter of a million dollars from a score of Issei-headed families. Eventually the California Supreme Court in *Fujii* v. *State* (1952) declared the Alien Land Acts, which dated back to 1913, unconstitutional. A case challenging the acts had gone all the way to the United States Supreme Court, but that body, although it found for the Japanese plaintiff on technical grounds, had refused to strike the law down. Four justices how-

---

[48] Cited by Girdner and Loftis, *The Great Betrayal*, pp. 436–37.

ever, Black, Douglas, Murphy, and Rutledge, indicated in their angry concurrences that they were ready to do so, and, surely, had such action not been forestalled by the California decision, the alien land law would not have survived a test by the Warren Court.[49] Perhaps even more significant than the change in judicial opinion was that shown by the California electorate. In 1948 an anti-Japanese proposition that would have made the alien land laws harsher was placed on the ballot and was decisively rejected by the electorate, with almost 59 percent of the voters opposing it. Never before in California history had an anti-Oriental measure been rejected at the polls, but, it should be noted, better than four voters out of ten still favored harsher treatment for Asian immigrants.

Much of the legal basis for discrimination against Asians in the United States, although it flourished at the state level, was based on national law. As long as Asians were "aliens ineligible to citizenship" by national statute, state and local discrimination would have legal standing. It is ironic that the real death blow to legal discrimination resulted neither from Presidential or Congressional liberalism nor from an increasingly libertarian Supreme Court, but from one of the most reactionary pieces of national legislation, the McCarran-Walter Act of 1952. This act, passed over President Truman's veto, perpetuated the racism of the National Origins Act of 1924, made deportation and revocation of naturalization much simpler (for example, if a naturalized citizen were convicted of contempt of Congress within ten years after his naturalization, his citizenship could be summarily revoked), subjected visiting scholars to all kinds of indignities, and was in many other ways a typical measure of the era of Senator Joseph R. McCarthy and cold war hysteria. But within this abominable piece of legislation was a significant redeeming principle: total exclusion of Asians from immigration and naturalization was ended. Every part of the world got some kind of quota—Japan's was 185 a year—and all racial barriers to citizenship were dropped. Actually, because of complications in the law—wives and close relatives of American citizens were classified as nonquota immigrants—some 40,000 Japanese were admitted to the United States in the eight years after 1952; many, if not most of them, have become citizens, as have thousands of long-resident Issei.

The year 1952 thus marks the end of an era for the Japanese Americans. Just ten years after the evacuation the last legal discrimination against Americans of Japanese ancestry disappeared. This victory, whatever its price, was surely the last and most significant decoration won by the men of the 442nd.

---

[49] The federal case was *Oyama* v. *California*, 332 US 633. There is a good discussion in C. Herman Pritchett, *Civil Liberties and the Vinson Court* (Chicago: University of Chicago Press, 1954), pp. 118–22.

9
EPILOGUE

In the quarter century since the evacuation the position of the Japanese Americans has changed significantly: from a pariah group which some wanted to expel from American soil, they have become, in the words of one sociologist, a "model minority." An important symbolic recognition of this change came at the otherwise disastrous 1968 Democratic National Convention in Chicago, where the keynote speech was given by Senator Daniel Inouye of Hawaii who had lost an arm fighting with the Japanese American troops in Italy. Even within California, where anti-Japanese feeling was the strongest, one Japanese American, S. I. Hayakawa, the hard-line president of San Francisco State College, has become a kind of culture hero as a result of his apparently successful battle against what he termed student anarchy. The roles of these two individuals are strikingly similar, and represent, I think, the major tendency of the Nisei generation: an alignment with dominant middle-class institutions and an opposition to what is felt are disruptive elements within American society. To a very great degree the Japanese Americans have achieved middle-class status, a status reflected not only by their attitudes but by the census data as well.

By 1960, for example, Japanese Americans in California had a distinctly higher degree of educational attainment than did the general population—college graduates are 11 percent more likely to be found among Japanese males than among white males—and if figures were available for the native-born alone, the disparity would be much greater. Yet despite this impressive educational attainment, income figures for Japanese Americans are surprisingly low: for every $51 received by a white Californian, a Japanese gets $43. If we look only at the relatively affluent, the income disparity is much greater: a white man's chances of having an annual income of $10,000 or more are 57 percent greater than those of a Japanese. What these figures mean is that although education and income are usually directly correlated in American society, there are enough vestiges of discrimination against Japanese Americans to prevent them from gaining that degree of affluence that usually accompanies high educational attainments. As opposed to the prewar situation, when Nisei college graduates could look forward only to careers as "professional carrot washers," most can now find jobs appropriate to their education, but once in those jobs they often do not have the degree of upward professional mobility that would be theirs if they were white. What is most often crucial is the failure to obtain promotion to positions in which they can supervise, hire, and fire white people. In housing, too, Japanese Americans and other Orientals still encounter difficulties with white owners, landlords, and real estate brokers, but not to the degree to which such discriminations are encountered by blacks and Mexican Americans; at the same time urban Japanese Americans, once found largely in compact central city ghettoes, are, like lower-middle-class white Americans, fleeing to suburbs as the growing black and brown ghettoes abut and encroach upon their neighborhoods. In Los Angeles, still the chief concentration point for Japanese Americans, this phenomenon can be most easily observed in the suburb of Gardena.

Politically, except in the new state of Hawaii where they are the largest single group and have obtained, in Congress at least, a disproportionately high representation, the Japanese Americans have been, until very recently, relatively passive. The major political activities of the JACL have been directed at destroying the vestiges of discrimination—it mounted a highly successful attack against the immigration and naturalization laws, and the "liberalism" of the McCarran-Walter Act is at least partially a fruit of that campaign—rather than at gaining political power. Part of this was a reflection of the tiny size of the Japanese population—in California, the largest mainland concentration, it was 1 percent—but also represented the conscious and understandable desire of most Nisei to maintain a low social profile and not "make waves." To what degree this accommodationist posture has been influenced by their wartime experience and to what degree it is the result of strong submissive tendencies present within the Japanese American character cannot be calculated, but it seems apparent that each has been a significant factor.

By the end of the 1960s however, it was clear to most close observers of the Japanese American community that the winds of change stirring other ethnic groups were not without their effect on the Nisei and particularly upon their children, the third, or Sansei, generation. A distinct but articulate minority of the latter, particularly those in college or of college age, have become radical and militant to a degree that shocks their elders even more perhaps than does similar behavior by their white and black peers. The most radical see themselves as natural allies of lower-class minorities and have, on some California campuses, coalesced with them in organizations like the Third World Liberation Front, which has a distinct Maoist hue. Much more characteristic is an increased awareness of their ethnic heritage on both sides of the Pacific, with the result that courses in Asian-American history and culture and Asian-American Study Centers have arisen in West Coast colleges and universities. The mimetic effect of the black and brown power movements has produced a half-serious, half-comic yellow power movement. Its rhetoric too is imitative: a popular third-generation joke styles accommodationist Japanese as "bananas," that is, "yellow on the outside but white on the inside."

Despite (or is it because of?) these examples of rebellion, there is every probability that this third generation of Japanese Americans will be even more middle class, more professionalized, more Americanized than its predecessor. That this is true less than a quarter century after the last concentration camp closed is remarkable testimony to the resiliency of both the Japanese Americans and the society in which they live. Yet, what happened to the Japanese Americans should be a constant reminder that the elasticity of our multiethnic, democratic, racist society can stretch both ways. If there are powerful forces within it for ameliorative social change, there are also almost equally powerful atavistic forces. If, as the late Morton Grodzins put it, the evacuation betrayed all Americans, its history stands as an equally grim warning of democracy at its worst, the discarding and abusing of due process in order to work the will of the majority. No serious student of the twentieth century can any longer believe that old tag line, *vox populi, vox Dei*, either in Latin or in its modern translation, "Power to the People." The real problem, at least at certain crucial times, is how to keep the majority, silent or otherwise, from wreaking its often mindless will on minorities, ethnic, political, or generational.

A NOTE ON SOURCES

Materials for the study of Japanese Americans during World War II are numerous, as are the published studies. On the West Coast, major manuscript collections are in the Bancroft Library at Berkeley, the Japanese American Research Project at UCLA, the University of Washington, and in the Hoover Institution Archives at Stanford. Although there are some federal materials stored at both Berkeley and UCLA, the major repository is the National Archives in Washington. Particularly relevant are the records of the United States Army, especially those of the Secretary and Assistant Secretary of War, the Provost Marshal General, the Adjutant General, and the Western Defense Command; and the records of the War Relocation Authority. Less pertinent, but revealing, are records of other government agencies associated with the relocation: the Office of War Information, the Office of Government Reports (at the Records Center, Suitland, Md.), the Department of Agriculture, and the Department of the Interior. The major group of papers not fully accessible to scholars are those of the Department of Justice; happily, there are enough materials from Justice in the papers of other agencies so that an accurate outline of departmental decisions can be sketched, but we know little of the internal history of those decisions. There are few materials about the relocation in the Franklin D. Roosevelt Library at Hyde Park, but those few are quite revealing.

As for the published literature, only key works can be listed here: the fullest bibliographies appear in Edward H. Spicer et al., *Impounded People* (Tucson: University of Arizona Press, 1969) and Audrie Girdner and Anne Loftis, *The Great Betrayal* (New York: Macmillan, 1969) but many useful items are not in either of these works. The most influential popular accounts are, in chronological order, Carey McWilliams, *Prejudice: Japanese Americans: Symbol of Racial Intolerance* (Boston: Little, Brown, 1944); Allan R. Bosworth, *America's Concentration Camps* (New York: Norton, 1967); Bill Hosokawa, *Nisei:The Quiet Americans* (New York: Morrow, 1969); and Girdner and Loftis, *The Great Betrayal*, cited above.

Scholarship has focused on a number of topics. On the question of the causes of the evacuation, the leading works are Morton Grodzins, *Americans Betrayed: Politics and the Japanese Evacuation* (Chicago: University of Chicago Press, 1949) and Jacobus tenBroek, Edward N. Barnhart, and Floyd W. Matson, *Prejudice, War, and the Constitution* (Berkeley and Los Angeles: University of California Press, 1954). Each poses a different erroneous "theory of responsibility," and both need to be corrected by Stetson Conn, "Japanese Evacuation from the West Coast" in Stetson Conn, Rose C. Engleman, and Byron Fairchild, *The United States Army in World War II: The Western Hemisphere: Guarding the United States and Its Outposts* (Washington: Government Printing Office, 1964).

Life in the camps was treated in numerous monographs and pamphlets published by the War Relocation Authority during and shortly after the war. Although these contain much valuable information, they are, without exception, written from the point of view of "sympathetic keepers," as is the memoir by WRA director Dillon S. Myer, *Uprooted Americans: The Japanese Americans and the War Relocation Authority during World War II* (Tucson: University of Arizona Press, 1971). More valuable, but questionable because of their perspective and methodology, are two early works published by the University of California Japanese American Evacuation and Resettlement Study: Dorothy S. Thomas and Richard S. Nishimoto, *The Spoilage* (Berkeley and Los Angeles: University of California Press, 1946) and Dorothy S. Thomas, *The Salvage* (Berkeley and Los Angeles: University of California Press, 1952). These should be supplemented by Harry H. L. Kitano, *Japanese Americans: Evolution of a Subculture* (Englewood Cliffs, N.J.: Prentice-Hall, 1969); Leonard J. Arrington, *The Price of Prejudice: The Japanese-American Relocation*

Center in Utah during World War II (Logan, Utah: Utah State University, 1962); and Douglas W. Nelson, "Heart Mountain: The History of an American Concentration Camp," unpublished M.A. thesis, University of Wyoming, 1970.

The legal aspects of the evacuation have attracted much attention. Most useful are Eugene V. Rostow, "The Japanese-American Cases—A Disaster," *Yale Law Journal* (June, 1945); Milton R. Konvitz, *The Alien and the Asiatic in American Law* (Ithaca, N.Y.: Cornell University Press, 1946); C. Herman Pritchett, *Civil Liberties and the Vinson Court* (Chicago: University of Chicago Press, 1954); Alpheus Thomas Mason, *Harlan Fiske Stone: Pillar of the Law* (New York: Viking, 1956); Sidney Fine, "Mr. Justice Murphy and the Hirabayshi Case," *Pacific Historical Review* (May, 1964); and J. Woodford Howard, Jr., *Mr. Justice Murphy: A Political Biography* (Princeton, N.J.: Princeton University Press, 1968).

On other topics Thomas D. Murphy, *Ambassadors in Arms* (Honolulu: University of Hawaii Press, 1954) tells of the Japanese American combat units; Robert W. O'Brien, *The College Nisei* (Palo Alto: Pacific Books, 1949) tells of the education of the relocated students; T. A. Larson, *Wyoming's War Years* (Laramie: University of Wyoming, 1954), contains the best account of a state's reaction to the evacuated people; and John Modell, "The Japanese in Los Angeles: A Study in Growth and Accommodation, 1900–1946," unpublished Ph.D. dissertation, Columbia University, 1969, has the best account of the return of the West Coast Japanese to a particular locality.